P9-CRK-736

THE ESSENCE OF CHOCOLATE

SCHARFFEN BERGER

CHOCOLATE MAKER

THE ESSENCE OF CHOCOLATE

Recipes for Baking and Cooking with Fine Chocolate

By John Scharffenberger and Robert Steinberg
with Ann Krueger Spivack and Susie Heller

Photography by Deborah Jones

HYPERION

NEW YORK

ISBN-10: 1-4013-0238-6
ISBN-13: 978-1-4013-0238-2

Hyperion books are available for special promotions and premiums.

For details contact Michael Rentas, Assistant Director, Inventory Operations,

Hyperion, 77 West 66th Street, 12th floor, New York, New York 10023, or call 212-456-0133.

FIRST EDITION

10 9 8 7 6 5 4 3 2

THIS BOOK IS DEDICATED TO THE GROWERS OF CACAO AND THE FUTURE OF CACAO AGRICULTURE.

CONTENTS

CHAPTER 2

Intensely Chocolate

CHAPTER 8

CHAPTER 9

CHAPTER 10

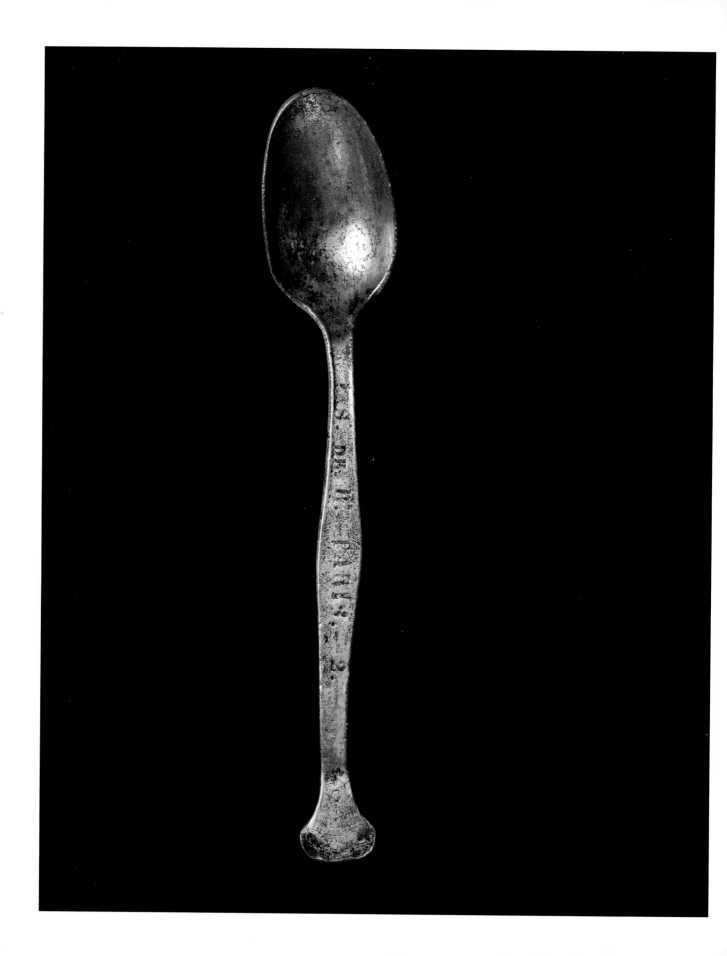

INTRODUCTION

A NOTE FROM SUSIE HELLER

Writing about chocolate seems like a dream job to most people, but when this book began, I wasn't so sure. When faced with a restaurant dessert menu, I tended to order a fruit dessert. I also wasn't sure about having mountains of chocolate in my house as I tested and wrote these recipes. Wouldn't this mean a giant weight gain? The answer, surprisingly, is no. When I first met Robert Steinberg and John Scharffenberger, I saw two very lean men. What was their secret?

The secret is the quality of the chocolate. Working with great chocolate has changed how I bake with and eat chocolate. There is such a satisfying feeling when you taste a true artisanal chocolate. The question became, how could we translate this experience into the recipes chosen for this book? We began by choosing recipes that focused on the flavor of the chocolate. This book doesn't call for a lot of fancy embellishments or difficult methods; it's about the "essence" of the chocolate. For these recipes, we dug into the Scharffen Berger files, asked top chefs from around the country to give us their favorite ideas for Scharffen Berger chocolate, and even went back a few generations in my own recipe file to find recipes that you'd want to make again and again.

The interesting thing about chocolate is that almost everyone loves it, but not in the same way. Some people want a dessert that is as rich and dense as possible, while others prefer something light and airy with just a hint of that wonderful flavor. We have divided the recipes into three sections, "Intensely Chocolate," "Essentially Chocolate," and "A Hint of Chocolate," according to the intensity of chocolate in each dessert.

When I started as a cook, the choices available to me were unsweetened, semisweet, and milk chocolate. Today part of the fun of using chocolate is to experiment and find your favorite one. The chocolate I use most often now is 70% bittersweet, because I prefer desserts that are less sweet than those made with 62% semisweet, and I love the intensity of the 70% used as chips in cookies.

The 82% chocolate was new to me when I began working on these recipes, and I found I like its darker flavor as a highlight—to brush on a tart shell before filling it, for example, or as a ribbon in fudge.

The richness of Scharffen Berger milk chocolate changed my perception of milk chocolate as something best eaten out of hand. Of course it's perfect for S'mores (page 188), but try it in Brown Butter Blondies (page 191) or White Velvet Cake with Milk Chocolate Ganache (page 212). This milk chocolate is very kid friendly, but we found that kids actually liked the darker chocolates too. Don't assume that children like only milk chocolate.

My kitchen is now well stocked with 62%, 70%, 82%, and 99% chocolate as well as milk chocolate and what I think is the most wonderful cocoa available. And I now put cacao nibs into and on everything imaginable. I love the variety of intensity they add to desserts. Once you taste nibs, you'll want to experiment with them. Try them in recipes that call for nuts, substituting nibs for some or all of the nuts. You will be amazed at the flavor and interest they add.

When I was a kid, my mother baked daily, and I would wake up to the smell of her baking my favorite Hungarian Kuchen (coffee cake). The Pull-Apart Kuchen (page 221), Layered Crepe Torte (page 215), and Apricot Hazelnut Squares (page 239) are all my mother's recipes, and I am thrilled to share them.

There are also savory recipes included in the "Hint" chapter, many of them based on the idea of a Mexican mole, a fragrant, savory combination of chocolate and spices. A traditional mole is complicated, requiring at least two dozen spices added in a precise order. We have translated the concept into dishes that require less time to prepare, such as John's Cocoa Rub (page 274), and offered ideas for using chocolate in savory recipes that you already make.

While we were writing this book, many of the contributors, as well as friends and neighbors, offered their favorite ways of satisfying a chocolate craving. These appear throughout the book as "Quick Fixes."

All of these recipes were tested in my home kitchen using standard home equipment. Working with two dozen pastry chefs for this book made it clear that there are as many cooking techniques as there are cooks. Most of the time, there isn't a single correct method: the trick is to find the one that works best for you. We included a separate section on some of the simple techniques we use most frequently; see page 22.

There are many variables in baking. My friend Jacques Pépin says, "A recipe is what happened with a particular piece of equipment on a particular day." Circumstances can change, especially when you're baking. Altitude, humidity, the type of chocolate or flour or butter you use, the temperature of your oven, the temperature of your kitchen, your equipment—all of these things affect baking.

Trust your instincts. Use the baking times we list as a general guideline, and use your own judgment too. If you think something is overcooking, it probably is. I give this advice here because years ago, I never used to trust my instincts. I would follow a recipe exactly, even while thinking to myself, "This isn't going to work." But, in fact, usually my instincts were right. The tendency to follow a recipe as written, even when you have doubts about it, is natural, and very hard to overcome.

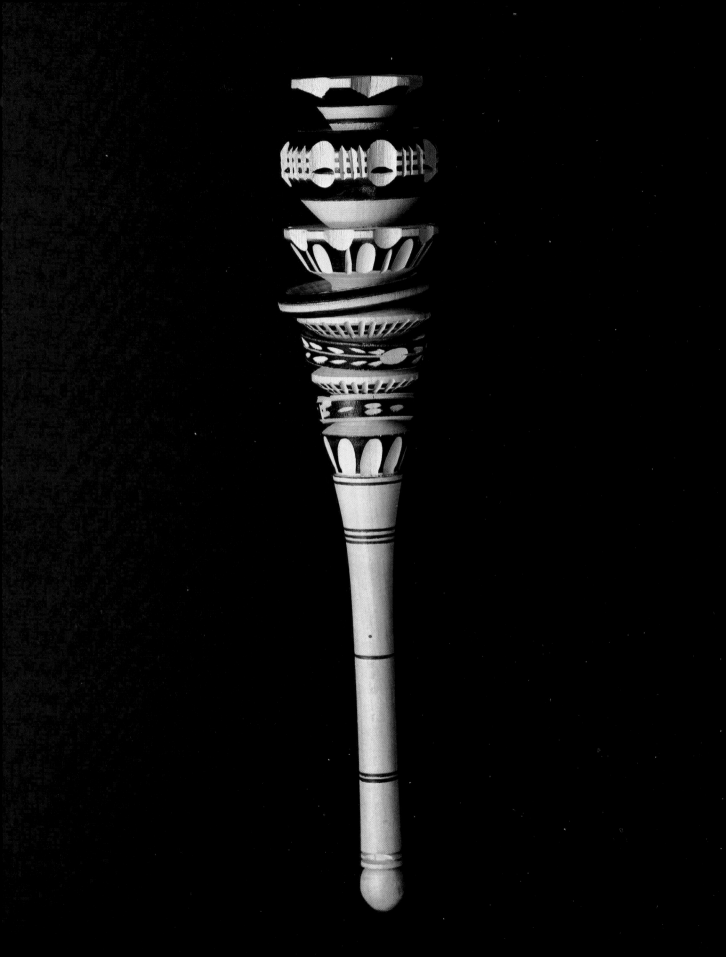

This book calls for very little special equipment, but in my kitchen, there are certain tools I find indispensable; see page 25 for our list. You probably already own most of these tools, but if you don't, they are definitely worth adding to your kitchen. They can be found at specialty shops, housewares departments, and sometimes even supermarkets. They can also be purchased from the Culinary Institute of America at Greystone, Sur La Table, and Williams-Sonoma.

I'm often asked which chocolate recipes are my favorites. Cooking with artisan chocolate has taught me that choosing a favorite chocolate dessert is a little like choosing a favorite wine. Just as you have favorite red wines and favorite wines from France, you'll find that your favorite recipe for an 82% chocolate will be different than your favorite recipe for 70% or milk chocolate.

We wrote this book to give a glimpse into the world of chocolate making and to provide recipes that showcase high-quality chocolate. Robert Steinberg and John Scharffenberger have opened a door with Scharffen Berger Chocolate Makers, and chocolate lovers, as they taste the artisan chocolates now available, will find a new excitement in eating and cooking with these distinctive flavors.

Enjoy!

Favorite Techniques

MELTING CHOCOLATE

Before you begin, there are some general rules about melting chocolate that you will want to keep in mind.

- Take your time. Dark chocolate can withstand higher temperatures than milk or white chocolate, but it's always best to heat chocolate gently.
- Chopping chocolate before melting it means the heat will be more evenly distributed, and the chocolate will melt quickly, with little fuss.
- Be very careful to keep liquid away from melting chocolate. Chocolate is composed of solids suspended in cocoa butter. Melting the chocolate transforms the cocoa butter to a liquid, and the solid particles glide easily through this cocoa butter base. But just a few drops of water, or any liquid, will be absorbed by the solids and cause them to cling to each other. When this happens, the chocolate seizes, or becomes stiff and difficult to stir. Once chocolate has seized, your only option is to add more liquid and make John's Simple Chocolate Sauce (page 310).

We use three different methods for melting chocolate on its own and a fourth method for melting chocolate with cream.

Method 1: Water Bath

One of the most knowledgeable cooks we know, Alice Medrich, melts chocolate in a water bath, setting a metal bowl in the center of a wide deep skillet half full of simmering water. With this arrangement, you can easily see if the water is becoming too hot and turn down the heat as necessary. However, you do need to be cautious that no water splashes into the chocolate.

Method 2: Double Boiler

You don't have to own a standard double boiler to use this method: You can simply set a metal bowl over a saucepan, as long as there's no gap (such as a pour spout on the pan) for steam to escape through. (Steam can cause condensation on the bowl, so that water runs into the chocolate.) Many cooks believe that the bowl holding the chocolate should not touch the water, but that's actually a myth: It's fine for the bowl to touch the hot water beneath. The steam rising under the bowl is actually hotter than boiling water. But the water doesn't have to reach a boil; the bowl just needs to be warm to melt the chocolate. To avoid being burned by trapped steam, be careful when you remove the bowl or the top of a double boiler.

Method 3: Microwave

The microwave works wonderfully for melting chocolate as long as you heat it for very short periods of time and stir well after each one. The problem with microwaving is that the chocolate will retain its shape when melted. This means you can't determine whether or not the chocolate is melted by how it looks. Microwave in short bursts of 10 to 30 seconds (depending on the wattage of your microwave), and stir the chocolate after each burst until just melted.

Method 4: Heated Cream

When you're working with chocolate and cream—making a ganache, for example—most recipes tell you to put the chopped chocolate in a bowl, heat the cream, and pour it over the chocolate. But if the cream isn't hot enough or the chocolate isn't finely chopped, the chocolate may not melt completely. Pastry chef Jim Dodge uses this foolproof method: Finely chop the chocolate and have it in a bowl next to the stove. Heat the cream in a heavy saucepan. When the cream comes to a simmer, remove the pan from the heat. Add the chocolate to the pan, let stand, then stir until melted and smooth. The residual heat from the pan keeps the cream at the right temperature while the chocolate melts.

CHOCOLATE CURLS AND SHAVINGS

Begin with a thick chunk of chocolate, which is easier to grasp and creates better curls. The chocolate should be at room temperature. If it's too cold, the curls will break easily. You can warm it by placing it under a table lamp for several minutes.

Using a vegetable peeler, work in short, quick strokes to make shavings or move the peeler more slowly and press slightly harder for large curls. Let these drop onto a sheet of parchment or waxed paper. For shavings, pick up the paper and use it to dust the shavings over a dessert. Pick up the curls with a small spatula or butter knife. Don't use your fingers, as their heat can melt the chocolate.

LINING A BAKING SHEET WITH PARCHMENT

Lifting brownies and other baked goods out of a pan can be a challenge. Sometimes you lose a portion of the bottom of the brownie or cake, and often you end up scratching your pan. We found a clever way to avoid this: Line the pan with parchment paper that extends about 2 inches over two opposite sides of the pan. For example, for an 8 by 8 by 2-inch pan, the parchment paper should be 8 by 16 inches long. Place the parchment paper in the pan before you pour in the batter. The ends of the paper become handles that allow you to lift the entire brownie slab or cake from the pan in one easy motion. Then place it on a cutting board and slice neatly.

BAKING IN A WATER BATH

A water bath means simply setting your cooking container inside the oven within a large pan partially filled with water. Many of our recipes call for a water bath, which offers a gentler way of cooking by moderating an oven's heat. To bake with a water bath, in most cases you can use very hot tap water. Unless otherwise stipulated in a recipe, you don't need to boil the water.

It can be difficult to fill the pan with water and then maneuver it into the oven. An easier method is to fill a pitcher with hot water and set it next to the stove. Open the oven door, set the pans on the rack, and quickly but carefully pour the appropriate amount of hot water into the larger pan. Close the door as quickly as possible so you don't cool down your oven.

When it's time to remove the pan from the oven, the water will be very hot, so be careful. We've found that it's easiest to use a turkey baster to remove some of the water before lifting the smaller pan (or ramekins or mold) from the water bath.

ROTATING BAKING PANS IN THE OVEN

When we call for rotating pans in a recipe, we mean to turn each pan around, from front to back (180 degrees) and, if you are baking on two racks, switch the baking sheets from one rack to the other. This allows baked goods to cook as evenly as possible.

USING RAMEKINS AND SOUFFLÉ MOLDS

Ramekins and soufflé molds are not always measured in the same way. Some manufacturers give an ounce capacity that's equal to the number of liquid ounces it takes to fill the ramekin to the brim, while others list the capacity as the number of liquid ounces it takes to fill to one ounce below the brim.

The measurements given in this book follow the first method. When we call for 6-ounce ramekins, for example, we mean ramekins that hold 6 ounces when filled to the brim. If you're in doubt as to the size of your ramekins, fill them with water and then measure how many ounces of water each ramekin holds.

A good way to fill ramekins or molds is to pour the batter or other mixture into a large measuring cup with a spout. This not only helps you fill each container more easily, it also gives you an idea of how many ounces you're pouring into each one.

Favorite Kitchen Tools

STAND MIXER

When we refer to a stand mixer, we mean a heavy-duty mixer such as a KitchenAid that's equipped with a whisk, a paddle, and a dough hook. Many of these recipes can be made with a smaller hand mixer, but when a recipe requires some power during mixing, we use a stand mixer.

SCALE

When baking, we weigh our chocolate. Depending on the size of the pieces you are using, cup measurements can vary significantly. Using a scale guarantees an accurate measure and consistent results. However, just as a rule of thumb, we did find when using chunks of chocolate for cheesecake and some cookies that ½ cup of ¼-inch pieces is equal to 2½ ounces.

PASTRY BAGS

A traditional pastry bag is fine, but we love the convenience of disposable pastry bags. And very often a pastry tip is not necessary with these bags—you can just cut an opening of the right size in the end of the bag.

OFFSET SPATULAS

A thin offset baking spatula with an angled blade gives you the correct angle to spread batters and other mixtures evenly (see the photo on page 157). We use both full-size and mini offset spatulas.

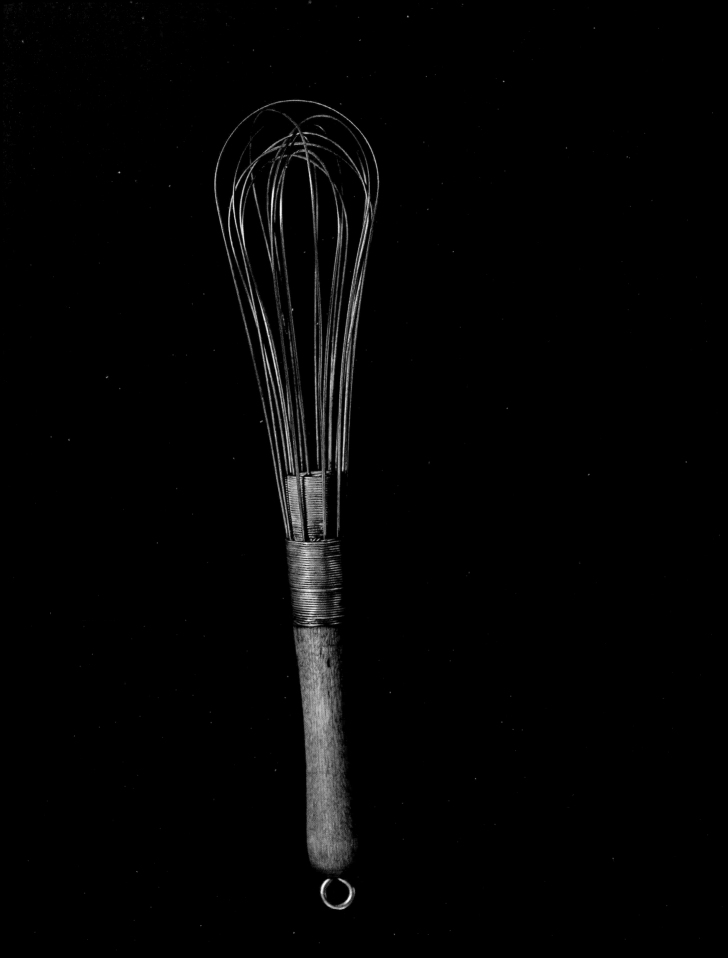

HEATPROOF SPOONS AND SPATULAS

We love heatproof spoons and spatulas for everything from combining melted butter and chocolate to stirring an ice cream base as it cooks.

MICROPLANE

A rasp grater that gives a fine grating of chocolate or fruit zest, Microplanes may be the best cooking invention of the last twenty years.

LIQUID AND DRY MEASURING CUPS AND SPOONS

The liquid measuring cups made by Oxo are very clever. They give the measurements both inside the cup, on an angled ledge set with numbers, as well as the standard way, with numbers on the outside of the cup.

For dry ingredients we use measuring cups made of heavy-duty metal that won't warp in the dishwasher, like those from Cuisipro. The same goes for measuring spoons.

COFFEE OR SPICE GRINDER AND SMALL CHOPPER

Some jobs are too small for a full-size food processor. We use small grinders for the smaller jobs, and tend to rely on the Minimate Plus Chopper Grinder by Cuisinart.

THERMOMETERS

Although often overlooked, an oven thermometer is an important tool. You may believe your oven's temperature is correct, but if it's off by as little 25 degrees, your baking won't be consistent.

Some of these recipes require a candy thermometer. Be sure to get one with a sturdy clip that attaches to the side of the pan.

SILPATS

A Silpat, a reusable baking pan liner, is a thin sheet of woven fiberglass coated with layers of food-grade silicon. It offers a nonstick surface that's easy to work on and cook on, as well as to clean (but don't cut on a Silpat). Silpats are now widely available in cookware/gourmet shops. We recommended having at least two.

....

Using Scharffen Berger Chocolate in Your Own Recipes

By Alice Medrich, pastry chef, founder of Cocolat,
and award-winning author of Bittersweet

Most standard semisweet chocolate is 55 to 60% cacao. When you want to use Scharffen Berger chocolate or another premium chocolate in a recipe that you've always made with standard baking chocolate, you can avoid unexpected, and unwanted, results by doing just a little math. First, check the percentage of the chocolate you plan to use. Scharffen Berger 62% semisweet can often be used instead of standard semisweet or bittersweet chocolate without any adjustment. However, if you find the results too intense or too dry, or if the sauce or ganache curdles, try adding 10 percent less chocolate than the recipe calls for the next time, and add 1 teaspoon sugar for every ounce of chocolate called for in the original recipe.

For example, if the original recipe calls for 10 ounces of chocolate, use 9 ounces of chocolate labeled 62% and add 10 teaspoons of sugar (3 tablespoons plus 1 teaspoon) to the recipe.

To substitute Scharffen Berger 70% bittersweet, use 30 to 35 percent less chocolate than the recipe calls for, and add up to 1½ teaspoons sugar for every ounce of chocolate called for in the original recipe.

If the original recipe calls for 10 ounces of chocolate, use 7 ounces of chocolate labeled 70% and add 15 teaspoons (5 tablespoons) of sugar. But taste what you've made, and then use your own judgment. If you want a little more bittersweet chocolate flavor, add slightly more chocolate the next time you make it. If you find, as I do, that a great chocolate requires less sugar, add slightly less than the amount given in the adjustment and see what you think of the results.

....

CHAPTER

1

BEFORE WE MADE CHOCOLATE

FROM MEDICINE TO CHOCOLATE: ROBERT STEINBERG

"Why did you leave medicine for chocolate?" People have asked me this question countless times, and I'm still not sure how to answer. The truth is, I never gave up practicing medicine. I just stopped being a full-time doctor, and my leaving medicine had nothing to do with chocolate. In fact, almost four years passed between the time I left my medical practice in San Francisco and the moment in 1994 when I first thought about making chocolate.

The major change in my life occurred in May 1989, when I was diagnosed with chronic lymphocytic leukemia. For a year and a half after the diagnosis, I continued to see patients. Although it became harder physically to go to work as symptoms of the leukemia began to emerge, I faced another challenge that was the result of the similarity between one aspect of my illness and that of some of my patients—a compromised immune system. In 1989, San Francisco was in the middle of a full-blown AIDS epidemic, and ten to fifteen percent of my patients either had AIDS or were HIV-positive. I attended to some extraordinarily ill patients and was present at the death of several of them. Looking at these patients felt at times like looking into a mirror, because I had been told when I was diagnosed that the leukemia was incurable and that I had a fifty percent chance of dying within ten years as a result of a weakened immune system. The combined effect of my waning energy and the feeling that I was torn between worrying about how to take care of myself and how to take care of my patients led me to sell my practice. At the end of my last day at the practice, when I'd transferred the care of my patients to another physician, I walked out into the cold air of a late November night with a feeling I can only describe as a mixture of relief and elation. Paradoxically, the apparent nearness of death gave me permission to try just about anything.

Free of a rigid daily schedule, I took piano lessons and life drawing classes and tried to improve my Spanish and French. Although hardly a moment passed when I wasn't conscious on some level of my illness, this period of my life strengthened a resolution I had made shortly after my diagnosis: that the leukemia would not monopolize my life. I went each morning to the Zuni Café, where I would order a double espresso and linger over a book or my journal for hours. I became such a fixture at Zuni that Sylvie Darr, the manager and sommelier, included me when arranging wine-tasting trips to Napa and Sonoma for the staff. I was lucky to be invited on those trips, because they introduced me to the intellectual side of tasting. I began to understand the importance of attaching words to a sensory experience.

. . . .

Living with an Illness

Since we began Scharffen Berger, I've received many letters from people who are coping with an illness of some sort. Whenever I can, I write back. Many of these letters praise my openness about my leukemia as "courageous." But I don't see myself as courageous. Cancer is such a charged topic in our society, it's easy for an illness to become a sort of dramatic event, but not very easy to shrug off the kind of stigma that we assign to people with cancer. To talk openly about my illness is simply to talk about an integral part of my being. It's hard for me to imagine trying to direct a conversation away from the topic without being closed and mysterious in a way that is foreign to my sense of self. Being open about my leukemia also lets me acknowledge what I know for sure from my years of practicing medicine: every one of us has challenges to face. The deeply felt and beautifully written letters that have been sent to me connect me to people in an unusually personal way. For those who have asked me how to approach life with an illness, I can say this: there are no useful generalizations, but to the extent that your illness and life circumstances allow, try to be yourself and understand that in accepting who you are, you are likely to become more accepting of others. It may not be readily apparent, but that sort of compassion is often a reward in itself.

. . . .

When I felt well enough, I traveled, first to Bologna, Italy, and then to France. During a stay in Paris, I walked past a small tailoring shop in the Marais late one night and stopped to admire a jacket that hung in the shop window. When I returned a day or two later to try on the jacket, the tailor who owned the shop engaged me in conversation, and eventually he asked if I would help him import a line of eyeglasses that he'd designed. The idea of selling eyeglasses might have seemed a bit odd, but at that moment in my life, I wanted to be open to every possibility. Besides, I wasn't beyond looking for an excuse to visit Paris more often.

I returned to San Francisco and arranged to meet my friend Bob Voorhees for lunch. Bob, a restaurateur and coffee roaster, was the only businessman I knew, and he listened while I described the tailor and his idea. When I asked for his advice on my admittedly eccentric idea to import eyeglass frames, Bob sat forward in his chair, looked at me, and asked, "Robert, if you want to take up a business, why not start with something more familiar?" Bob felt that my intense interest in food and cooking as well as my background in basic science qualified me to help him with a business he had looked into a number of years earlier: making chocolate.

When Bob first thought about making chocolate, he enrolled in a brief industrial chocolate-making course, but his unfamiliarity with scientific terms frustrated him. He thought I would have an easier time grasping the chemistry involved. He loaned me a textbook from his course, a heavy six-hundred-page book called *Chocolate, Cocoa, and Confectionery: Science and Technology*, by B. W. Minifie. As I began reading, I felt as though the door to the underground world of chocolate had opened. I started to see a food that I had taken entirely for granted in a completely different light. The more I read, the more the challenge of chocolate making appealed to me. That chocolate crossed many fields of interest—history, science, agriculture, and archaeology—fueled my enthusiasm. I read the relevant parts of the book and then, while looking for other books about chocolate making, I began calling U.S. chocolate experts and manufacturers to see what they thought about making chocolate on a small scale. Every person I spoke with told me that I couldn't make chocolate without costly equipment and millions of dollars in capital—and many seemed amazed that I was even considering the idea.

It soon became clear to me that there was more than one way to make chocolate—there are actually many different machines that could be used—and that I couldn't learn chocolate making from a book. One fortuitous event occurred a month after Bob and I had our first conversation about chocolate. A pastry chef friend gave me a book called *A Passion for Chocolate*, which Rose Levy Beranbaum had translated from the original, *La Passion du Chocolat*. The authors of the book, Maurice and Jean-Jacques Bernachon, were chocolatiers who owned and ran a legendary chocolate company in Lyons.

In 1993, Bob Voorhees and I decided to meet in Paris and visit Bernachon together. We spoke with

Matthieu Barès, the person who managed Bernachon's store and public relations department. On an afternoon when no one was making chocolate, Matthieu walked us through the tiny factory. The Bernachons were unusual in several respects: Despite a large following, which might have led other chocolate makers to expand, the Bernachon family had kept their shop and factory virtually the same size over the course of decades, and their chocolate-making equipment was housed in a single large room.

Months later, as my frustration grew over not being able to really understand how to make chocolate, I decided to write a letter to the Bernachons, explaining that I was a physician interested in chocolate making, but that I was not in the business. I said that I spoke French and asked if they would let me work at their factory for a month. I had a friend help me phrase it in very polite French, and then mailed it to Matthieu, nearly certain that the answer would be no. They faxed me back a letter saying I was welcome to come for two weeks. I still don't understand why they agreed to let me spend two weeks there, but I know that I glowed when their response came through. It's safe to say that without Bernachon, there wouldn't be a Scharffen Berger.

Working at Bernachon seemed almost like a dream. I didn't absorb many technical details. I didn't, for instance, learn such things as the optimal micron size to which cacao beans had to be ground or exactly how much cocoa butter should be added. I didn't even learn to roast cacao. Instead, I absorbed a philosophy. The key idea behind chocolate making at Bernachon is attention to the ingredients that go into chocolate and an understanding of the role each ingredient plays.

During my first week at Bernachon, I was asked to fill in for one of the workers who was away on vacation—an incredible stroke of luck. I did whatever I was asked, sorting beans, scooping chocolate from one container to another, and scraping bits of stray chocolate off the floor at the end of the day. During the second week, spent in the confection-making area, I was more observer than contributor, although I did learn about enrobing and hand dipping, and I got to put the pistachios on top of the little bonbons as they went down the line.

Maurice Bernachon, who was eighty years old and lived in the apartment upstairs, came down every morning at 6:30, went to his table, and began making pastries. Every day at noon, the workers began sitting down in shifts at a large table to have lunch together. The company provided a bottle of wine, a big salad, and some kind of meat for the meal. I felt that I was sharing a way of life and an atmosphere from an era that had virtually passed. The workers could not have been more gracious or accepting of me. I was, after all, an American who'd appeared out of nowhere, asking dozens of questions and providing little help in exchange. (Their references to ganache, the center of every truffle, made no sense to me until I'd had a chance to consult a dictionary after I'd gone back to the hotel for the evening.) When my two weeks ended, I sat down and had a conversation with Jean-Jacques and Maurice. After thanking them profusely for their openness and generosity, I suggested that they open a factory in California. Bob and I would help them, I said. They laughed. "This is much too hard," Maurice replied, smiling. "We couldn't possibly start at the beginning and do all this again."

In 1999, I returned to Bernachon, bringing Scharffen Berger chocolate for the Bernachon family and the workers. I was greeted warmly, and many of the workers said, half-jokingly, "Maybe I could come to California and make chocolate with you in your factory!" Jean-Jacques sent us a letter saying that our chocolate was quite good and congratulating us on our success. Both John and I have always been open about our chocolate-making techniques and we've encouraged factory tours. I think this is due partly to the Bernachon family, who shared their ideas so generously and influenced the course of my life.

When I returned from Lyons, eager to begin making chocolate, Bob was busy with other business matters and I wasn't sure what our next step should be. John and I had met through mutual friends in 1979, when both of us lived in Ukiah. John came to see me as a patient during the late eighties, when I opened my practice in San Francisco. In the years after I'd become ill, I'd run into him from time to time, usually at restaurants, and we casually talked about what we were doing. It was probably at Zuni Café in the fall of 1995 that I first mentioned the fact that Bob and I were thinking about making chocolate.

Around the same time, I began hunting for chocolate-making equipment like the machines used at Bernachon. One visit to a used-equipment company stands out in my mind because it felt almost surreal. The warehouse was set in what seemed like the most desolate corner of the Bronx, on a street of old industrial buildings with few cars and no pedestrians. Once I walked into the building, I had to follow a long, fluorescent-lit corridor, making several sharp turns, until I finally reached the reception area, where miniature candy-making machines were set out on display. I was led inside their warehouse, filled with old machines that, not having been restored or cleaned, looked, to me, unusable.

I was beginning to wonder how Bob and I would turn our idea into reality. Uncertain about whether we were going in the right direction, I remember calling John one evening to ask if he, as someone who had started a business to make a similar affordable luxury, thought our plan was reasonable from the perspective of customer acceptance. Yes, he said, he thought it was. I had no idea at the time that John had sold his interest in his winery, Scharffenberger Cellars, so it was a surprise when I received a call from him in December 1995, asking if I was still interested in making chocolate.

In early 1996, John met with Bob and me, and the three of us agreed to explore working together. We incorporated under the name SVS—for Steinberg, Voorhees, and Scharffenberger—but agreed to call our company Scharffen Berger Chocolate Maker. To use Scharffen Berger made sense given that Scharffenberger Cellars was familiar to many people who knew food and wine. We decided on the "Chocolate Maker" part of our name while considering how to best translate *chocolatier* into English.

Months passed and still nothing happened, until the day I saw an ad in *The Manufacturing Confectioner*, a trade magazine I'd subscribed to. The ad announced a trade show in Düsseldorf for confectioners and chocolate manufacturers. I called John and told him I thought we ought to go and see what kind of equipment they had displayed at the show. John agreed. By that point, Bob had bowed out, citing other business ideas he wanted to pursue. John and I met in Düsseldorf, drove to the convention together, and bought our first piece of equipment.

FROM WINEMAKING TO CHOCOLATE: JOHN SCHARFFENBERGER

When Robert spoke to me about chocolate, it seemed like a natural thing for us to do together. I had been growing food and making food products for most of my life, and chocolate seemed a logical step after I sold my winery.

I might never have become a farmer if my family hadn't moved from New Jersey to a ranch house on Warner Ranch, a two-thousand-acre spread of open land in Woodland Hills, California, when I was nine years old. It seemed like the end of the world. I went from riding my bike in the suburbs with my friends to being stuck in the middle of a huge farm with only my siblings for company.

My father was a businessman who loved country life. He kept bee-hives and planted fruit trees. His idea of a really great weekend was putting in a new irrigation line or making a barbed wire fence (until he realized that putting in electric fences was even more fun). Gradually, though, I grew to love having a vast place to explore.

My dad had bought a farm for himself right out of college, and quickly lost his shirt trying to make it work. He'd had the sense to rent out the farm and return to business and finance to pay off the relatives who lent him money. For him, that was the end of farming and the beginning of a very good business career. But even though he succeeded in business, I think at heart he always thought of himself as a farmer.

When I began school at the University of California, it was the first time I'd lived in an apartment house, my first time living in an urban setting. I liked Berkeley, but I kept thinking, "What's wrong? What am I missing here?" I realized I missed the open spaces I'd grown up in and I couldn't stand the thought of not having my hands in the dirt for a whole year. I took a job as a live-in gardener tending a really good, big garden in the Oakland Hills. The woman who hired me was eighty-five years old. Her garden, which had once been terrific, had been on the decline for years. Her incredible collection of plants had completely grown together, and I spent a lot of time trying to sort them out. That was my first serious gardening job, and it made me acutely aware of my lack of knowledge about plants. From my upbringing, I understood things like watering systems, trimming, and mowing, but the rest I had to teach myself.

At the time I was studying landscape design but I decided to create my own major combining botany, geography, cultural anthropology, and food history. I kept up with school, but farming and gardening occupied most of my thoughts. My school friends and I were constantly coming up with schemes to buy land. This was during the height of the "back to the land" movement, and I was ready to stop attending classes and start working on a farm, a plan that my parents fought pretty effectively.

At the end of my junior year, I landed an internship with the Stony Hill Winery. I lived up in the wine country during the crush, and met more people who were doing the things that I dreamed of doing. The owners of Stony Hill were famous horticulturalists as well as winemakers, and this made a big impression on me; it was enlightening to see people pursuing the same things I was interested in and making it work.

After I graduated, I worked at Château Souverain as a cellar rat. My job lasted up through the crush, and while there, I just happened to spot a real estate sign. I called the phone number on the sign, thinking about land for my father.

My father had finally decided to sell the New Jersey farm he'd bought after college but not lived on for twenty years. He wanted to buy a ranch in California where he could grow grapes, and he had asked me to look for the right piece of property. So far nothing I'd seen had made sense for him, but when I called Paige Mailliard, the Realtor, just by chance, he convinced me to drive to Ukiah to look at a property. We went up a four-mile dirt road and suddenly came out on a hidden plateau with rolling hills and oak trees and lots of water—it looked like Virginia.

My parents came to take a look at it and saw its potential. There was an offer in on the farm in New Jersey, so the timing was perfect. They bought it and put me in charge. My experience with horticulture and small irrigation projects seemed a drop in the bucket compared to all that was needed to run a two-thousand-acre ranch. I had to find tractors, arrange for miles of fencing to be built, and plant and graft tens of thousands of vines.

After our first harvest, I began selling our grapes. I got involved in a community of winemakers and other growers and was invited to participate in various wine-tasting groups. One of the groups was made up of well-known professional winemakers; I was the only "pedestrian." This group was where I learned how to taste properly. Paul Dolan, the winemaker at Fetzer winery and one of the first winemakers in California to champion organic grapes, gave me a primer on how to taste, and that was my first exposure to flavor as a dynamic experience. After tasting some great Champagne at a friend's wedding, I decided that I wanted to try to make a French-style sparkling wine.

Flavor as a Dynamic Experience

Think about the amount of time that elapses when you taste a dark chocolate (or a wine). It takes about six seconds to experience all the flavors and sensations, and something different happens during each of those seconds.

In the first second, you feel the chocolate melt on your tongue. A tartness or sourness becomes obvious, followed quickly by wonderful fruity flavors. The fruit notes continue but another note appears—you begin to experience the mid-palate sensations of smoothness and richness as the fat begins to coat your tongue.

At this point the chocolate's sweetness begins to react with the fruitiness, which results in a crescendo of flavors. As that tapers off, soft tannins excite your tongue, allowing some of the broader low notes to come through. At the finish, a slow drying sensation combines with a final note of sugar.

If you can imagine these six seconds of tasting as a very short symphony, you grasp what we're trying to do when we blend various beans to make our chocolate. We're assembling notes—putting together high fruity notes and lower, broader base notes to try to make those six seconds that you taste a bite of chocolate as wide-ranging and intensely flavorful as possible. The flavor notes come first of all from the beans we choose, but we can affect the notes in our chocolate by how long we roast the beans, how long we grind the nibs, and by the proportions of the various beans we use in our blends.

. . . .

I borrowed the money I needed to start and found an open Butler building made of corrugated galvanized steel with flat floors, a tilt-up. I hired a winemaker. I was able to get great contracts from Anderson Valley vineyards because nobody else would buy their grapes. I could secure long-term supplies of grapes at a decent price. All I had to do was learn how to make Champagne.

I went to France three times over a period of six months, looking at equipment and learning everything I could about the *champenoise* process. I found out that the official information offered by the various companies—the "front of the house" information—differed, sometimes radically, from what the young winemakers working in back told me. Years later, I would remember those winemakers when trying to pry information from industry professionals in the chocolate world. I remembered how the official word often wasn't as well-informed as the advice I got from individuals actually *doing* the work, and that perspective served me well in learning about chocolate making too.

I bought some equipment in France at auctions, but most of it I scrounged up in California, buying really old pieces and cobbling them into working order. This was winemaking on a shoestring, but I preferred to spend my real capital on great grapes, because I knew they were the key to the flavors I was looking for.

In hindsight, this was sort of like diving into the water above Niagara Falls—it was actually pretty stupid to just jump in and think I could put together a champagne-making process with very little money. But it worked. In 1994, when chocolate making came up and we were thinking about equipment, our situation was so similar to the way I'd started my winery I felt as if I'd done it before, and that gave me confidence, even when things didn't go smoothly in the beginning. It seemed obvious to me that if you could make something taste great, success would follow.

Just by chance, the people who ran Pommery and Lanson Champagnes were visiting the Fetzer family in California. John Fetzer didn't speak much French, so he called and invited me to join them for lunch. I went, and I brought my wines. They thought my wines were good and wanted to come and see my winery. Patrice Bruneau took one look at our little tilt-up and said, "You made *that* wine in *this* old garage? If you had a really good winery and your own vineyards, I bet you could make really good wine."

That's how our collaboration began. Pommery and Lanson bought my company, and began working with me to build a real winery. Before the building was completed, the Berlin Wall fell. Danone, parent

company to Pommery and Lanson, sold many of the small companies they'd bought, including Scharffenberger Cellars. Moët Hennessy Louis Vuitton bought us and assigned the winery to Veuve Clicquot, making us an American arm of their Champagne works. The best part of that arrangement was working with tasters from Veuve Clicquot. I worked with LVMH for six years, the company grew, and we hit the goals that I wanted to achieve—basically, I could take my wines to France, and nobody there would suspect they weren't French. In 1995, our brut won Wine of the Year from *Wine Magazine*, a major British publication. We were where we wanted to be creatively, and the wines had grown a following.

I knew that I would be leaving the winery, and I was ready to leave. The creative part—producing that flavor I'd had in my mind—was finished. The vines and trees were planted, the ponds, roads, and winery built. People were appreciating the flavor of our wines and they seemed happy to pay a decent amount for them. I had learned from building Scharffenberger Cellars, and I began thinking about what I'd do next. When I ran into Robert, and he mentioned chocolate making, it seemed like a great idea. It felt that the timing was right, that Americans would be receptive to a chocolate with great flavor. I figured we could follow the same steps I'd used to build a winery: rent a building, build the machines, find the flavor we wanted to produce, make the product, and sell it. I'd done it with the winery, and felt confident we could do the same with chocolate. I asked Robert if I could be a part of it.

CHAPTER 2

Intensely Chocolate

Chocolate Orange Fondue, page 61.

IGNORE THE TEMPTATION TO SAVE THE GOOD
CHOCOLATE FOR ORNATE DESSERTS.
There are some very formal desserts in these pages, but most of our favorites are very simple. With
good dark chocolate, the less you add to it, the better. The subtler flavors of chocolate come through
most clearly in desserts with fewer ingredients.

THAT CHOCOLATE CAKE

If you could only have one recipe for chocolate cake, this would be the one. It's the quintessential chocolate cake with chocolate frosting, rich and moist, completely satisfying, glorious without being the least bit formal. The best recipes are passed along, gaining fans each time they're given to somebody new, and this one was given to Susie Heller by her friend Jackie, who was given the recipe by a different Susie, who got the recipe from a chef in the Caribbean. Grown-ups love it, kids love it. This one is hard to beat.

FOR THE FROSTING:
In a small saucepan, combine the sugar and cream and bring to a boil over medium heat, stirring occasionally. Reduce the heat and simmer for 6 minutes. Add the chocolate and butter and stir until melted. Pour into a bowl and stir in the vanilla.

Let the frosting cool, whisking gently from time to time. Don't overwhip, or you'll create air bubbles.

FOR THE CAKE:
Position a rack in the center of the oven and preheat the oven to 350°F. Lightly butter the bottom of two 9-inch round cake pans. Line the bottom with parchment paper, then butter and flour the parchment and the sides of the pans.

In the bowl of a stand mixer fitted with the paddle attachment, combine the sugar, flour, cocoa, salt, baking powder, and baking soda, mixing on low speed. Mix in the eggs, oil, and milk.

Increase the speed to medium and beat for 2 minutes. Reduce the speed to low and mix in the water. The batter will be soupy.

Divide the batter evenly between the cake pans. Bake for 30 to 35 minutes, or until a skewer inserted in the center comes out clean.

Remove from the oven and cool on a cooling rack for 5 minutes, then turn the layers out onto the rack and cool completely.

When the cakes have cooled, check the frosting. It should have the consistency of mayonnaise. If it is still too thin, allow it to cool longer.

TO FROST THE CAKE:
Place one cake layer on a serving plate. Spread the frosting with a hot palette knife or icing spatula to give the frosting a beautiful shine: Run the knife under hot tap water and dry with a towel. Spread about ¾ cup of the frosting over the top of the first layer. Top with the second layer. Spread the remaining frosting over the top and sides of the cake, heating the knife again as necessary.

SERVES 8 TO 10

FROSTING
1¼ cups granulated sugar

1 cup heavy cream

5 ounces 99% unsweetened chocolate, finely chopped

8 tablespoons (4 ounces) unsalted butter, cut into ½-inch pieces

1 teaspoon pure vanilla extract

CAKE
Unsalted butter and flour for the pans

2 cups granulated sugar

1¾ cups all-purpose flour

¾ cup unsweetened cocoa powder

1 teaspoon salt

1½ teaspoons baking powder

1½ teaspoons baking soda

2 large eggs, lightly beaten

½ cup canola oil

1 cup whole milk

1 cup boiling water

CHOCOLATE ALMOND CAKE

CONTRIBUTED BY JIM DODGE

Pastry chef, author, and teacher Jim Dodge has an expert touch with chocolate. His recipes are easy to follow and include some of our best-loved desserts. This Chocolate Almond Cake is a perfect example. The cake stays moist and flavorful, and it is extremely versatile. You can bake it, then cut it into rounds, diamonds, or even petit fours; fill it with jam, buttercream, whipped cream, or, as we do, melted chocolate; and top it with nuts, fruit, or anything you like. Made with 70% chocolate, 82% chocolate, and cocoa powder, it is the perfect melding of dark chocolate and rich almond paste.

CAKE

12 ounces unsalted butter, at room temperature, plus more for the pan

Flour for the pan

1 pound almond paste

1¾ cups granulated sugar

¾ cup plus 2 tablespoons unsweetened cocoa powder

8 large eggs

FILLING AND GLAZE

4 ounces 82% extra dark chocolate, melted

12 tablespoons (6 ounces) unsalted butter, cut into cubes

8 ounces 70% bittersweet chocolate, finely chopped

FOR THE CAKE:

Position a rack in the middle of the oven and preheat the oven to 350°F. Lightly butter the bottom and sides of a 17 by 12 by 1-inch baking sheet (half sheet pan). Line the bottom with parchment, butter the parchment, then flour the parchment and the sides of the pan. Set aside.

In the bowl of a stand mixer fitted with the paddle attachment, mix the butter and almond paste on medium speed, scraping down the sides as necessary, for 3 to 5 minutes, until the mixture is light and creamy. Add the sugar and cocoa and blend on low speed. Increase the speed to medium and add the eggs one at a time, beating after each addition until incorporated. Continue to mix for 2 to 3 minutes, or until lightened, scraping down the sides as necessary.

Pour the batter into the prepared pan and spread it evenly, making certain to get in the corners. Bake for 25 minutes, or until just set: the surface should still be slightly spongy to the touch, but a skewer inserted in the center will come out clean, and the cake will begin to pull from the sides of the pan.

Remove from the oven and cool on a cooling rack for 5 to 10 minutes. Turn out onto the rack and cool completely.

Place the cake in the refrigerator for 20 minutes or the freezer for 10 to 15 minutes so it will be easier to cut.

TO FILL THE CAKES:

Using a 2½-inch round cutter, cut 24 disks from the cake. Brush the top of 12 of the disks with the melted chocolate, and top with the remaining 12 disks. Place a cooling rack over a baking sheet. Arrange the cakes on the rack, leaving ample room between them. Let the cakes come to room temperature before glazing.

TO GLAZE THE CAKES:

Scatter the butter over the bottom of a medium skillet and top with the chopped chocolate. Place over medium heat and let sit until about three-quarters of the chocolate is melted. Remove the pan from the heat and whisk just to combine and melt the remaining chocolate; whisk gently, to avoid creating bubbles. Transfer the glaze to a measuring cup with a spout. Slowly pour some glaze over the center of one cake, then use a small offset spatula to push the glaze over the sides, coating the top and sides of the cake. Smooth the sides to cover if desired. Repeat with the remaining cakes. If you use all the glaze, remove the rack from the pan, remove any crumbs from the glaze that has dripped into the baking sheet, and, if necessary, reheat the glaze before using it.

Let the cakes sit at room temperature until the glaze sets, then transfer to a platter or individual plates.

MAKES 12 INDIVIDUAL CAKES

ORBIT CAKE

CONTRIBUTED BY DAVID LEBOVITZ

This is our adaptation of David Lebovitz's Chocolate Orbit Cake from his book *Room for Dessert*. This recipe is a favorite of Sam Evans, the son of our national sales director, Nancy Arum. With some urging from his mother's friend Rozanne Gold, Sam baked this himself at the age of fourteen, intrigued by the idea that the cake calls for just four ingredients. Sam claims he got his first job as an assistant pastry chef because he impressed the owners with this cake.

INGREDIENTS

14 tablespoons (7 ounces) unsalted butter, cut into ¼-inch cubes, plus more for the pan

10 ounces 62% semisweet chocolate, finely chopped

5 large eggs

1 cup granulated sugar

Whipped Cream (page 315)

Position a rack in the middle of the oven and preheat the oven to 350°F. Lightly butter a 9 by 2-inch round cake pan and line the bottom with parchment paper.

Place the butter and chocolate in the top of a double boiler set over gently simmering water. Whisk occasionally until the chocolate has melted and the mixture is smooth. Remove from the heat.

In a large bowl, whisk together the eggs and sugar. Gradually whisk in the melted chocolate mixture, and continue whisking until thoroughly combined.

Pour the batter into the prepared pan. Place the pan in a larger baking pan, and cover the top of the cake pan with foil. Add enough very hot water to the baking pan to come halfway up the sides of the cake pan, and bake for 1 hour and 15 minutes to 1 hour and 30 minutes, or until the cake has set. To test, touch the center of the cake lightly with your fingers: the surface will be slightly tacky, but your fingers should come away clean.

Carefully remove the cake pan from the water bath and place on a cooling rack to cool completely.

Cover the pan with plastic wrap and refrigerate for at least 2 hours or up to 3 days.

To serve, run a knife around the edges of the cake to loosen the sides. Warm the bottom of the cake pan with a hot towel or over a gas burner, moving the pan constantly to heat the bottom evenly and loosen the cake. Invert onto a serving plate. Peel off the parchment paper.

Cut into thin slices and serve each slice with a dollop of whipped cream.

SERVES 12 TO 14

CHOCOLATE PUDDING CAKES

Each bite of these pudding cakes offers an intense hit of chocolate that's sumptuous and yet still warm and cozy. Instead of unmolding, serve them warm, right from the ramekins. It is easy to make a large batch of these. They can be prepared ahead and refrigerated for up to 2 days before baking.

Position a rack in the middle of the oven and preheat the oven to 325°F.

Butter ten 5- to 6-ounce ramekins (see page 25) and coat the insides with cocoa powder: The easiest and neatest way of coating them with the cocoa is to place about 1 tablespoon in one ramekin, rotating and tapping it until all sides are covered. Pour the excess into the next ramekin and repeat the process, adding additional cocoa as needed. Arrange on a baking sheet and set aside.

Place the chocolate in a medium bowl.

In a medium saucepan, bring the cream and butter to a simmer over medium heat. Turn off the heat, add the chocolate, and let sit for 1 minute to melt the chocolate. Whisk until the chocolate has melted completely and the mixture is smooth.

Position a fine-mesh strainer over a large measuring cup with a spout. In a large bowl, whisk together the sugar, cornstarch, and salt. Whisk in the eggs. While whisking, gradually add the chocolate mixture. Strain into the measuring cup and divide the batter evenly between the ramekins. (The ramekins can be covered and refrigerated for up to 2 days. Bring to room temperature before baking.)

Bake until the surface is puffed and cracked, about 30 minutes. Let cool for 15 minutes before serving.

Serve warm, topped with a dollop of whipped cream, if desired.

SERVES 10

INGREDIENTS

Unsalted butter for the ramekins

¼ to ⅓ cup unsweetened cocoa powder for coating the ramekins

7 ounces 99% unsweetened chocolate, finely chopped

2 cups heavy cream

8 tablespoons (4 ounces) unsalted butter, cut into 1-inch chunks

1⅓ cups granulated sugar

2 tablespoons cornstarch

½ teaspoon salt

4 large eggs

Whipped Cream (page 315; optional)

Chocolate Chocolate Cupcakes, page 54.

CHOCOLATE CHOCOLATE CUPCAKES

CONTRIBUTED BY STEPHANIE HERSH

Stephanie Hersh made cupcakes over and over while developing this recipe for our chocolate. Stephanie is known for making very elaborate cakes; here she has simplified the steps so even nonbakers will have no trouble. Ideal for a child's birthday party, these cupcakes will please both adults and children.

FROSTING

1 cup heavy cream

8 ounces 62% semisweet chocolate, coarsely chopped

CUPCAKES

1 cup all-purpose flour

½ cup unsweetened cocoa powder

10 tablespoons (5 ounces) unsalted butter, at room temperature

¾ cup granulated sugar

½ teaspoon baking soda

⅛ teaspoon baking powder

⅛ teaspoon salt

1 large egg

¾ cup whole milk

FOR THE FROSTING:

In a small saucepan, heat the cream over medium-low heat, until it just begins to simmer. Add the chocolate and whisk until the chocolate has melted completely and the mixture is smooth. Transfer to a small bowl and let cool for about 2 hours, or until the ganache has thickened enough to frost the cupcakes. If you'd like it to thicken faster, place the ganache in the refrigerator. The ganache will thicken around the edges first, so be sure to stir it every 5 minutes once it has begun to set. Remove it as soon as it has thickened or warm to room temperature and stir.

FOR THE CUPCAKES:

Position a rack in the middle of the oven and preheat the oven to 350°F. Line 12 muffin cups (¾-cup capacity) with paper liners.

Stir together the flour and cocoa powder in a small bowl, and set aside.

In the bowl of a stand mixer fitted with the paddle attachment, combine the butter, sugar, baking soda, baking powder, and salt and beat on medium speed for about 5 minutes, or until pale, light, and fluffy. Scrape down the sides and bottom of the bowl as necessary.

Add the egg and beat until incorporated. Add the flour mixture and milk alternately in two batches each, scraping down the the bowl as necessary. Continue mixing until the batter is uniform in color.

Fill the muffin cups about two-thirds full. Bake for 15 to 20 minutes, or until the cupcakes spring back slightly when pressed in the center.

Let cool for 10 minutes in the pan on a cooling rack, then remove and allow to cool completely on the rack.

Once the frosting has thickened, dip the top of each cupcake in it and then twist as you lift it out, or spread a small amount of frosting on top of each cupcake. If the frosting becomes too firm to spread, warm it slightly in a microwave or over a double boiler, stirring gently.

MAKES 12 CUPCAKES

LEGENDS & LORE

Why Is It Called Devil's Food?

By the end of the seventeenth century, chocolate houses had spread from France and England to the Netherlands. By coincidence, the group of Pilgrims that would later sail to Plymouth Rock took up residence next door to one of Amsterdam's biggest chocolate houses in 1690. The Pilgrims, who stoned people for adultery and basically repudiated anything that looked enjoyable, watched as the chocolate-house patrons cavorted next door. A few nights was all it took to convince the Pilgrims that chocolate was the devil's work. They promptly christened chocolate "Devil's food," and outlawed chocolate in Plymouth Colony. Years later, when a cake made of chocolate gained popularity in Amsterdam, the bakers took one look at the dark, obviously sinful cake, and named it Devil's Food. The name has stuck through centuries.

Baked Hot Chocolate, page 58.

BAKED HOT CHOCOLATE

CONTRIBUTED BY HEIDI FRIEDLANDER

Baked hot chocolate is almost like having three desserts in one—the top layer has just a hint of crispness, the center has the texture of a warm chocolate pudding, and the bottom layer is just a shade thicker than the thickest hot chocolate you can imagine. Heidi developed this recipe for Moxie, a popular Cleveland restaurant, where it remains a signature dish.

Baked in mugs or cups, these can be topped with whipped cream and served as you would traditional hot chocolate, preferably in front of a fire.

INGREDIENTS

9 ounces 62% semisweet chocolate, finely chopped

6 tablespoons (3 ounces) unsalted butter, cut into cubes

4 large eggs

¼ cup granulated sugar

Cocoa Whipped Cream (page 315)

Position a rack in the middle of the oven and preheat the oven to 350°F. Arrange four 1-cup ovenproof coffee cups or mugs or 8-ounce ramekins (see page 25) in a baking or roasting pan.

Place the chocolate and butter in the top of a double boiler set over gently simmering water, and whisk occasionally until the chocolate has melted and the mixture is smooth. Remove from the heat and set aside. Stir the eggs and sugar together in the bowl of a stand mixer then set over the simmering water and stir until warm to the touch.

Place the bowl on the stand mixer and, using the whisk attachment, beat for 3 to 5 minutes, until light and fluffy. Remove from the mixer, and fold the eggs into the chocolate mixture until it is light and smooth.

Spoon the batter into the cups. Add enough very hot water to the baking pan to come halfway up the sides of the cups. Bake for 15 to 20 minutes. The baked hot chocolates will be done when the tops lose their glossy finish. A wooden skewer inserted in the top will emerge clean, but batter toward the bottom of the cup will still be very moist.

Carefully remove the cups from the pan. The cakes can be served warm, at room temperature, or covered and refrigerated for up to 1 day. To reheat, bring to room temperature and place in a preheated 350°F oven for 5 minutes, or until warm.

Serve topped with a dollop of cocoa whipped cream.

SERVES 4

MOLTEN CAKES

CONTRIBUTED BY CRAIG STOLL

Craig Stoll, the chef-owner of San Francisco's popular Delfina restaurant, says he likes his chocolate "unencumbered." Craig says these cakes, which are baked daily at Delfina by pastry chef Michelle Polzine, "are all about the flavor of the chocolate. In the mid-1990s, every restaurant had a version of this recipe because it's the ultimate chocolate dessert—but this is still one of the most popular items on our menu. Honestly, if you have a great chocolate, I can't imagine a better way to use it."

It is best to bake these on the floor of the oven. If that is not possible, position a rack on the lowest level of the oven. Preheat the oven to 400°F. Generously butter or spray the sides of four 5- to 6-ounce ramekins or six 4-ounce ramekins (see page 25). Line the bottom of each ramekin with parchment and lightly butter or spray the parchment. Arrange the ramekins on a baking sheet.

Place the chocolate and butter in a large heatproof bowl and set it over a pot of gently simmering water. Stir occasionally until melted and smooth. Remove from the heat.

In the bowl of a stand mixer fitted with the whisk attachment, combine the eggs, yolks, sugar, and salt and beat on high speed for 4 to 5 minutes, or until the mixture is thick and pale. When the whisk is lifted and the batter is run back and forth over itself, it will hold a slowly dissolving ribbon.

With the mixer on low speed, sprinkle the flour over the batter, and mix until combined.

Fold the egg mixture one-third at a time into the chocolate mixture.

Fill the ramekins with batter to within ¼ inch of the top. (At this point, the ramekins can be covered with plastic wrap and refrigerated for up to 2 days. Bring to room temperature before baking.)

Bake for 8 to 10 minutes, until the sides of the cakes are firm. The centers will be soft to the touch but set.

Let stand for 1 minute, then unmold each cake onto a serving plate. Serve immediately, topped with custard sauce or ice cream.

SERVES 4

INGREDIENTS

Unsalted butter or nonstick cooking spray for the ramekins

6 ounces 70% bittersweet chocolate, coarsely chopped

8 tablespoons (4 ounces) unsalted butter, cut into 1-inch cubes

2 large eggs

2 large egg yolks

¼ cup granulated sugar

Pinch of salt

1½ tablespoons all-purpose flour

Custard Sauce (page 313) or ice cream

CHOCOLATE ORANGE FONDUE

CONTRIBUTED BY CAROLE BLOOM

In the seventies, fondue meant melted chocolate in a pot surrounded by pound cake, bananas, and strawberries. This contemporary version from teacher and cookbook author Carole Bloom is served in individual portions or family style accompanied by a variety of interesting dippers.

Place the cream and orange peel in a small saucepan and bring to a boil over medium-high heat. Remove from the heat, cover, and let stand for 30 minutes to infuse the cream with the flavor of the orange. Remove the orange peel.

Place the milk chocolate in a medium bowl.

Reheat the cream until simmering. Pour the cream over the chocolate and let stand for 30 seconds, then whisk gently until the mixture is very smooth. Whisk in the Grand Marnier.

SERVE WARM EITHER FAMILY-STYLE OR IN INDIVIDUAL PORTIONS, WITH A SELECTION OF DIPPING INGREDIENTS.

MAKES ABOUT 1 CUP; SERVES 3 TO 4

INGREDIENTS

½ cup heavy cream

3 strips orange peel

7 ounces 41% milk chocolate, very finely chopped

1 tablespoon Grand Marnier or other orange liqueur (optional)

FOR DIPPING

Honeycomb (page 308)

Mini Madeleines (page 243)

Marshmallows (page 307)

Orange segments

Fresh cherries, berries, figs, or other fruit, sliced or cut up for dipping

Chocolate and Olive Oil Fondue

CONTRIBUTED BY MARVIN MARTIN

TRUST MARVIN MARTIN, who's an olive oil producer as well as a chef, to come up with this simple but innovative fondue: drizzle three parts melted chocolate (either 62% semisweet or 70% bittersweet) with one part olive oil. For example, 6 ounces of chocolate and 2 ounces of olive oil make enough fondue for 2 to 4 people. Don't stint on the oil—a really fine, fruity olive oil is crucial here.

Melt the chocolate on the stove and transfer to a serving bowl or use a fondue pot. Set out small bowls of sea salt and platters of crusty bread, sliced or torn into chunks, orange and tangerine sections, fresh figs or strawberries. Just before serving, drizzle the olive oil over the chocolate.

Have guests dip the bread or fruit in the chocolate, sprinkle with a pinch of sea salt, and taste. Try this fondue with both Spanish and California olive oils to see which you prefer.

ORANGE CHOCOLATE GANACHE TART

CONTRIBUTED BY CAROLE BLOOM

Carole Bloom's ganache tart reminds us of the refined, sophisticated tarts we tasted in Vienna and in Paris. A sweet pastry shell holds a velvety ganache made from 70% bittersweet chocolate and orange zest. You can garnish the tart with either ground toasted hazelnuts or grated orange zest. Because this tart can be cut into very thin slices, it's a wonderful addition to a buffet table or a dessert platter.

PASTRY

1 large egg yolk

1 teaspoon pure vanilla extract

1 teaspoon finely grated orange zest

1⅓ cups all-purpose flour

½ cup confectioners' sugar

⅛ teaspoon salt

8 tablespoons (4 ounces) cold unsalted butter, cut into small pieces

GANACHE FILLING

12 ounces 72% bittersweet chocolate, very finely chopped

1¼ cups heavy cream

1 tablespoon finely grated orange zest

FOR GARNISH

2 tablespoons finely ground toasted hazelnuts or finely grated zest of 1 large orange

FOR THE PASTRY:

In a small bowl, lightly beat the yolk with the vanilla. Add the orange zest, and set aside.

Place the flour, sugar, and salt in the bowl of a food processor and pulse briefly to blend the ingredients. Add the butter and pulse for about 30 seconds, or until it is cut into tiny pieces. With the processor running, add the yolk mixture through the feed tube. Mix for about 1 minute, or until the dough forms a ball and wraps around the blade.

Transfer the dough to a board and shape into a 6-inch disk. Wrap in a double layer of plastic wrap and refrigerate until firm, about 3 hours. (The dough can be refrigerated for up to 4 days or frozen for up to 2 months. If frozen, defrost the dough overnight in the refrigerator.)

Roll the dough between two sheets of lightly floured parchment paper into a 13-inch circle. Flour the dough as necessary to keep it from sticking. Remove the top sheet of parchment paper and brush off any excess flour. Roll the dough up around the rolling pin and unroll it into a 9-inch fluted tart pan with a removable bottom. Gently lift the edges to ease the dough into the corners of the pan, then push down gently. Trim the dough to a 1-inch overhang. Fold the overhang over and press it against the sides of the pan to form a secure double layer. Place the tart pan on a baking sheet and refrigerate for 20 minutes.

Position a rack in the center of the oven and preheat the oven to 375°F.

Prick the bottom of the tart shell with a fork. Line the shell with aluminum foil or parchment paper and fill with pie weights or dry beans. Bake for 12 minutes.

Remove the parchment and weights, prick the bottom of the crust again, and bake for 12 to 14 minutes longer, or until golden. Remove the pan from the oven and cool completely on a rack.

FOR THE GANACHE:

Place the chocolate in a medium bowl and set a fine-mesh strainer over the bowl.

In a small saucepan, bring the cream to a boil over medium-high heat. Add the zest to the cream, turn off the heat, and cover the pan. Let steep for 15 minutes.

Remove the lid and bring the cream back to a boil over medium-high heat. Strain onto the chocolate. Let stand for 30 seconds, then use a whisk, rubber spatula, or immersion blender to blend the mixture until very smooth.

Pour the ganache into the tart shell and spread it evenly. Sprinkle the top with the hazelnuts or zest. Let stand at room temperature for 3 to 4 hours, or refrigerate for about 1 hour, or until the ganache is set. (The tart can be made ahead and stored at room temperature for up to 2 days.) Once the garnache is set, cover the top with a piece of parchment paper and wrap the entire tart tightly with aluminum foil.

To serve, remove the ring of the tart pan and cut the tart into thin slices.

SERVES 12

CHOCOLATE PECAN PIE

CONTRIBUTED BY STEPHANIE HERSH

Don't think of this as a pecan pie with a little chocolate, think of it as a sinfully rich chocolate pie studded with pecans. There's no need to prebake the piecrust but do use a traditional 9-inch pie plate for this recipe. This isn't a deep-dish pie.

CRUST

4 tablespoons (2 ounces) unsalted butter, at room temperature

3 ounces cream cheese, at room temperature

Pinch of salt

1 teaspoon ground cinnamon

2 tablespoons granulated sugar

½ cup all-purpose flour

FILLING

1½ cups lightly toasted pecans, coarsely chopped

4 ounces 70% bittersweet chocolate, finely chopped

2 tablespoons (1 ounce) unsalted butter

5 ounces 70% bittersweet chocolate, coarsely chopped

¼ cup firmly packed light brown sugar

1 cup light corn syrup

3 large eggs, lightly beaten

1 teaspoon pure vanilla extract

FOR THE CRUST:

In the bowl of a stand mixer fitted with the paddle attachment, cream together the butter and cream cheese until there are no lumps. Add the salt, cinnamon, and sugar and beat until the mixture is uniform in color. Add the flour and mix until just combined.

Turn the dough out and shape it into a 6-inch disk. Wrap in plastic wrap and refrigerate until thoroughly chilled, about 2 hours.

On a lightly floured board, roll out the dough to a 12-inch circle, flouring the dough and board as necessary to keep it from sticking. Roll the dough up around the rolling pin and unroll into a 9-inch pie plate. Gently lift the edges to ease the dough into the corners of the plate, then push down gently to ensure an even thickness throughout. Trim the edges and crimp as desired. Cover with plastic wrap and refrigerate for 1 hour.

Position a rack in the lowest level of the oven and preheat the oven to 350°F.

FOR THE FILLING:

Place the pie plate on a baking sheet. Sprinkle the pecans and the 4 ounces of chocolate evenly over the bottom of the piecrust.

In a medium saucepan, melt the butter and the 5 ounces of chocolate over low heat, stirring occasionally until smooth. Remove from the heat and stir in the brown sugar, corn syrup, eggs, and vanilla. Pour over the pecans and chocolate in the pie shell.

Bake for about 45 to 50 minutes, or until the crust is golden and the filling is set. Remove to a cooling rack to cool completely.

SERVES 8 TO 10

LEGENDS & LORE

Chocolate and Amorous Pursuits

Does chocolate enhance ardor? Throughout history, chocolate has been linked with the love lives of historical figures ranging from Montezuma to Casanova. In his autobiography, *The Memoirs of Jacques Casanova de Seingalt,* Casanova notes that chocolate fans the flame of desire. "Chocolate is my favorite breakfast dish," he states, "and all the more so when it was made by a friend." A careful reading of his memoirs shows that Casanova offers chocolate as a bribe more often than he uses it as an aphrodisiac; he is able to get past chaperones quite effectively by offering "a dozen pounds of capital chocolate: I had brought it with me from Genoa."

Is there any scientific proof that chocolate flames desire? No, science has not been able to definitively prove chocolate is an aphrodisiac, although it does appear that several compounds in chocolate stimulate the same portions of the brain stimulated by an infatuation. Does chocolate—like Champagne—seduce the senses through its complex flavors and silken texture, and set the scene for romance? Perhaps that's a question best answered on an individual basis.

CHOCOLATE MOUSSE

CONTRIBUTED BY DAVID LEBOVITZ

Few people are as passionate about chocolate as David Lebovitz. His recipes reflect both his years of experience in the pastry department at Chez Panisse and his great skill as a teacher—they're straightforward and produce impressive results. David says, "Forget light and ethereal. A real chocolate mousse should be thick and rich." Its richness comes not from uncooked eggs but from a silky custard base.

You can pour the mousse mixture into goblets, but David prefers to refrigerate it in a single large bowl. To serve, he scoops the mousse into individual glasses on top of a light layer of whipped cream.

INGREDIENTS

12 ounces 70% bittersweet chocolate, finely chopped

4 large egg yolks

1 cup whole milk

3 tablespoons granulated sugar

⅔ cup heavy cream

Whipped Cream (page 315)

Chocolate shavings, cacao nibs, or cocoa powder, for garnish (optional)

Place a medium bowl and a whisk in the refrigerator or freezer to chill.

Place the chocolate in a large bowl, and set a fine-mesh strainer over the bowl.

In a medium bowl, stir together the egg yolks.

In a medium saucepan, bring the milk and 2 tablespoons of the sugar to a simmer, stirring until the sugar has dissolved. Slowly pour the milk into the egg yolks, stirring constantly with a heatproof rubber spatula or wooden spoon. Pour the mixture back into the saucepan and cook, stirring constantly, over medium heat for 6 to 10 minutes, or until it is thick enough to coat the back of a wooden spoon. Remove from the heat and strain the custard onto the chocolate. Stir gently until the chocolate has melted completely. Let cool to room temperature.

In the chilled bowl with the chilled whisk, whip the cream until it holds soft peaks. Whip in the remaining 1 tablespoon sugar and whip just until the cream holds a shape. Do not over-whip, or the mousse may be grainy.

Fold the whipped cream into the chocolate mixture. Cover with plastic wrap and refrigerate for 4 hours, or until set.

To serve, place a dollop of whipped cream in the bottom of each goblet or bowl. Dip an ice cream scoop in hot water, dry it, and scoop the mousse onto the cream. Garnish with a sprinkling of shaved chocolate, cacao nibs, or cocoa powder.

SERVES 6

DARK CHOCOLATE ICE CREAM

For lovers of chocolate ice cream, this is the final word. This dark chocolate ice cream is deeper and richer than any ice cream you can buy. What's especially intriguing is the hint of dark caramel flavor you'll taste beneath the chocolate.

Serve unadorned, or top with Dulce de Leche (page 312), Candied Almonds (page 314), and Whipped Cream (page 315).

Place the chocolate in a large bowl. Set a fine-mesh strainer over the bowl, and set aside.

In a medium bowl, whisk the yolks and ¾ cup of the sugar until slightly paler in color. Add the cocoa and whisk until a paste forms.

In a medium saucepan, bring the milk to a boil over medium heat. Whisking constantly, slowly pour the milk into the cocoa mixture, and whisk until smooth. Return the mixture to the saucepan and cook over medium heat, stirring constantly with a wooden spoon, until the mixture is thick enough to coat the back of the spoon, about 3 minutes.

Strain the hot mixture onto the chocolate. Stir until the chocolate is completely melted.

Place the remaining 2 tablespoons sugar and the water in a small saucepan and bring to a boil over high heat, stirring to dissolve the sugar. Continue to cook, without stirring, until the caramel is dark brown, swirling the pan occasionally so the caramel colors evenly. If sugar crystals form on the sides of the pan, brush with a wet pastry brush. Test the color of the caramel by drizzling a few drops onto a white plate. When the color is medium to dark amber, remove the pan from the heat. Immediately pour the caramel into the chocolate mixture, whisking constantly. If any of the caramel solidifies into small chunks, strain the mixture.

Let cool, cover with plastic wrap, and refrigerate for at least several hours, or overnight.

Place the ice cream base in an ice cream maker and freeze following the manufacturer's instructions. Because the mixture is so thick to begin with, it may take less time than most ice cream to freeze to the desired consistency. For a firmer texture, transfer to a covered container and freeze for at least 2 hours before serving.

MAKES ABOUT 2 CUPS; SERVES 4

INGREDIENTS

3½ ounces 62% semisweet chocolate, finely chopped

4 large egg yolks

¾ cup plus 2 tablespoons granulated sugar

¼ cup plus 3 tablespoons unsweetened cocoa powder

2 cups whole milk

2 teaspoons water

Ice Cream Shooters

HOMEMADE CHOCOLATE ICE CREAM AND YOUR FAVORITE LIQUEUR whipped up in a blender, these sophisticated smoothies make a dinner party a little more fun. Blend them in batches using the liqueur each guest prefers—Kahlúa, Bailey's Irish Cream, Frangelico, or any liqueur you like. We think this tastes best with our Dark Chocolate Ice Cream (page 71) but you can use store-bought ice cream too. If you like, float a layer of liqueur or heavy cream on top of each smoothie. (See page 101 for tips.) For a completely different smoothie, try using vanilla ice cream with our Chocolate Liqueur (page 101).

Combine 1 cup of ice cream with 1/4 cup liqueur in a blender. Blend until smooth, pour into shot glasses, and serve immediately.

MAKES 10 TO 12 SHOOTERS

CHOCOLATE SORBET

This recipe is simple but the chocolate flavor of the sorbet is deep, clear, and addictive. Wonderfully smooth as well as low in fat, this recipe is ideal for those avoiding dairy products. You won't miss the cream at all.

Serve alone or with fresh or Macerated Berries (page 314), TKO cookie crumbs (see page 174), and Whipped Cream (page 315).

For a refreshing drink, scoop the sorbet into a tall glass and top with sparkling water.

In a medium saucepan, combine the cocoa powder and sugar with a whisk. Whisk in 1 cup of the water until any large lumps of cocoa are broken up but there are still some dry streaks, then whisk in the remaining 3 cups water 1 cup at a time until all of the dry ingredients are dissolved. Make sure to scrape the sides and bottom of the pan.

Place the pan over medium heat and whisk occasionally until the mixture just begins to simmer. Remove from the heat and add the vanilla. Pour into a bowl and refrigerate for at least 3 hours, or overnight.

Place the sorbet base in an ice cream maker and freeze following the manufacturer's instructions; stop the machine from time to time and scrape the sides of the freezer bowl to ensure an even consistency. Store tightly in a covered container in the freezer.

MAKES ABOUT 1 QUART

INGREDIENTS

2 cups unsweetened cocoa powder

1¾ cups granulated sugar

4 cups water

1 teaspoon pure vanilla extract

Cocoa Ice Bars

These are just like the treats you used to buy from the ice cream vendor's truck, but with a darker cocoa flavor. Finding molds in the traditional shape is the hardest part about making these frozen confections. Look in cookware stores such as Sur La Table for decorative molds such as the Donvier molds we used here (or order them online at www.donvier.com). This recipe will make 6 bars in molds with a ½-cup capacity and 9 bars in molds with a ⅓-cup capacity.

In a medium saucepan, whisk together the cocoa powder, sugar, and about ½ cup of the milk to make a smooth paste. Whisk in the remaining milk and water, ½ cup at a time.

Place the saucepan over medium heat and and stir with a heatproof spatula or wooden spoon just until the cocoa powder and sugar have dissolved. Do not overheat or the mixture could lose flavor.

The sugar should be dissolved and steam will be rising from the surface. Pour into a pitcher or a large measuring cup with a spout. Cool to room temperature, then refrigerate until cold.

The cocoa will have settled on the bottom of the container. Stir to recombine the mixture, and pour into the molds. Add the sticks and cover according to the directions provided with the molds. Freeze for at least a few hours, until solid.

If you want to unmold the ice bars and serve them from a bowl, chill the bowl beforehand in the freezer.

MAKES 6 TO 9 BARS

INGREDIENTS

¾ cup plus 2 tablespoons unsweetened cocoa powder

⅔ cup granulated sugar

1⅓ cups whole milk

1⅓ cups water

LEGENDS & LORE

Brownies Appear

Brownies are an American creation, but they've changed quite a bit in the past century. When Fannie Farmer made brownies in 1896 in fluted marguerite molds, molasses accounted for much of the flavor and color of the cookie-like treats. Named after the "Brownies" or tiny elfin characters of Palmer Cox's popular cartoons and poems, chocolate brownies appeared in the 1897 Sears, Roebuck & Co. catalog—but those brownies more closely resembled candy than the brownies we know.

By the 1920s, the dense chocolaty squares would become popular across the United States. Blondies, brownies made with butterscotch, appeared in the 1950s, and since then we've seen every sort of brownie—mint, caramel, and brownies with fruit and every variety of nut. Still, for most of us, the straightforward classic brownie remains a sentimental favorite.

FUDGY BROWNIES

Robert developed this recipe, but when the brownies came out of our test kitchen oven, they didn't have their usual glossy, crackled top and fudgy texture. The cookbook crew asked Robert to make the brownies while they watched. We realized that an electric mixer doesn't work for this recipe. The batter must be beaten by hand until it pulls from the sides of the bowl. This sounds like a task but it's not; there's something homey and satisfying about stirring this thick, glossy batter yourself.

Position a rack in the lower third of the oven and preheat the oven to 325°F. Cut an 8 by 16-inch piece of parchment paper. Lightly butter an 8 by 8 by 2-inch pan and line it with the parchment, allowing it to extend evenly over the opposite sides. Butter the parchment including the paper on the sides of the pan.

Place the chocolate and butter in a large heatproof bowl set over a pot of gently simmering water and stir occasionally until melted and smooth. Remove from the heat.

With a large rubber spatula or wooden spoon, beat the sugar and salt into the chocolate mixture. Beat in the eggs one at a time. Add the flour and mix vigorously until the batter is very glossy and pulls away from the sides of the bowl.

Break the nuts into large pieces over the batter and fold them in.

Pour the batter into the prepared pan and tap the pan bottom on the countertop to level the batter. Bake for 30 to 35 minutes, or until a skewer inserted in the center comes out moist but clean.

Let cool in the pan on a cooling rack for 10 minutes. Remove the brownies from the pan using the parchment "handles," and cool completely on the rack before cutting into 2-inch squares.

MAKES SIXTEEN 2-INCH BROWNIES

INGREDIENTS

6 tablespoons (3 ounces) unsalted butter, cut into cubes, plus more for the pan

8 ounces 70% bittersweet chocolate, coarsely chopped

¾ cup plus 2 tablespoons granulated sugar

¼ teaspoon salt

2 large eggs

⅓ cup all-purpose flour

½ cup toasted walnut halves

CAKEY BROWNIES

CONTRIBUTED BY JIM DODGE

People have strong opinions about which is better: fudgy or cakey brownies. For fudgy, see Robert's recipe just before this one. This recipe produces intensely chocolate brownies that have both a cakey texture and a creamy quality, thanks to a special meringue technique developed by Jim Dodge. If you like, add coarsely chopped nuts or chunks of chocolate just before baking.

INGREDIENTS

8 tablespoons (4 ounces) unsalted butter, plus more for the pan

⅓ cup cake flour

⅓ cup unsweetened cocoa powder

1 teaspoon baking powder

4 ounces 70% bittersweet chocolate, finely chopped

1 cup granulated sugar

4 large eggs, separated

½ cup coarsely chopped nuts or chocolate (optional)

Position a rack on the lowest level of the oven and preheat the oven to 325°F. Lightly butter a 9 by 9 by 2-inch baking pan.

Sift together the flour, cocoa, and baking powder. Set aside.

Melt the butter in a small heavy saucepan over medium heat. Remove from the heat and add the chocolate. Let stand, stirring occasionally, until the chocolate is melted and evenly blended with the butter.

Add ½ cup of the sugar and stir until it is dissolved. Stir in the yolks. Pour the mixture into a medium bowl and add the dry mixture, stirring just until incorporated.

In the bowl of a stand mixer fitted with the whisk attachment, whip the whites at high speed until a loose froth with large bubbles forms. While continuing to whip, gradually add the remaining ½ cup sugar in a slow, steady stream. If sugar builds up on the sides of the bowl, stop the mixer and quickly scrape the sugar into the whites. Continue whipping until the whites form firm peaks.

Remove the bowl from the mixer and, using a rubber spatula, fold in the chocolate mixture. Fold in the chopped nuts or chocolate, if using. Scrape into the prepared pan and smooth the top with a few strokes of the spatula. Don't spend a lot of time trying to make the top perfectly even, because that could overwork and deflate the batter.

Bake for 30 to 35 minutes, or until a skewer inserted in the center comes out clean. Transfer to a cooling rack and let cool completely before cutting.

MAKES EIGHTEEN 1½ BY 3-INCH BROWNIES

CHOCOLATE DROP COOKIES

Robert is not really a cookie eater, but when he was put in charge of developing recipes for our 99% chocolate, he began experimenting. He found that using less sugar in the dough actually made the cookies more flavorful. When people taste this cookie, they say, "This is a cookie for adults," but children really like them as well.

Don't cut short the beating time or the cookies' texture will be affected. The batter will be thick and fluffy after about 10 minutes.

It's easy to overbake these cookies. Keep a sharp eye on them and take them from the oven as soon as they lose their glossy finish and begin to show cracks along the tops.

Position the racks in the lower and upper thirds of the oven and preheat the oven to 350°F. Line two baking sheets with Silpats or parchment paper.

Stir together the flour and baking powder in a small bowl, and set aside.

Place the chocolate and butter in the top of a double boiler set over gently simmering water and stir occasionally until the chocolate has melted and the mixture is smooth. Remove from the heat.

In the bowl of a stand mixer fitted with the paddle attachment, combine the eggs, sugar, salt, coffee, and vanilla and beat on medium speed for 10 to 12 minutes, or until the batter is thick and fluffy. Reduce the speed to low, add the chocolate mixture, and mix for 2 to 3 minutes, or until incorporated, scraping the sides of the bowl as necessary. Remove the bowl from the mixer and fold in the dry ingredients, and then the nuts, if desired.

Drop the dough by heaping tablespoons onto the prepared pans, 12 per sheet. Bake for 10 to 12 minutes, rotating the pans halfway through. When the cookies are done, they will begin to crack on top; do not overbake. Transfer to a cooling rack to cool completely.

The cookies can be stored in an airtight container at room temperature for 2 days or frozen for up to a month.

MAKES 2 DOZEN COOKIES

INGREDIENTS

⅓ cup all-purpose flour

¼ teaspoon baking powder

6 ounces 99% unsweetened chocolate, coarsely chopped

4 tablespoons (2 ounces) unsalted butter

2 large eggs, at room temperature

1⅓ cups granulated sugar

¼ teaspoon salt

1½ teaspoons finely ground coffee beans

1 teaspoon pure vanilla extract

½ cup coarsely chopped toasted walnuts or pecans (optional)

CHOCOLATE CRINKLE COOKIES

Deep chocolate crinkles are the original black-and-white cookie. They go into the oven as unimpressive balls rolled in confectioners' sugar and emerge with an appealing contrast between the fissures of dark chocolate and the sugar.

The crinkles can be soft and chewy or crisp, depending on how long you bake them. The dough freezes well, so you can roll it into balls (don't dip them in sugar), place on a baking sheet, and freeze until firm, then store in an airtight container or plastic freezer bag. To bake, remove as many balls as you need from the freezer and let thaw for 30 minutes, then roll in the sugar and bake.

Combine the flour, baking powder, and salt. Set aside.

In the bowl of a stand mixer fitted with the paddle attachment, combine the oil, chocolate, and granulated sugar and blend on medium speed. With the mixer running, add the eggs one at a time, followed by the vanilla, scraping the sides of the bowl as necessary. There may be some small clumps of sugar in the batter at this point. Add the dry ingredients and mix on low speed, stopping once to scrape down the sides. Mix until just incorporated, 2 to 3 minutes. The dough will be sticky.

Gather the dough into a disk, wrap in plastic wrap, and chill for at least 2 hours or overnight.

Position the racks in the lower and upper thirds of the oven and preheat the oven to 350°F. Line two baking sheets with Silpats or parchment paper.

Pour the confectioners' sugar onto a plate or into a shallow bowl. Roll the dough into 1-inch balls, drop onto the sugar, and roll each ball so that all sides are covered. Place 2 inches apart on the prepared sheets.

Bake for 10 minutes for soft, chewy cookies, or 12 minutes for crisp cookies, rotating the pans halfway through baking. The cookies are done when the edges are set (but the tops still have a little give to them). Let cool completely on cooling racks.

The cookies can be stored in an airtight container for 3 to 4 days.

MAKES 5 DOZEN COOKIES

INGREDIENTS

2 cups sifted all-purpose flour

2 teaspoons baking powder

½ teaspoon salt

¼ cup canola oil

4 ounces 99% unsweetened chocolate, melted

2 cups granulated sugar

4 large eggs

2 teaspoons pure vanilla extract

1 cup confectioners' sugar

CHOCOLATE SHORTBREAD WITH CACAO NIBS AND SEA SALT

CONTRIBUTED BY ELIZABETH FALKNER

If you like salt with your chocolate, this will be your favorite cookie, hands down. While other shortbread may have a hint of salt, these are salty with a hint of sweetness. Nibs and sea salt are an ideal combination—the nibs add crunch and the sea salt brings out the deep cocoa flavor. Only Elizabeth Falkner could come up with a cookie this hedonistic.

Try a variety of salts with this shortbread. Choose finer salt crystals for a more subtle approach, or coarse sea salt if you want a shock of salt. You can also garnish the top of each baked cookie with a few grains of salt or set out small bowls of different salts and let your guests choose their favorite.

INGREDIENTS

1 cup all-purpose flour

¾ cup unsweetened cocoa powder

¼ cup plus 2 tablespoons cacao nibs, crushed with a rolling pin

1 teaspoon fine or coarse sea salt

12 tablespoons (6 ounces) unsalted butter, at room temperature

½ cup granulated sugar

1 teaspoon pure vanilla extract

Position the racks in the lower and upper thirds of the oven and preheat the oven to 325°F. Line two baking sheets with Silpats or parchment paper.

Combine the flour and cocoa powder in a small bowl. Combine the nibs and sea salt in another small bowl.

In the bowl of a stand mixer fitted with the paddle attachment, cream the butter and sugar on medium speed for about 5 minutes, or until light and fluffy, stopping as necessary to scrape the sides and bottom of the bowl. Mix in the vanilla. Add about half of the flour mixture and mix on low speed. Add the remaining flour-cocoa mixture, stopping as necessary to scrape the bowl. Once incorporated, mix on medium speed for 1 to 2 minutes. Mix in the nibs and salt. (The dough can be refrigerated, well wrapped, for up to 1 week or frozen for up to 2 months.)

On a lightly floured board, or between two pieces of parchment paper, roll the dough into a square ¼ inch thick. Cut into 1 by 2½-inch rectangles or other desired shape, by hand or with a cookie cutter, and place on the prepared pans about 1 inch apart.

Bake for 15 minutes, rotating the pans once halfway through baking. It is sometimes difficult to know when chocolate cookies are done. One of the best indications is the scent of baked cookies in the air. And when these shortbread cookies are gently nudged, they shouldn't feel soft but the bottoms should seem crisp.

REMOVE THE PANS FROM THE OVEN AND TRANSFER THE SHORTBREAD TO A COOLING RACK TO COOL COMPLETELY.

The cookies can be stored in an airtight container for up to 1 week.

MAKES ABOUT 3 DOZEN 1 BY 2½-INCH SHORTBREAD

Chocolate-Dipped Potato Chips and Pretzels

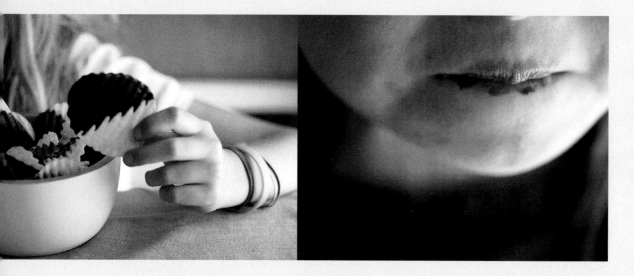

CHIPS AND PRETZELS DIPPED IN CHOCOLATE have a yin and yang sort of appeal. The crisp saltiness sets off chocolate's rich, dark flavor very well. Use gourmet chips and hand-rolled pretzels for a distinctive treat or use your standard grocery-store variety of chips and pretzels.

Simply choose your favorite chocolate and melt it (see page 22 for methods). You can either use the chocolate as a dip, eating as you go, or submerge the chips and pretzels either halfway or completely into the chocolate and then place them on a Silpat or a sheet of parchment paper until the chocolate has set.

ROBERT'S TRUFFLES

      This truffle recipe uses a coating of untempered chocolate, an optional coating of cacao nibs, and a dusting of cocoa powder. But if you temper the chocolate for the coating, the truffles may be either left plain or rolled in nibs, then coated with two layers of the tempered chocolate. I think it's worth the extra effort to temper, because tempered truffles don't need to be refrigerated and they remain beautifully glossy.

      One final note: Don't be in a hurry to melt the chocolate. Slower is always better where chocolate is concerned.

Place the chopped chocolates in the top of a double boiler set over gently simmering water. Let the chocolate melt three-quarters of the way, then remove from the heat and stir until smooth. Return the pan to the bottom of the double boiler, off the heat, to keep warm.

Meanwhile, heat the cream in a small saucepan to between 115° and 120°F. The goal is to have the chocolate and cream at the same temperature.

Slowly drizzle the melted chocolate into the cream, stirring with a heatproof spatula to blend and emulsify (this emulsification is called a ganache). Stir gently, and do not overmix.

Pour the ganache onto a baking sheet and spread into a layer about ¼ inch thick. Once it has reached room temperature, cover with plastic wrap and let it stand overnight at room temperature to solidify.

Scoop up a teaspoon of ganache on a spoon or with a melon baller and shape the chocolate gently into a ball. Place on a sheet of parchment paper. Do not roll the truffles in the palms of your hand at this point; it will compress them too much and make them hard. They don't need to be regular in size or shape. Scrape up any remaining bits of ganache with a pastry scraper and form into truffles.

Place the cacao nibs, if using, in a small bowl and the cocoa powder in another. Place about a teaspoon of melted chocolate in the palm of one hand, and roll a truffle between your palms to coat it lightly with chocolate. (Rolling the truffles between your hands at this point will create a very thin layer of chocolate that will prevent the cocoa from soaking into the truffle.) You can roll the truffle in the cacao nibs, and then coat in the cocoa powder or just roll the coated truffles in the cocoa powder.

The truffles can be kept in an airtight container at room temperature for 2 days or refrigerated for up to 2 weeks. Allow the truffles to come to room temperature before serving.

MAKES ABOUT 3 DOZEN TRUFFLES

INGREDIENTS

3 ounces 62% semisweet chocolate, chopped

3 ounces 70% bittersweet chocolate, chopped

½ cup heavy cream, preferably not ultra-pasteurized

⅓ cup chopped cacao nibs (optional)

¼ cup cocoa powder

5 ounces 70% chocolate, melted

. . . .

Tempering Chocolate

To be sure chocolate solidifies properly—that is, with a glossy sheen and good "snap" when broken—it must be tempered. Chocolate is tempered as a step in chocolate making but may fall out of temper due to improper storage, heat, or humidity.

What Happens During Tempering?

When chocolate's temperature is raised to above 92° or 93°F and then lowered, the triglyceride molecules in the cocoa butter bond together to form crystals. Imagine the crystals as stacking chairs. In the right formation, these crystals form a stable, tightly linked unit. But if chocolate melts and then hardens without tempering, the crystals aren't neatly stacked but instead tossed together every which way, which means you don't have the same stability—and you don't have the same beautiful glossiness, snap, and smoothness you find in tempered chocolate.

Even professional pastry chefs can approach tempering with trepidation. But if you keep in mind that tempering is just a matter of time, temperature, and stirring, you won't feel intimidated. Here are several methods you can follow, based on how much chocolate you'd like to temper.

Methods

Whichever method you use, work slowly and do not rush the process.

THE BASIC METHOD OF TEMPERING

Place the chopped chocolate in the top of a double boiler set over simmering water. When the chocolate is three-quarters melted, remove the bowl from the water and stir slowly but constantly. Stirring will distribute the still-tempered crystals throughout the chocolate and cause the other crystals to temper. The melted chocolate will be at around 95° to 96°F. Because the melting point of chocolate is actually below body temperature, it will feel slightly cool to the touch. When it is lifted on a spatula and drizzled onto itself, tempered chocolate will form ribbons on the surface of the chocolate. You can also test by dipping a knife blade in the chocolate and setting it on a plate to cool for about 5 minutes. When the chocolate on the knife is set, it shouldn't have any streaks.

If the process of tempering goes too far, the chocolate may start to solidify in the bowl. Return it to the double boiler and stir briefly over warm water just long enough to remelt it. A workable temperature for tempered chocolate is 89° to 91°F.

THE SEEDING METHOD OF TEMPERING

You can temper a large quantity of chocolate easily by adding solid chocolate to already melted chocolate.

Put aside one-quarter to one-third of the chocolate you are going to temper, leaving it in a solid block. Chop the rest of the chocolate. Place the chopped chocolate in the top of a double boiler set over simmering water. Stir the chocolate slowly but constantly. Use an instant-read thermometer to gauge the temperature, and as soon as the temperature reaches 95° to 100°F, remove from the heat, add the solid chocolate you set aside, and stir slowly until the entire mass is melted.

. . . .

SCOTCH TRUFFLE HEARTS

CONTRIBUTED BY ALICE MEDRICH

Since we began Scharffen Berger Chocolate Maker, Cocolat founder Alice Medrich has been a constant help, ready to lend a hand with everything from bean tasting to recipe testing. We're especially honored to have Alice's chocolate recipes in our book because both of us are fans of her chocolate confections, which she first began selling in Berkeley in the 1970s.

These chocolates have a thin dark shell around a decadently soft center underscored with the warmth and fragrance of a single-malt Scotch. Alice recommends that you mix this ganache gently with a spatula rather than vigorously with a whisk. Because the chocolate coating is not tempered, the hearts must be stored in the refrigerator to keep them from discoloring or blooming. Enjoy them cold, right from the refrigerator, or let them sit at room temperature for a half an hour or so, to bring up the flavors of the chocolate and the Scotch.

INGREDIENTS

7 ounces 62% semisweet chocolate, finely chopped

1 cup heavy cream

2 tablespoons single-malt Scotch

12 ounces 82% extra dark chocolate, finely chopped

2 tablespoons unsweetened cocoa powder (optional)

Line an 8 by 8 by 2-inch baking pan with aluminum foil, overlapping the top slightly, and set out a fine-mesh strainer.

Place the 62% chocolate in a medium bowl, and set aside.

In a small saucepan, bring the cream to a boil. Pour the cream over the chocolate, and stir gently with a heatproof spatula until the chocolate is completely melted and the mixture is smooth. Do not whisk or splash the mixture by stirring too briskly, or the texture of the chocolates will be cakey and granular. Add the Scotch and stir just to incorporate.

Strain the ganache into the prepared pan. Tilt the pan to level the ganache. Cover with plastic wrap and freeze for at least 4 hours or overnight.

Transfer the pan of ganache to the refrigerator to soften for 20 minutes. Choose a baking sheet or dish that will fit in your freezer and line it with parchment paper.

Place a sheet of foil about 12 inches long on your work surface. Remove the ganache, using the foil that you used to line the pan to help lift it. Invert it onto the clean sheet of foil. Peel the foil from the bottom.

Using a 1½-inch heart-shaped cutter, cut out hearts as close together as possible to avoid excessive amounts of scraps, and transfer to the prepared pan. If the ganache becomes too soft to work with, cover with plastic wrap and return to the freezer to harden. The scraps can be gently pushed together, spread to an even thickness, and used for more hearts, but they may need to harden first in the freezer.

Once all of the hearts are cut, cover with plastic wrap and freeze until very hard, at least 4 hours or overnight. (At this point, the hearts can be placed in an airtight container and frozen for up to 2 months.)

TO COAT THE HEARTS:

Choose a baking sheet or pan that will fit in your refrigerator and line with parchment paper.

Melt the 82% chocolate (see page 22) and stir until smooth. Cool to 100° to 105°F.

Put the bowl of melted chocolate next to the prepared baking pan.

Remove the hearts from the freezer one small batch at a time. Place a heart in the center of the bowl of chocolate and, using a dipping fork or table fork, flip it over and push it under the surface of the chocolate to coat completely. Slip the fork under the center and lift the heart out of the chocolate, tap the fork on the side of the bowl so any excess chocolate drips back into the bowl, and then wipe the bottom of the fork on the edge of the bowl and set the heart on the prepared pan. Repeat with the remaining hearts.

Use a small fine-mesh strainer or shaker to dust the hearts with the cocoa. Refrigerate for 1 hour, or until the chocolate has hardened.

The hearts can be stored in an airtight container in the refrigerator for up to 2 weeks or in the freezer for up to 3 months.

MAKES 30 TO 36 HEARTS

....

Chocolate with Scotch

A curious, almost magical thing occurs when dark chocolate is tasted with an aged Scotch (and you can try this with bourbon too). New, intense flavors emerge that seem to improve the taste of both the whiskey and the chocolate. To try this, choose a well-aged single-malt Scotch, avoiding brands with strong, smoky flavors.

Take a bite of the chocolate and wait until the final flavor note has peaked in your mouth. Then sip the Scotch. You'll notice a burst of flavor. The chemical components responsible for this phenomenon are a matter of speculation because chocolate (and probably Scotch as well) has more than four hundred flavor components. The chemical compounds in chocolate—which fall into the general classes of alcohols, aldehydes, acids, and esters—are directly related to the complexity of a chocolate's flavor. Most likely, similar compounds in Scotch have an additive or possibly synergistic effect. Vanilla, an ingredient of fine chocolate, is also a flavor Scotch acquires as a result of aging in oak barrels. The caramel notes that are common in Scotch can also appear in chocolate because of the way the beans are roasted or the effect of heating ground cacao beans during conching.

Until recently, the remarkable flavors that arise from this unlikely pairing have been a secret shared by a relatively small group of people. Try this with a variety of chocolates—all of which should be mellow and low in astringency—and your favorite single-malt Scotch.

....

FUDGE

This rich, creamy fudge has a thin layer of dark chocolate in the center. Developed by our own Norm Shea, Scharffen Berger's marketing coordinator, the recipe calls for homemade marshmallow cream. Because layering the dark chocolate requires a few well-timed steps, have all of the ingredients ready and read the entire recipe before starting.

Cut a 9 by 21-inch piece of parchment paper, and use it to line a 9 by 13 by 2-inch baking pan, allowing the paper to extend evenly over the two short ends of the pan.

MARSHMALLOW CREAM

¼ cup plus 2 tablespoons cold water

One ¼-ounce envelope gelatin

¾ cup granulated sugar

¼ cup light corn syrup

⅛ teaspoon salt

1½ teaspoons pure vanilla extract

One 12-ounce can evaporated milk

4½ cups granulated sugar

2 tablespoons (1 ounce) unsalted butter

⅛ teaspoon salt

1¼ pounds 70% bittersweet chocolate, finely chopped

4 ounces 99% unsweetened chocolate, finely chopped

1 tablespoon pure vanilla extract

8 ounces 82% extra dark chocolate, coarsely chopped

FOR THE MARSHMALLOW CREAM:

In the bowl of a stand mixer, combine 2 tablespoons of the cold water and the gelatin. With a small rubber spatula or wooden spoon, stir gently to combine. Set aside.

In a small heavy-bottomed pot combine the sugar, corn syrup, the remaining ¼ cup water, and the salt. Clip a candy thermometer to the side of the pot. Stir to dissolve the sugar and bring the mixture to a boil over medium to medium-high heat, washing down the sides of the pot as necessary with a brush dipped in water to remove sugar crystals. Continue to cook until the syrup reaches 236°F.

Meanwhile, fill a medium bowl with ice water. Remove the syrup from the heat and dip the bottom of the pan in the ice water for about 5 seconds to stop the cooking and allow the syrup temperature to drop to 210°F.

Pour the syrup into the gelatin and stir to combine. Place on the mixer and, using the whisk attachment, whip at medium-high to high speed for 5 to 7 minutes, or until thick and fluffy.

In a large heavy saucepan, combine the evaporated milk, sugar, butter, and salt.

Once the marshmallow cream has thickened, add the 1½ teaspoons vanilla extract and whip for an additional 30 seconds. Stir in the 70% and 99% chocolate. The marshmallow cream may begin to set slightly while sitting.

Place the saucepan with the butter mixture over medium-high heat and bring to a boil, stirring occasionally. Once it boils, stir constantly, and continue to boil for 5 minutes. Pour the mixture over the marshmallow cream. (The mixture and the mixing bowl will be very hot.) Turn the mixer to low and whip until the butter is incorporated. Increase the speed to medium and beat until thoroughly combined. Add the vanilla. Beat for 30 seconds to 1 minute.

Pour half of the fudge into the prepared pan. Sprinkle it evenly with the 82% chocolate. Top with the remaining fudge. Let the fudge stand overnight at room temperature, uncovered, to set up. Lift it out with the "handles," and cut six 1½-inch wide strips lengthwise and then cut thirteen 1-inch strips across.

MAKES SEVENTY-EIGHT 1½-INCH PIECES

FACTORY STORE HOT CHOCOLATE

We make this hot chocolate daily, fill a tall dispenser with it, and set it on a counter in our factory store so people waiting for a tour can pour themselves a sample. It's hard to believe how often we have to refill the container. This is very simple drinking chocolate, but it's so good there's no need for whipped cream or even a marshmallow.

In a small saucepan, whisk together the cocoa powder and sugar. Whisk in the milk and heat over low to medium-low heat, stirring until the sugar dissolves. Increase the heat to medium and continue to stir for another 3 to 5 minutes, or just until steam begins to rise from the top. Do not boil.

SERVES 2

INGREDIENTS

¼ cup plus 3 tablespoons unsweetened cocoa powder

1 tablespoon plus ½ teaspoon granulated sugar

2 cups whole milk

CHOCOLATE LIQUEUR

We've always liked the idea of crème de cacao, but the bottled liqueurs available in the United States don't have the pure taste we like. Making this liqueur yourself allows it to really absorb the flavor of chocolate.

We like to serve this in shot glasses topped with cream and sprinkled with a few cacao nibs. Substitute this for standard chocolate liqueurs in your favorite drink recipes and try it in our Chocolate Martini (page 103).

In a medium bowl, combine the cocoa powder and boiling water, stirring to dissolve the cocoa. Set aside.

In a small saucepan, combine the sugar and water and bring to a simmer over medium heat, stirring until the sugar has dissolved. Stir the sugar syrup into the cocoa mixture and add the vodka. Strain through a fine-mesh strainer into a container with a lid.

Refrigerate overnight. The liqueur will keep for several weeks, but the flavor of the vodka will weaken as time goes on.

To serve, stir the liqueur well, then strain it again through a fine-mesh strainer. Fill each shot glass two-thirds full with liqueur. Top with whipped cream or "float" unwhipped heavy cream on the liqueur. Hold a spoon over the glass, just above the liqueur with the bowl of the spoon facing down. The spoon will diffuse the cream. Slowly pour until a ⅛- to ¼-inch layer of cream rests on top of the liqueur. Sprinkle with 3 to 4 nibs.

MAKES 3 CUPS

INGREDIENTS

¼ cup unsweetened cocoa powder

1 cup boiling water

1 cup granulated sugar

1 cup water

1 cup vodka

Heavy cream for topping

Cacao nibs for garnish

CHOCOLATE MARTINI

A traditional martini is made with gin and vermouth. So as not to overwhelm the flavor of the chocolate, we make this martini with vodka. For a very dry martini, swirl the glass with dry vermouth and empty it before pouring in the liqueur and the vodka.

A rim of ground dark chocolate makes this drink look especially enticing. To get this consistency, grind chunks of chocolate in a coffee or spice grinder.

Pour ¼ inch of vermouth, vodka, or water into a rimmed saucer. Place ¼ inch of the ground chocolate on a second saucer slightly larger than the rim of the glass.

Swirl each glass with a splash of vermouth, and pour it out. To create the chocolate rim, dip the rim of the glass in the vermouth, vodka, or water, then in the ground chocolate.

For each drink, pour 2 parts chocolate liqueur to 1 part vodka into a shaker with ice. Shake and pour into the glass.

INGREDIENTS

Dry vermouth

Vodka (kept in the freezer)

Ground 62% semisweet or 70% bittersweet chocolate

Chocolate Liqueur (page 101)

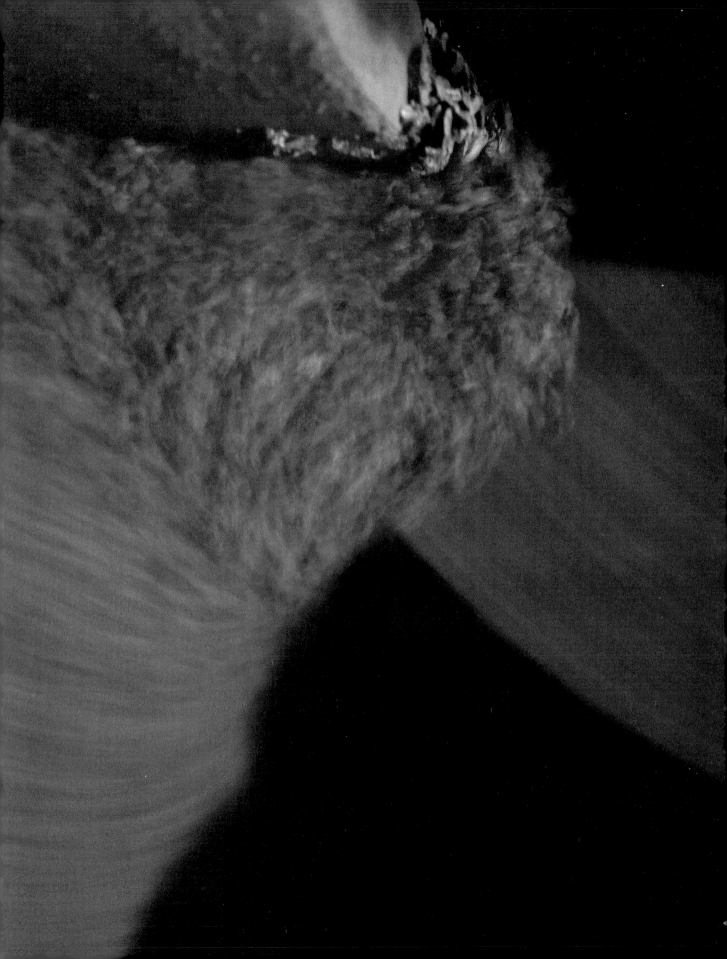

LEGENDS & LORE

Chocolate as a Ritual Drink

Bernal Díaz del Castillo, the Spanish soldier who recorded Cortés's conquests, claimed that Montezuma would order fifty cups of chocolate prepared just before he'd visit his harem. Most likely Montezuma wanted to be sure that he and all his companions would not lack for chocolate, but some historians believe that Montezuma would go from cup to cup, sipping just the foam from each.

Many ancient cultures considered the chocolate foam the essence of the drink. It was believed to contain chocolate's vital properties, and early Mesoamericans never drank chocolate without frothing it up first. Even today, in parts of Mexico and Central America, chocolate is never served without a good head of foam. In Guatemala, while visiting some of the people who grow cacao beans, we learned that Mayan growers ritually consume chocolate drinks prior to planting corn, to celebrate the birth of a child, and on all feast days.

The earliest method of frothing was to pour a mixture of chocolate and water from one vessel into another from a height of three or four feet. Archaeologists have found pottery, such as the Princeton Vase, which dates back to A.D. 750, depicting people frothing their chocolate this way. The *molinillo* (shown on page 21), probably devised by the Spanish, came into vogue in the sixteenth century. A slender wooden rod with carved wooden cylinders at one end, a molinillo whips air into a cup of hot chocolate very quickly when you twirl it between your palms.

JOHN'S CLASSIC DRINKING CHOCOLATE

Everywhere I go—the bookstore, the farmers' market, every single cocktail party—people ask me, "What's your favorite dessert?" I *hate* the question, because people expect me to say a mile-high chocolate cake or something really ornate. Instead, I like to make really good, thick hot chocolate and serve it at the end of a meal. I use my favorite demitasse cups, and place a few slices of a perfect pear or two pieces of shortbread on the plate next to the cup. That's my favorite dessert. During the holidays, I add rum or brandy and serve it instead of eggnog.

Personally, I'm not a fan of cinnamon or other spices in hot chocolate, because I think it diverts attention from the chocolate's flavor, but for an authentic Mexican-style chocolate, add the cinnamon and cayenne.

INGREDIENTS

2½ cups whole milk

4 ounces 99% unsweetened chocolate, coarsely chopped

⅓ cup granulated sugar

1½ teaspoons pure vanilla extract

¾ teaspoon ground cinnamon (optional)

⅛ teaspoon cayenne pepper (optional)

Heat the milk in a medium saucepan over medium heat until it is hot to the touch. Whisk in the chocolate and sugar and continue whisking for 1 to 2 minutes until the sugar has dissolved. Whisk in the vanilla and the cinnamon and cayenne, if using. Reduce the heat to low. The chocolate may be made ahead; it will thicken as it sits.

Serve in demitasse cups or mugs depending on desired portion.

SERVES 6 TO 12

Note: For a lighter, airy consistency, remove the hot chocolate from the heat and mix with a hand blender on low speed just before serving. Or make ahead and use the frother of an espresso machine to reheat it. Individual servings can also be topped with frothed milk.

This can be made up to 3 days ahead and refrigerated, but if you use the spices, keep in mind their flavor intensifies over time.

CHAPTER
3

A NEW AMERICAN CHOCOLATE COMPANY

JOHN

The 1996 candy equipment show in Düsseldorf was really when our company began. When Robert and I first spoke about chocolate making, I was intrigued by the idea but felt it would be a massive endeavor.

One photograph of Bernachon changed my ideas about making chocolate. Bernachon made their chocolate in one L-shaped room, and the entire factory wasn't much larger than a thousand square feet. That photograph made Bernachon seem more like a workshop than a factory, and that was very appealing to me. Suddenly, the idea of chocolate making—experimenting and teaching ourselves how to do it—seemed very exciting. We could start the chocolate-making equivalent of a garage winery.

Robert thought Düsseldorf would be the best place to see as many chocolate machines as possible. I agreed, thinking that if all the other chocolate manufacturers would be at this show, then we'd better be there too.

We walked into the convention not knowing what to expect. The hall was immense, packed with more than two thousand exhibitors and the latest equipment. My first impression was of bright lights, guys in suits, and lots of stainless steel. After a few hours of wandering through the show, looking at the high-tech systems, it became clear that none of them would apply to the chocolate we wanted to make. We planned on making chocolate one batch at a time, and selling all the chocolate before starting a new batch. The machines at the convention were designed to crank out candy bars by the millions. We wouldn't be able to fit even one of those machines in the space we had envisioned for our factory. And the cost was beyond what we could afford, even if we had wanted to make chocolate on such a large scale.

We talked with a few of the salespeople on the floor, describing the type of machines we wanted. They'd look at us as if we were crazy and say, "You should buy chocolate from somebody else. You can *buy* chocolate liquor instead of making your own chocolate." Robert had gotten the same reaction when he'd called American chocolate manufacturers a year earlier. Every single chocolate maker he'd reached had told him that he couldn't possibly start a chocolate factory without millions of dollars, and they strongly suggested he give up the idea and just buy liquor from an existing chocolate maker.

....

What Is Chocolate Liquor?

Chocolate liquor is neither liquid nor alcohol. It is the mass that results when cacao beans are roasted, shelled, and then ground. Grinding releases the cocoa butter from the rest of the bean. Once the cocoa butter is released through grinding and then heated, it becomes a liquid in which all the tiny solid particles of ground cacao bean become suspended. Transforming the roasted cacao beans into chocolate liquor is the first step in chocolate making.

....

ROBERT

Because obtaining the beans, then roasting and grinding them are the most difficult steps in chocolate making, most chocolatiers buy chocolate liquor that is ready to be melted and further refined. We had no interest in starting with liquor. If we bought the same chocolate liquor as everyone else, then how would our chocolate be different from everybody else's?

Luckily I spotted an acquaintance at the show, Jimmy Greenberg. Jimmy sold used equipment; I'd met him a year earlier when I'd visited his warehouse in the Bronx. His company's presence at the convention consisted of a small table and a folding chair, a modest setup compared to the corporate-looking, professionally designed displays of the other machinery vendors. After we'd spoken for several minutes, Jimmy told us the same thing everybody else had said. "You don't *need* to make your own chocolate. Buy liquor and do whatever you want with that."

But when John and I both shook our heads, Jimmy gave us advice that proved to be crucial. "If you really want to do it yourselves, there's a guy who travels around the world getting old equipment up and running. I think he's helped a few small chocolate companies get off the ground. His name is Karl Bittong," Jimmy said. "You should call him. Also, have a look at these pictures. These were taken in a chocolate factory not far from here that we're dismantling."

JOHN

Jimmy handed us a binder, and we flipped through Polaroids in plastic sleeves. Robert stopped at one photograph. "John," he said, holding up the binder, "this is it. This is exactly like the mélangeur used at Bernachon." This was the first time in a year of searching that Robert had seen equipment like Bernachon's. Both of us looked at the photo and looked at Jimmy.

"How do we know this mélangeur works?" Robert asked him.

"Well, it *was* just working," Jimmy replied. "They closed the entire factory, but until the last day all this stuff was running."

"How much does it cost?" I asked.

"Six thousand dollars," Jimmy answered. The new equipment displayed at the convention cost $350,000 and up, so Jimmy's price seemed pretty reasonable.

Robert and I looked at each other, thinking the same thing. We had to start somewhere, and this machine seemed like a good place to start.

A week later, we were back at home in the Bay Area and a check for the mélangeur was on its way to Jimmy. Buying that machine was like writing the first sentence in a story. We had a long way to go until we could taste our first chocolate, but at least our story now had a beginning.

ROBERT

A dinner party led to finding exceptional cacao beans. The friend who gave the dinner party seated me next to his mother because I was the only other person in the room who could speak Spanish. My friend's mother, Ana Estrella, who knew of my interest in chocolate, put me in touch with a friend of hers in Caracas, Carmen Elena Ótengo de Wallis. I visited Carmen Elena in Caracas and she introduced me to some of the cacao growers in the surrounding areas. Some of them were large producers but most of them

were small-scale farmers. Among those who know cacao, Venezuelan beans have a reputation for being among the world's best. The anticipation of tasting beans that normally would be inaccessible to a first-time chocolate maker filled me with the same sense of possibility I'd felt when invited to spend time at Bernachon. The weeks in Caracas were magical, both for the excitement of accessing the beans and because there was a kind of gentility and graciousness to every social interaction.

I flew back to California from Venezuela with five pounds of cacao beans tucked away in my suitcase. I sourced beans from other regions and soon had a small mountain stacked against one wall in my kitchen—an assortment of brown paper bags, small hand-sewn burlap sacks, and clear plastic bags with samples of cacao beans from Brazil, Indonesia, Trinidad, and Ghana, in addition to the Venezuelan beans—all destined to be turned into crude homemade chocolate.

....

Kitchen Chocolate

Clearly, making chocolate in a home kitchen is different from how it's made in a factory, but you follow the same basic principles. If you start with cacao beans, you must roast them, remove the husks, grind the nibs, grind sugar, refine the paste, add cocoa butter, and conch the chocolate (knead it until the cacao particles are small enough so the chocolate feels smooth on your tongue).

As cacao beans can be hard to come by unless you live near the equator, you can make chocolate at home starting with nibs, the dark, intensely flavorful, nut-like chunks that result when cacao beans are roasted and shelled. Don't expect the chocolate to be smooth. Kitchen chocolate will be much closer to the coarse product made by hand before the Industrial Age.

First decide how sweet you want your chocolate to be. Most bittersweet chocolate is about two-thirds nibs and one-third sugar. Using a clean coffee grinder (not a burr grinder), grind a mixture of nibs and granulated sugar until it becomes a paste. When the paste is as fine as possible, remove it from the grinder and warm it in a bowl set over a pot of water, or warm at a low temperature in a microwave for a few seconds at a time. This step melts the cocoa butter that the grinding released from the nibs. If you're feeling ambitious, you can temper your chocolate at this point. (See page 92.) If you choose not to temper, just spoon the chocolate into a bowl or a chocolate mold and refrigerate for 15 to 20 minutes. Then taste the chocolate you made.

....

After trying to roast beans in a popcorn air popper (which burned the beans because they were too heavy for the air stream), I decided to roast them in my oven on an aluminum pizza screen. I set the oven to

275°F and put a handful of beans on the screen. Although I knew my method could be only a rough approximation of a roaster that continuously tossed the beans in a heated stream of air, I stirred the beans periodically with a wooden spoon in an effort to roast them as evenly as possible.

I checked the beans by pulling one off the screen and breaking the hull quickly with my fingers. I tasted a portion and found it to be a little chewy, with a flavor that reminded me of undercooked broccoli or the smell of hops cooking. (I was familiar with the smell of hops because of the odors wafting from the brewery six blocks from my house.) A few minutes later, I tested another bean. The bean tasted slightly nutty and a little less bitter. I didn't yet know what it meant for a cacao bean to be "done," so I was merely following my sense of taste. The beans, which were too hot to hold for more than a second or two, had expanded in the oven and become plumper and more uniform than they had been before roasting.

When they were cool, I separated the shells from the cacao nibs in what turned out to be the hardest, slowest step in the process. The shells, which are surprisingly hard and sharp, leave tiny cuts in your fingertips, and tiny pieces of them would fall into the bowl of nibs and have to be painstakingly separated out. I finished that first batch and one or two more, but after that I began hiring anyone I could convince to help me. My housekeeper carried bags of roasted beans home from my apartment; she and several members of her family would shell the beans, and then she would bring them back. I even convinced two young French tourists whom I met in a café to help me winnow cacao beans.

The rest of the process evolved over time. I settled on a handheld blade coffee grinder to turn the roasted beans into a rough paste, although this step, like the others, required several adjustments before it worked well. As the paste generated by the grinding became increasingly fine, it also became increasingly thick. The heat generated by the friction of grinding also melted the cocoa butter, so to make sure the mass was being ground evenly, every thirty seconds or so I had to stop and scrape the bottom of the grinder, which had begun to slow down, whine, and overheat.

When I added sugar to the beans at the beginning of this step, I found it helped prevent the paste from sticking. After trying several different methods, I ground the sugar first and then put it and the nibs in the grinder. The stiff, coarse paste that came from the grinder wouldn't be easy to melt or temper. I had decided, following Bernachon's example, to add cocoa butter to the crude chocolate. This meant I needed a way to melt the cocoa butter while making certain it was well mixed into the chocolate. At a gourmet store in my neighborhood, I came across a heavy cream-colored mortar and pestle made out of clay and measuring about a foot across. I set this on a trivet over my gas stove, lit a tiny flame underneath, added the cacao and sugar paste and then the cocoa butter, and began to refine the mixture with the pestle. With a little heat, the chocolate began to take on the irresistibly seductive sheen that must account, at least in part, for the craving so many people have for chocolate. As the chocolate became liquid, there was something breathtaking about the glossy, dark mass at the bottom of the cream-colored mortar. I was beginning to grasp chocolate's remarkable capacity to transform itself.

JOHN

The same skills that make Robert such a great physician made him really good at figuring out the blends for chocolate. He approached chocolate making the way he'd approach seeing a patient—by taking in every fact he could and mulling over every possibility before reaching a conclusion. His diagnostic skills are so good because he keeps an open mind, and this worked for chocolate making too.

All of the beans that we'd acquired so far were stacked up in Robert's kitchen, and with them, he had acquired a serious moth infestation. The first batch of beans that he brought back from Venezuela hadn't been fumigated, so the insects took over. There were tiny worms wriggling through the cacao beans and moths perpetually hovering overhead (the worms and the moths were generally the same insect, just in different stages).

Robert is fond of wandering through a big restaurant supply house in San Francisco called Economy Restaurant Fixtures. When he went there looking for storage containers to keep the bugs in check, he picked up a trade paper, *West Coast Restaurant News*. We placed an ad in the *WCR News* that led to hiring our first employee, Peter Kocaurek.

Peter had a very eclectic background: a chemistry degree from U. C. Davis, experience as a pantry manager at Stars, and manager of the seafood department at Safeway. During his years with us, Peter would

work on everything from equipment repair to bean tasting to payroll at Scharffen Berger Chocolate Maker. But what really made Peter so valuable is that he has a great palate, and he understood right away what we were trying to do with our chocolate making.

While waiting for the mélangeur to arrive from Germany, we hunted for a space to make chocolate, someplace simple and open, and big enough to drive a forklift through. The dot-com explosion had begun in San Francisco, making rental properties hard to find, even in industrial areas.

We finally found a place in South San Francisco, a stripped-down building that had been used for storage and didn't even have light fixtures. When the mélangeur arrived, it wasn't in one big crate, as we'd expected, but disassembled and strapped to several pallets. I had to borrow a forklift from the owner of the factory next door to bring the pallets inside. The pallets were heavy and the forklift small, so while I drove it, the guy that we'd hired to paint hung off the back of the forklift as ballast; without him, the forklift would have tipped over.

We bought a few lights from a nearby hardware store and plugged them in along the floor, hoping to get a better look at the mélangeur pieces. Peter and I lifted the heavy, grimy parts as best we could while Robert held up a light to peer underneath. The parts were covered with layers of cocoa butter, caked chocolate liquor, machine grease, and oil, as well as a good amount of rust. We had no idea what the different pieces were or how they fit together. Much later, when we began looking at serial numbers, we realized that one part had one number and another part had a different serial number, so the pieces weren't even all from the same machine.

Looking over those crud-coated parts, my first reaction was, "Well, great. *Now* what do we do?" Years before, when I'd built my winery from vintage equipment bought at auction, I'd at least had enough experience with the machines to get everything running. But I'd never seen a working mélangeur and knew we couldn't put these heavy, encrusted pieces together without some help.

Because the mélangeur was bought and paid for, and because we had a relatively small budget, there was no going back. It was either get the mélangeur up and running, or surrender the idea of chocolate making. Robert and I began calling anyone we could think of who might have some idea of how to repair a machine that was decades old and practically unheard of except among chocolate makers.

ROBERT

We were lucky to hear about Conhagen, a company in Benicia that overhauls commercial equipment, primarily for the shipping and petroleum industries. They had lathes big enough to machine the parts we needed. The mélangeur seemed to interest the machinists who worked there, both because they'd never seen one before and because of its size. Our mélangeur was three tons and four feet high—normally, these guys worked on forty-ton hundred-foot-high ship's engines, steam turbines, enormous pumps, and compressors. By comparison, our mélangeur was a small, fairly simple machine, appealing because of its size and the fact that it was a novelty.

Conhagen was so different from the places I had worked that it fascinated me. The cavernous work

space, bigger than any warehouse I'd seen, had a thick concrete floor, and I could feel the bumpiness and coolness of that floor through my shoes. I would see some of the guys assigned to the mélangeur sitting over a brown bag lunch, drinking coffee from a Thermos. Most of them were burly, bearded, and covered with tattoos. They didn't look as if they would be enthusiastic about cleaning and fixing an old chocolate machine. Yet they took such care with the mélangeur, down to the final, painstaking paint job. They'd call me periodically to explain what they'd done, and to ask if I wanted to come and see the work in progress. I drove up as often as I could because I was genuinely touched both by the craftsmanship of the people who worked on the mélangeur and by the pride they took in their work.

For me, seeing the mélangeur arrive in a state of disrepair hadn't been particularly worrisome. I felt confident that we'd find someone who could fix it. My worst moment came when we opened the shipping container containing our beans from Venezuela.

The Venezuelan beans had flavors that we hadn't found anywhere else, and these flavors were essential to the blend we'd agreed was our favorite among all the small batches of chocolate made in my kitchen. Normally a shipping container had to be filled with one type of cacao, about twelve tons of beans. I'd convinced the Venezuelans who'd sold me the beans to pack four types of beans into our first shipment: Sur del Lago, Ocumare, Rio Caribe, and Carenero Superior.

We unlocked the doors to the shipping container, swung them open, and were met by the smell of wet burlap sacks. The bags near the door felt damp, and at first it seemed that the entire shipment of beans might have been ruined. The beans had been a substantial financial investment, much more than we'd paid for the mélangeur, but I was more concerned by the thought that we couldn't easily replace these beans.

JOHN

When the container from Venezuela finally cleared customs at the Port of Oakland and arrived at our factory, we couldn't wait to open it. We were expecting the same beans that Robert had used in his kitchen. But when we pulled open the doors, we found sodden bags of beans, some totally soaked. The whole container had a wet, jungle sort of smell—what you'd imagine beans would smell like if locked in a hot, damp place for weeks on end. The smell was not good. When we'd first tasted the beans, from the small bag that Robert had carried home from Venezuela, they'd had such pronounced notes of fruit. I hadn't ever tasted such deep, luscious, dark cherry flavors in cacao. We'd planned for these beans to be the key flavor components in our first batches of chocolate. Looking at all those damp burlap bags, all I could think was, "We can't make chocolate with these beans. We've paid for them, we can't return them, they were crucial for our first batch, and they're ruined."

That moment marked a change in how I thought about chocolate making. It wasn't until we opened the container that I realized not just intellectually, but viscerally how far these beans had to travel, and how little control I had over them before they reached our factory. All the years I'd made wine, I'd used grapes grown within driving distance. I could jump in my VW and check on how the grapes were growing; I had some control over what happened to the fruit before winemaking began. Chocolate making wasn't going to offer the same luxury.

ROBERT

That shipment taught us about bean conditioning. While trying to locate a tool called a thief, I had the good fortune to find someone who could help us condition the beans. A thief is a long hollow rod with a tip sharp enough to pierce a sack of beans. The thief "steals" a few beans, giving you a random sampling of the beans inside without requiring that you open the sack.

I found a thief by looking under "coffee" in the Yellow Pages and calling a variety of places that dealt with coffee beans. I finally reached a person who understood what it meant to receive a shipment of damp beans. He offered to pick up the beans, dry them, rebag them, and return them to us "conditioned." He spoke of this service as though he performed it routinely, and didn't seem surprised to hear that we had cacao beans instead of coffee beans.

We did lose some of the beans from that batch to mold, but not terribly many. And even the beans that were moldy weren't wasted. We put them aside to use as test batches when we first turned on our machinery.

In addition to the four Venezuelan bean types, now newly conditioned, we had bean shipments arriving from Ghana, Papua New Guinea, Bahìa, and Madagascar. Our first blend would have eight types of beans. Bernachon had used eleven types of beans for their blends, but based on the flavors of the chocolate batches made in my kitchen, this blend would work well for us.

At this point, we wanted input from people who knew something about chocolate. John and I invited Alice Medrich, Narsai David, and Elizabeth Falkner to my apartment for a tasting. Alice was a chocolate celebrity. When she opened her dessert shop, Cocolat, in Berkeley in 1976, she singlehandedly changed how people thought about chocolate. I'd known Alice for two years, had lots of conversations with her, and respected her opinion. Narsai was an elder statesman of food in the Bay Area, and people really looked up to him. Both John and I admired the way he built and ran his businesses, as well as his ideas about food. Elizabeth I knew from Rubicon, and at that time, she was just beginning Citizen Cake in San Francisco. Elizabeth has always been terrifically encouraging, and I thought her work was so creative; she has an artist's background and her desserts were so different from what was available in bakeries at that time. The cake Elizabeth baked for my fiftieth birthday party was an amazing piece of art that was almost six square feet and looked like Frank Gehry's work done in chocolate.

The sun poured in through the windows of my apartment, and the five of us sat around my wooden dining table, each person with his or her own small stack of crudely made chocolate bars. The bars didn't have the smoothness or sheen of the bars we'd go on to make in our factory—they looked like I'd made them in my kitchen, which I had. Because of his experience in starting and running a food business, Narsai was skeptical about building a chocolate factory. Although he would be extraordinarily supportive when our chocolate came out, at the first tasting he asked us difficult questions about marketing and our competition. His questions forced us to think more strategically about our business. How could a doctor and a wine-maker with a tiny budget hope to compete in a market that was composed primarily of huge corporations?

Alice and Elizabeth, on the other hand, weren't concerned about how we would make a company work. Both of them tasted the chocolate and told us what they thought about the chocolate's flavor. Both of them said they couldn't wait for the day that our factory would begin producing chocolate. I wasn't thinking about the future at all, but just about that moment. I was completely caught up in the excitement of having these three people whom I admired tasting our chocolate. That moment—the light from the windows, the smell of the chocolate, the sound of their voices—is imprinted on my memory to the smallest detail.

JOHN

While the mélangeur was being put together and the beans were being reconditioned, we called Karl Bittong. Jimmy Greenberg's recommendation was good advice. At that time, there was no other person who could have helped us as much as Karl did.

Born in Germany, Karl still speaks with an accent, even though he's lived in Florida for decades with his five kids. When Karl was a teenager, he went to a food school in Berlin, then made bonbons by hand for a well-known shop there after graduating. But he decided he wanted to expand his horizons and learn more about chocolate making, so he moved to Holland, where he worked for Van Houten in their development department. Van Houten was and still is one of the world's top cocoa companies, begun in 1828 by Conrad Van Houten, who invented a press that squeezed the cocoa butter from cacao beans to make cocoa powder. The Van Houten company required all employees to train for three years, learning every aspect of the company. When Karl left Van Houten in 1971, he knew chocolate and the machinery very well.

By the time we met Karl, he'd spent most of his career finding old machinery and making it work. He knows machinery well enough to assemble just the right machine—or sometimes create an entirely different machine—from old equipment or even just parts of machines.

Initially Karl told us the same thing that everybody else had: "There are easier ways to start up a chocolate factory." But, fairly quickly, Karl came to appreciate what we were trying to do. Because he knows chocolate making and because he understands what each machine is capable of doing, we relied on his experience. We'd explain to him what we were looking for, he'd recommend a few options, and then he'd go out and find the used machines we needed.

The first machine Karl found for us was a winnower. A winnower removes the shells from the roasted cacao beans by running the beans through metal rollers that gently crack the shells. The machine drops the cracked beans onto vibrating tiered screens that separate the shell fragments from the nibs, and strategically aimed blasts of air shoot the shell bits away while allowing the heavier nibs to fall into chutes. We'd been working with a French company that wanted to make us a winnower for $65,000. Karl found an old one that cost $20,000. We bought the old one, which Karl called "museum quality." When the winnower arrived, it looked ancient. There was a leather belt driving it, and every moving part of the machine ran off that belt.

Once we got the winnower functioning properly, we sat down and mapped out on paper very specifically how we wanted to make our chocolate. We had a clear sense of the steps involved because of the dozens of batches made in Robert's kitchen: roasting, removing the shells, grinding the nibs, grinding the sugar, refining the paste, adding cocoa butter and just a little vanilla and lecithin, before finally conching the chocolate and tempering it. We just had to scale up those steps and decide which set of machines made the most sense. With chocolate making, it's not the same as, say, bread baking, where you can replace one oven fairly easily with another type of oven. Chocolate making can be separated into steps, and there are a lot of different ways, and different sets of machines, to accomplish those steps. We spent hours analyzing machines for refining and conching before deciding on a Macintyre.

Karl was set on the Macintyre and he talked us into buying one, even though we would use it differently from the way it's normally used. Traditionally chocolate makers use a Macintyre when they want to mix chocolate liquor with something else. We would be using the Macintyre at a slightly earlier stage, putting cacao into it that wasn't as finely ground as chocolate liquor, although the nibs would have gone through an initial grinding in our mélangeur. We would give the Macintyre a sort of semi-liquor to refine and conch. Karl knew the Macintyre's capabilities, and he was convinced it was the best machine for us. Karl was right. At our scale—for the size of the batches we make—the Macintyre is uniquely good.

The Macintyre isn't a traditional machine in any case. It conchs and refines in a way that isn't done by a lot of other machines. Most conches use rollers, which squish the cacao particles in the chocolate. By using steel knives that scrape against the metal walls of the machine, the Macintyre gave us a different shape of cacao particle. Before we bought the machine, the four of us—Karl, Peter, Robert, and I—talked at length about particle shape and the idea that you can't really know how particle shape will affect a chocolate's flavor.

Finally, *finally*, the machines were in place—the winnower, the mélangeur, and the Macintyre were assembled, fine-tuned, and ready to fire up. We used the moldy beans that we hadn't been able to salvage from the first Venezuelan shipment, roasted and shelled them, and then poured them into the mélangeur. The dark brown, gravelly nibs started out dusty-looking, and there was a dry, raspy sound when the granite wheels of the mélangeur began turning, but in just a few minutes, the nibs became glossy as they were coated with the cocoa butter released by grinding.

ROBERT

Perhaps out of sheer luck, the first batch we made (after the test run with the moldy beans) was very good. The machines worked smoothly, the beans had been evenly roasted, the flavors in that first batch of chocolate were everything we'd hoped for. We set aside the batch, which was 400kg or a little more than 800 pounds of chocolate, and we began roasting beans for the second batch. From batch two through batch eight, a smoky, burnt-rubber taste pervaded the chocolate, and we couldn't figure out how to replicate the success we'd had with the first batch. Finally I took samples of the faulty batches to a lab I'd worked with as a physician, and had them test it with a gas chromatograph, an instrument that separates the various chemical components in a given material and breaks it down into its specific parts. The chromatogram showed bizarre chemical components that shouldn't have been a part of the chocolate. Although the results of the test weren't a very good diagnostic tool for what was going wrong, we finally adjusted the roasting and were able to produce a few subsequent good batches.

At the same time, we began to consider the size and shape of our chocolate bars, and how we wanted to package them. Initially we didn't even consider candy-bar-sized molds. Because we saw food professionals as our primary customers, we crafted molds for 3.3-pound chocolate bars, large by any standard.

From the beginning, John and I agreed on a few basic rules about the wrap. We felt that the tones of the paper and its texture were important. Our wrap had to be elegant but simple, and the paper had to convey an artisanal quality. Both of us felt strongly that the packaging could not overshadow the chocolate—the dark, glossy bar of chocolate was the primary attraction, which meant the packaging had to have matte finishes, nothing shiny, and no gold.

JOHN

Every time I lead a tour, someone asks where our mountain goat logo originated. The ibex image was literally handed to me years before I thought about chocolate making. A man named Horst Scharfenberg appeared at my winery on a foreign press junket. He worked for the German equivalent of *Gourmet* magazine, and he claimed to be a cousin of mine. He said, "I brought you our family crest," and he pulled out a photo of a simple, stylized image of an ibex balanced on a mountain peak. He and I talked, and what he said coincided with what I already knew about the Scharffenberger family. After some research, I found that the ibex *was* the crest for part of my family. Because this image has been around for centuries, the goat has had some mileage. Occasionally people e-mail me goat sightings, reporting that they saw the same ibex as a statue on a mountaintop in Slovenia, set into a tile floor of a Bavarian castle, or as part of a wrought-iron

gate of a German estate.

I liked the image right from the start, but I already had labels for my wine, so I filed it away. When Robert and I first talked about our logo, I found the photo and showed it to him. Both of us liked the fact that the goat had a real history, that there was substance behind the image. For both of us, the ibex evoked something rare and maybe even noble. We liked the idea that it wasn't some graphic made up by a designer, but an image that had existed and had meaning long before we came on the scene. I framed the photo that Horst brought me, and the day we moved to our Berkeley factory, I hung it on the wall of our gift shop, where it still hangs today.

The ibex has gone through many small changes over the years. If you look at the wrappers of our older bars, you'll see that some goats have longer horns, and some have more peaks under their hooves. One goat appeared to be smirking, so he was ousted pretty quickly. The ibex has evolved gradually, just as we have.

ROBERT

Our bars were still a bit rough looking, but John wanted to unveil our chocolate at the annual food and wine show in Aspen, Colorado. We hurried to make the bars and wrapped them by hand, then carried the boxes with us on the plane. John had attended the show for years as a winemaker, and he was convinced that the people who attended it were our target audience. He was right. People returned repeatedly to sample another bite, many of them commenting that they'd never tasted a dark chocolate like ours.

JOHN

Both Jacques Pépin and Julia Child were at the Aspen show, and I couldn't resist the impulse to push some of our chocolate into their hands. Jacques said that the chocolate reminded him of the chocolate from his childhood in France, and Julia told us it was the best chocolate she'd ever had from the United States. The Aspen show convinced me that we were ready to sell our chocolate.

We'd made the chocolate we wanted to make. We'd designed packaging that both of us really liked. Our chocolate had been praised by both Jacques Pépin and Julia Child. All in all, we were happy with the product we created. The only problem was that not many food professionals were buying it. All along, our plan had been to focus on restaurants and pastry chefs, and then later see if there was any interest from serious home cooks. But during those first three months, sales to restaurants and chefs were slow.

Robert and I traveled to Los Angeles, New York, and Chicago; both of us visited restaurants and pastry chefs all over California. Some chefs did buy from us, but not enough of them bought to make the business work.

Part of the reason for this was distribution. Restaurants buy from distributors. Most chefs don't go to the farmer for carrots, and most pastry chefs don't go to the chocolate makers for baking supplies. It took time before we found someone—Bill Wilkinson from Greenleaf—who was willing to take a chance on us and offer our chocolate.

ROBERT

The other reason sales weren't as rapid as we'd anticipated was the chefs themselves. Many pastry chefs already had a favorite brand of chocolate that they relied on to make the one chocolate dessert listed on the menu every night. Although they would taste our chocolate and like it, most weren't eager to switch from the chocolate they'd always used. There's a risk in changing to an unheard-of brand of chocolate—it's not as simple as switching from romaine to red leaf lettuce in a salad, for example. The risk is compounded by the fact that chocolate is one of the more expensive items a pastry chef has to buy.

Although our aesthetically pure, beautiful bars of chocolate weren't an immediate hit among food professionals, we soon realized that our chocolate had found its own group of customers. During those first months, we received a lot of press coverage. The handcrafted aspects of our chocolate—the fact that our machines were old and refurbished, that we made very small batches and hand-wrapped each bar—all this interested the press. The magazine and newspaper articles created a kind of link directly to our first consumers, who weren't chefs, but instead ordinary home cooks like us. While we were jetting back and forth across the country, puzzled as to why we weren't getting anywhere with distributors and restaurateurs, thousands of people who read about our chocolate began calling us.

JOHN

People phoned the factory, asking if they could come and see how we made chocolate. "Of course," we'd always answer. "When would you like to come?" Both of us know people in the wine and food industries, and many of our friends began dropping by as well. Although we were a bit surprised that these spontaneous tours began before we'd had a chance to plan them, from the beginning we knew we wanted our factory to be open, a place where we could demonstrate how we made our chocolate. This runs against the prevailing wisdom among chocolate manufacturers. Most of the big names in chocolate work behind a veil of secrecy. Tours of the major chocolate-making plants—those that allowed tours at all—were light in content, and were kept separate from the chocolate manufacturing.

It wasn't that we set out to be different from the other chocolate makers. It was just that the idea of secrecy never occurred to us. We *wanted* people to see how we made our chocolate. The only way I knew how to do this was to *show* people: I love answering questions with way too much information, and Robert is the same way. I'd seen how having an open winery had given me access to my customers. Early on, I'd realized that seeing the steps involved in wine making added to the experience of drinking that wine. I thought the same would be true of chocolate, and Robert agreed with me. If you're willing to let your customers see every step of the process, then it's obvious that you stand behind your ingredients and your craftsmanship.

Beyond those reasons, both Robert and I like to explain how we do what we do. Both of us believe that if you understand the steps involved in chocolate making—as well as a little about the history of the cacao, the geography, the cultural context—there's more depth to the experience when you finally put the chocolate in your mouth.

To have the press and the public respond so positively to our open policy was a little surprising, but very encouraging. Intuitively, both of us felt that welcoming customers into our factory was a good idea. To have people excited about touring our factory—as small as it was in those days—made us feel that we were on the right track.

ROBERT

The San Francisco Farmers' Market marked a turning point in how we sold our chocolate. The market has strict rules about what can be sold there, because they want to encourage local farmers. Obviously cacao can't be grown locally, but because we made our chocolate nearby, we received a special dispensation to set up a table. We took dozens of our smallest bars and sample-sized bars that we'd never sold previously.

We had never intended to sell chocolate in increments as small as these five-gram bars. The big molds we used initially had small indentations set between the dividing lines between bars, and these indentations filled with chocolate. After unmolding the big bars, we picked up the squares, wrapped them, and kept them on hand as samples for pastry chefs and restaurateurs. Peter, John, and I had a price discussion the night before the first market because we weren't sure how much we should charge.

JOHN

I got the first farmers' market shift, and it turned out to be a seminal day for us. I had brought a small table, a large wooden chopping block, and a big chef's knife to cut small pieces as samples. I expected to sell a few of our 1.5-kilogram bars to serious home chefs and a small number of our crude 3-ounce bars that we usually gave away as samples. But the moment I set out the chocolate, a mob surrounded the table. The smaller bars flew off the table so fast I barely had time to put the money in a cash box. We went through all the chocolate I had in less than two hours. I called Peter, who was working at the factory that day, and said, "We need more of the bars. Wrap up everything you can and bring it here, fast!" We sold more than a thousand dollars' worth of chocolate in one afternoon.

Robert went to the market the following week, and it was the same wild scene. After those two days at the market, Robert, Peter, and I sat down and regrouped. The farmers' market proved that there was a strong consumer demand for our chocolate. It was time to change direction and make products for that market as quickly as we could.

ROBERT

We began making smaller bars, and we seemed to reach a production level that worked, in terms of selling what we made fairly quickly. Within three years, though, it was clear that we had outgrown our South San Francisco factory.

During this time, I received a letter from a businessman named Peter Wais. Peter had just sold his family's steel-finishing business, and, after having bought our chocolate for a year, he asked if he could be involved in the company. Peter's letter caught my attention: he called our chocolate "uniquely pure among American-made chocolate" and said he was "motivated by a love of chocolate, not chutzpah." Peter became our first big investor and a partner—he came along at a time when John and I knew we needed to grow. With Peter's help, we began to look around the Bay Area for a bigger factory space.

We could have relocated a few hours from the city and paid less rent, but we preferred to be close to the city and accessible to our customers, as well as to the people who had worked with us since our inception. We looked at dozens of spaces, but few suited our logistical requirements as well as our sensibilities. We seriously considered one factory in Oakland, but we held off because the building wasn't centrally located.

As soon as we saw the factory in Berkeley, we knew it was the right place. It had been built to be a sulfur factory in 1906, and the same qualities required in sulfur manufacturing made it ideal for chocolate making. The thick brick walls served as insulation, keeping the factory cool even on hot days. The high ceilings gave us space to put in overhead tempering equipment without making the rooms feel crowded. The building was right off the freeway, with parking nearby. And both of us loved the building. Its age and character seemed to match perfectly what we were trying to do with our chocolate—to create something that we believed in, something authentic that stayed true to its long history.

JOHN

Along the way, we hired more people like Peter Kocaurek—people who didn't necessarily have a background in chocolate making, but who added to Scharffen Berger Chocolate Maker just because they believed in the product. A key hire was Jim Harris, who took over the job of chief operating officer and chief financial officer in 2004. We knew Jim because he worked for one of our investors, Jim Kohlberg. Jim Harris recognized the importance of flavor and bean selection in determining Scharffen Berger's success; he immediately began attending our tasting meetings because he wanted to learn more about how we chose our beans. Within a few months, Jim was able to identify the key flavors and characteristics of cacao and we found him to have a fine palate.

As we grew, we needed help managing the company. It was obvious that neither Robert nor I had the skills required to stay on top of the constant changes. We interviewed people for months without finding anyone who seemed right for the job. At one point, one of us commented offhandedly that we needed a guy like Jim Harris. One of our board members said, "Why not ask Jim?" We offered him the job, and he took on the responsibility of managing the business, freeing Robert and me to focus on cacao development projects.

ROBERT

I'm not a businessman and John takes a big-picture approach to running a company. Jim Harris loves business, and he took on the day-to-day challenges and actually enjoyed resolving them, something John and I never did.

Without a word from John or me, Jim understood how important it was to know our chocolate, to learn about tasting, and to grasp how our machines work. When we bought a new mélangeur, Jim drove to Conhagen to see for himself how they repaired it.

Even more important, Jim is interested in people and he's insightful about assessing personalities and how they fit into the company. When he joined us, a lot of the organizational issues of a rapidly growing company were taken off our hands, and it was such a relief. Jim suits Scharffen Berger so well because he loves chocolate and beneath the strict, efficient businessman's exterior, he is a very caring person.

Ultra Thin Chocolate Chunk Cookies, page 182.

CHAPTER 4

Essentially Chocolate

THE RECIPES IN THIS CHAPTER DON'T HAVE LESS
FLAVOR THAN THE RECIPES IN CHAPTER 2 BUT THEY
OFTEN TAKE A LIGHTER APPROACH.

Texture is key. You'll see that the same chocolate can show a completely different character when used in an airy mousse, a light soufflé, or a silken crème brûlée. This chapter also highlights ingredients that pair well with chocolate, such as sour cream, ginger, bananas, marshmallow, and a variety of nuts.

Chocolate Chunk Cheesecake, page 136.

CHOCOLATE CHUNK CHEESECAKE

Every bite of this cheesecake gives you a double hit of chocolate, first in the cocoa wafer crust and then in the chunks of bittersweet strewn throughout the cheesecake. The chocolate chunks register on your tongue a half instant after the cream cheese and sour cream flavors, so you get a layered effect that pleases both chocolate lovers and cheesecake lovers.

This cheesecake is made in an 8-inch springform pan. The cake will puff over the rim of the pan. To prevent batter from spilling over the rim, mound it slightly in the center before baking.

CRUST

2½ cups fine chocolate wafer cookie crumbs made from store-bought cookies

8 tablespoons (4 ounces) unsalted butter, melted

OR

TKO cookie crumbs (from 1 full recipe; see page 000)

FILLING

Three (8-ounce) packages cream cheese, at room temperature

1 cup granulated sugar

Pinch of salt

2 large eggs

2 cups sour cream

1 teaspoon pure vanilla extract

10 ounces 70% bittersweet chocolate, chopped into ¼-inch pieces

FOR THE CRUST:

If using chocolate wafer cookie crumbs, in a medium bowl, stir together the crumbs and melted butter. The TKO crumbs do not need additional butter. Press the crumbs into the bottom and at least halfway up the sides of an 8-inch springform pan. Refrigerate for 20 minutes.

Position a rack in the middle of the oven and preheat the oven to 375°F. Bake the crust for 10 minutes, remove from the oven and cool on a rack. Lower the oven temperature to 350°F.

FOR THE FILLING:

In the bowl of a stand mixer fitted with the paddle attachment, beat the cream cheese, sugar, and salt on medium speed about 1 minute, or until fluffy. Scrape down the sides of the bowl, add the eggs, and beat for 2 minutes. Add the sour cream and vanilla and mix for an additional 2 minutes, or until the batter is smooth and creamy. Scrape the bowl and paddle as necessary. Remove the bowl from the mixer and fold in the chocolate.

Pour the batter into the crust. Spread it evenly with a small offset spatula, then mound it slightly higher in the center. Bake for 55 minutes to 1 hour, or until lightly browned and set. There may be a few cracks around the edges. Turn off the heat, prop open the oven door with a wooden spoon, and let the cake rest in the oven for 30 minutes.

Remove the cheesecake from the oven and cool on a cooling rack for 30 minutes, then refrigerate for at least 4 hours to chill and firm or preferably overnight.

Run a palette knife or icing spatula around the edge of the pan, remove the springform ring, and carefully transfer the cake to a serving plate. Cover with plastic wrap and refrigerate until serving. (If you want to remove the springform bottom from the cheesecake, run the spatula carefully between the crust and the bottom of the pan.)

The cheesecake can be refrigerated up to 3 days or frozen up to 1 month.

SERVES 10

COCOA CHIFFON CAKE

CONTRIBUTED BY FLO BRAKER

Flo is a charter member of the Baker's Dozen, a San Francisco group founded to bring together bakers. Her desserts are always simply, straightforwardly good. This chiffon cake is a good example. It has a very light texture for a cake with such a rich cocoa taste.

We like this moist cake served plain with a cup of coffee or topped with ice cream or very softly whipped cream.

Position a rack in the lower third of the oven and preheat the oven to 350°F. Set out an ungreased 10 by 4-inch round angel-food tube pan, and have a long-necked bottle nearby. (After baking, you will invert the baked cake onto the neck of the bottle to cool completely.)

Sift the flour, 1⅓ cups of the granulated sugar, the baking powder, and salt into a large bowl.

In a medium bowl, whisk the cocoa powder and hot water until blended. Let cool, then stir in the oil and egg yolks until smooth.

In the bowl of a stand mixer fitted with the whisk attachment, whip the egg whites at low speed until small bubbles appear. Increase the speed, add the cream of tartar, and whip until soft peaks form. Add the remaining 2 tablespoons granulated sugar in a steady stream, and continue whipping until stiff, but not dry, peaks form.

Make a well in the center of the flour mixture, add the cocoa-egg mixture, and mix with a rubber spatula until smooth. Scoop half of the meringue onto the cocoa mixture and fold it in. Fold in remaining meringue until thoroughly combined. Pour the batter into the ungreased angel-food tube pan, and spread it evenly.

Bake for 50 to 55 minutes, or until the top of the cake is cracked and it springs back slightly when touched. Invert onto the long-necked bottle and let cool completely.

To remove the cake from its pan, gently tap around the edges of the pan on the work surface. When the cake appears almost free from the sides of the pan, place a sheet of waxed paper on the work surface, turn the pan upside down, and, with gentle force, hit the pan against the work surface. Lift the pan from the cake. With the aid of the waxed paper, lift the cake onto a serving plate, turning it right side up.

To serve, sprinkle the top of the cake with confectioners' sugar. Cut into slices with a long serrated knife. Accompany each slice with whipped cream or a scoop of a favorite flavor of ice cream.

SERVES 14

INGREDIENTS

1½ cups unsifted cake flour

1⅓ cups plus 2 tablespoons granulated sugar

1 tablespoon baking powder

¾ teaspoon salt

⅔ cup unsweetened cocoa powder

¾ cup hot water

½ cup canola oil

6 large egg yolks

1 cup egg whites (7 to 8 large)

½ teaspoon cream of tartar

About ¼ cup confectioners' sugar for dusting the cake

Whipped Cream (page 315), fresh strawberries or ice cream (optional)

CHOCOLATE CHINCHILLA

CONTRIBUTED BY SALLY SCHMITT

Sally has made this dessert in her cooking classes for more than thirty years, and she shared it with John when he helped teach at The Apple Farm, the orchards where Sally and her husband, Don, grow apples. There's nobody quite like Sally, and no other dessert quite like a chinchilla. This soufflé has a really intriguing, almost sticky texture.

Sally adds cinnamon to the batter, but we usually leave it out. She tops each slice of chinchilla with sherry-flavored whipped cream. She uses a ring mold or tube pan for a dramatic look, as the batter rises to the top of the mold and puffs over the top beautifully as it bakes.

Position a rack in the middle of the oven and preheat the oven to 325°F. Butter an 11-inch ring mold or a 12-cup (10-inch) Bundt pan, and place in a deep roasting pan.

Sift together the sugar and cocoa into a medium bowl. Sift in cinnamon, if using.

In the bowl of a stand mixer fitted with the whisk attachment, whip the whites on medium speed until soft peaks form, 5 to 7 minutes. Do not overbeat.

Meanwhile, bring a medium saucepan of water to a boil for the water bath.

Remove the bowl from the mixer, and top the whites with the cocoa mixture. This will look like a lot to incorporate, but the batter will come together. Slowly and gently fold the ingredients together, reaching to the bottom of the bowl to incorporate all the whites.

Pour the batter into the prepared pan. Spread the batter into the corners with a rubber spatula.

Pour enough boiling water into the roasting pan to come 2 to 3 inches up the sides of the mold. Bake for 45 minutes to 1 hour, or until a skewer inserted in the center of the cake comes out clean. The cake will puff up as it bakes, then shrink back as it cools.

Carefully transfer the mold to a cooling rack, and cool completely in the pan. Run a knife around the edges of the pan and unmold the cake onto a serving plate. Serve with whipped cream and, if desired, a sprinkling of cacao nibs.

SERVES 12 TO 16

INGREDIENTS

2 cups confectioners' sugar

1¼ cups unsweetened cocoa powder

1 teaspoon ground cinnamon (optional)

2 cups egg whites (about 12 large whites)

Whipped Cream (page 315)

Cacao nibs for sprinkling (optional)

CHOCOLATE ROULADE

CONTRIBUTED BY ALICE MEDRICH

A delicate soufflé cake subtly laced with ground toasted pecans lends itself to a wide variety of flavors. Add a splash of rum, brandy, or Scotch to the whipped cream, vary the type of nuts, or spread a pint of softened ice cream instead of whipped cream over the cake before rolling it.

CAKE

⅓ cup pecans

1 tablespoon all-purpose flour

½ cup plus ⅓ cup granulated sugar

½ cup unsweetened cocoa powder, plus 1 tablespoon for dusting the cake

⅛ teaspoon salt

4 tablespoons (2 ounces) unsalted butter, melted and still hot

2 tablespoons water

½ teaspoon pure vanilla extract

3 large eggs, separated

2 large egg whites

⅛ teaspoon cream of tartar

FILLING

1 cup very cold heavy cream

½ teaspoon pure vanilla extract

1½ tablespoons granulated sugar

Cocoa powder or confectioners' sugar for dusting

FOR THE CAKE:

Position a rack in the lower third of the oven and preheat the oven to 350°F. Line a 17 by 12 by 1-inch baking sheet (half sheet pan) with parchment paper or foil.

Spread the nuts in a pie pan or on a small baking sheet and toast in the oven for 5 to 8 minutes, or until fragrant and lightly colored. Transfer the nuts to a plate to cool completely.

Combine the pecans and flour in the bowl of a food processor or a mini processor, and pulse until the nuts are finely ground. Set aside.

In a large bowl, combine ½ cup of the sugar with the cocoa and salt. Whisk in the hot butter, water, and vanilla. Whisk in the 3 egg yolks. Set aside.

In the bowl of a stand mixer fitted with the whisk attachment, beat the 5 egg whites and cream of tartar at medium speed until soft peaks form. Gradually sprinkle in the remaining ⅓ cup sugar, then increase the speed to high and whip until the whites are stiff and glossy but not dry.

Fold about one-quarter of the egg whites into the cocoa mixture. Top with the remaining egg whites, pour the nut mixture over them, and fold until the egg whites and nuts are just incorporated into the batter. Spread the batter evenly in the prepared pan, making sure to push it into the corners.

Bake for about 10 minutes, or until the cake is slightly puffed and a tester inserted in the center comes out clean. Cool completely in the pan on a cooling rack.

Run a knife around the edges of the cake to loosen it from the pan. Using a very fine strainer (a tea strainer works well), dust the top of the cake evenly with 1 tablespoon cocoa. Cover the cake with a sheet of foil long enough to extend over the ends of the pan. Holding the foil at the ends of the pan, invert the cake onto a work surface. Remove the pan and peel off the pan liner. Set out a serving plate or platter for the roulade.

FOR THE FILLING:

In a large bowl, whip the cream with the vanilla until it begins to thicken. Sprinkle in the sugar and beat until the cream holds soft peaks.

Spread the cream evenly over the cake. Starting at a short end, use the foil to help you roll the cake. At first the cake will crack as you roll it. Don't worry; the cracking will get less severe as the roulade gets fatter (and a little cracking on the finished roulade ends up looking quite appetizing anyway). Roll the roulade seam side down onto the serving platter. Cover with plastic wrap and refrigerate until ready to serve. (The roulade can be refrigerated for up to 1 day.)

Just before serving, trim the ends of the roulade for a cleaner look, or leave as is for a more rustic presentation. Dust a little cocoa or confectioners' sugar over the top, slice at the table, and serve on individual plates.

SERVES 8

Sofia's Almond, Fig, and Chocolate-Shaving Sandwich

SOMETIMES VERY GOOD CHOCOLATE IDEAS come from unexpected sources. Sofia Alicastro, an eighth grader we know, came up with this novel sandwich when she was put in charge of making her own school lunches.

Sofia starts with a good artisan bread, never presliced. She cuts two thick slices of the bread, spreads one slice with almond butter, and carefully arranges sliced fresh figs or dried Medjool dates on top before drizzling on honey. Then she grates dark chocolate over the top and caps it with the second slice of bread. We know people four times Sofia's age who think her sandwich is the height of sophistication.

ONE-POT SOUR CREAM CAKE

CONTRIBUTED BY STEPHANIE HERSH

This incredibly moist chocolate cake has two distinct advantages. First, you'll most likely have every ingredient already on hand. Second, you'll need only one pot and one pan. This batter also makes excellent cupcakes.

INGREDIENTS

Unsalted butter and flour for the pan

½ cup water

2 tablespoons unsweetened cocoa powder

8 tablespoons (4 ounces) unsalted butter, cut into 1-inch cubes

1 cup granulated sugar

½ cup all-purpose flour

½ teaspoon baking soda

1 large egg

¼ cup sour cream

Whipped Cream (page 315)

Chocolate Curls (page 23)

Position a rack in the middle of the oven and preheat the oven to 350°F. Butter and flour an 8-inch round cake pan or a standard cupcake tin. (This recipe makes 9 cupcakes.)

Place the water, cocoa powder, and butter in a medium saucepan, bring to a simmer over low heat, and simmer gently until the butter is melted. Whisk to combine, then add the sugar, remove from the heat, and whisk until smooth and well blended. (At this point, there may still be some visible granules of sugar.)

Whisk in the flour and baking soda. Add the egg and sour cream, and whisk until the batter is uniform in color.

Pour the batter into the prepared pan. Bake for 25 to 30 minutes (15 to 17 minutes for cupcakes), or until the sides of the cake begin to pull away from the pan and the center springs back when pressed lightly. A skewer inserted in the center of the cake should come out clean.

Remove the cake from the oven and cool in the pan on a rack for 10 minutes (2 minutes for cupcakes). Invert onto the rack to cool completely.

To serve, transfer the cake to a serving plate and top with the whipped cream and chocolate curls.

SERVES 8 TO 10 OR MAKES 9 CUPCAKES

Natural Cocoa Powder

In 1828, Conrad Van Houten created a mechanical press that squeezed the roasted nibs, pressing out the cocoa butter, instead of grinding the nibs into a paste as you would to make chocolate. Squeezing out 75 percent of the cocoa butter left a powder that could be stirred more easily into a drink. The cocoa powder kept indefinitely in a tin, and because it contained less fat, it was also easier to digest.

Van Houten also came up with the idea of adding an alkali to the cocoa powder to soften the astringent flavors. This process also made the powder extremely dark—the key color component of a devil's food cake. But although Dutch-processed cocoa, as it is called, may have been a good idea for low-grade beans, we can't bear to add an alkali to cocoa powder made naturally from good beans, because the alkali removes much of the flavor and aromas, the good as well as the bad.

Convincing cooks to switch to natural cocoa powder has been challenging. During every tour, we bring out two glass dishes filled with cocoa powder. Both are considered "premium," but one is dark and velvety, while the other is an earthy reddish brown. We pass the dishes around and ask the group to taste and smell. Most people find that the light-colored cocoa—our cocoa, made without alkali—tastes and smells much better. And yet because many bakers and pastry chefs can't bring themselves to give up that devil's food darkness, they're reluctant to switch.

In fairness to pastry chefs, switching to a natural cocoa powder may not result in a lot more flavor in recipes made with ingredients that will muffle the taste of the chocolate. But in recipes that allow the flavor of the chocolate to really come forward, a natural cocoa powder makes a big difference.

It seems odd to us that a process invented to make beans taste less harsh would remain in place even when it was no longer necessary—solely to preserve a side effect of the process: the darker color of the resulting cocoa powder. Bakers tell us that their customers believe the darker the cake, the more chocolatey its taste. They feel their customers aren't yet ready for a reddish-brown devil's food cake—even if that cake tastes better than one made with alkalized cocoa powder.

CHOCOLATE SOUFFLÉ

CONTRIBUTED BY STEPHEN DURFEE

Making a soufflé is a rite of passage. Inexperienced cooks often don't realize that a soufflé is not all that difficult—and it just might be the best dessert for tasting a really fine chocolate. Stephen's splendid combination of egg whites and dark chocolate has all the flavor of chocolate eaten out of hand but a texture that is both ethereal and rich.

Brush a 1- to 1½-quart soufflé mold with melted butter and coat the bottom and sides with 2 tablespoons of the sugar. Tap out any excess sugar, and refrigerate the mold until ready to use.

In a small bowl, mix together the butter and flour with a fork to form a paste. In a small saucepan, bring the milk to a boil over medium-high heat. Reduce the heat to medium and whisk in the flour-butter paste until smooth. The mixture will thicken right away.

Remove from the heat, add the chocolate, and whisk to melt it. Add the brandy. Stir in the 2 egg yolks. Transfer the mixture to a large bowl. Place a piece of plastic wrap against the surface and let cool at room temperature for about 5 minutes. (The soufflé base can be refrigerated for up to 3 days. Before using, bring it to room temperature by whisking it over a bowl of warm water or microwave for 2 to 5 seconds, then whisk.)

Position a rack in the middle of the oven and preheat the oven to 400°F.

In the bowl of a stand mixer fitted with the whisk attachment, whip the 3 egg whites and salt until bubbly, slightly frothy, and opaque. Slowly add the remaining 2½ tablespoons sugar and whip to soft peaks.

Stir one-quarter of the egg whites into the soufflé base. Fold in the remaining egg whites and pour the mixture into the prepared soufflé mold. Level the surface by jiggling the mold slightly, and gently smooth the top with an offset spatula.

Bake for about 20 minutes, or until the soufflé has risen; there should be some resistance when the edges are gently touched. (It will feel very similar to the top of a sponge cake.) Dust the soufflé with confectioners' sugar and serve immediately. Present it in the mold, spoon into individual bowls, and serve with the custard sauce, if desired.

SERVES 4

INGREDIENTS

Melted unsalted butter for the soufflé mold

2½ tablespoons granulated sugar plus 2 tablespoons for coating the mold

1½ tablespoons (¾ ounce) unsalted butter, at room temperature

2 tablespoons all-purpose flour

½ cup whole milk

3 ounces 70% bittersweet chocolate, finely chopped

1 tablespoon brandy

2 large eggs, separated

1 large egg white

Pinch of salt

Confectioners' sugar for dusting

Custard Sauce (page 313; optional)

Chocolate Pecan Tart, page 150.

CHOCOLATE PECAN TART

This tart's caramel-nut filling rests on a thin, light crust that's been coated with a layer of dark chocolate. Try using this same technique of coating a crust with chocolate for other tarts and pies, such as a lemon tart, coconut cream pie, and banana cream pie.

CRUST

1⅓ cups all-purpose flour

1 tablespoon plus 1 teaspoon granulated sugar

¼ teaspoon salt

12 tablespoons (6 ounces) unsalted butter, cut into ½-inch cubes

About 3 tablespoons ice water

3 ounces 82% extra dark chocolate, finely chopped

FILLING

1⅓ cups granulated sugar

⅓ cup water

1 cup heavy cream, warmed

1½ teaspoons pure vanilla extract

1 large egg

1 large egg yolk

4 tablespoons (2 ounces) unsalted butter, melted and cooled

1⅔ cups lightly toasted pecan halves

2 tablespoons cacao nibs, chopped (optional)

Cocoa Whipped Cream (page 315)

FOR THE CRUST:

Place the flour, sugar, and salt in the bowl of a food processor and pulse two or three times to combine. Add the butter and continue pulsing until the mixture resembles coarse meal. Add the water by drizzling about 1 tablespoon at a time, pulsing after each drizzle. Stop once the dough begins to come together.

Transfer the dough to a board and use the heel of your hand or a pastry scraper to press it together. Pat into a disk approximately 6 inches in diameter, wrap in plastic wrap, and refrigerate until firm, about 2 hours.

On a lightly floured board, roll out the dough to a 13- to 14-inch circle, flouring the dough and board as necessary to keep it from sticking. Roll up the dough around the rolling pin and unroll it into an 11-inch tart pan with a removable bottom. Gently lift the edges to ease the dough into the corners of the pan, then push the dough down gently to be certain the dough around the sides is ¼ inch thick. Use a paring knife to cut excess dough from the rim of the pan. If necessary, pat a bit of the dough trimmings into any thin spots. Cover with plastic wrap and refrigerate for 1 hour.

Position a rack in the middle of the oven and preheat the oven to 375°F. Place the tart pan on a baking sheet.

Prick the bottom of the crust with a fork, line with aluminum foil or parchment paper, and fill with pie weights or dry beans. Bake for 15 minutes.

Remove the parchment and weights, and continue to bake for 15 to 20 minutes, or until the crust is golden. Sprinkle the chopped chocolate evenly over the bottom of the crust and bake for an additional minute, just to melt the chocolate. Remove from the oven and use the back of a spoon or a small offset spatula to spread the chocolate in an even layer. Let cool on a rack while you prepare the filling. Raise the oven temperature to 400°F.

FOR THE FILLING:

In a medium saucepan, combine the sugar and water and stir over medium-low heat until the sugar dissolves. Increase the heat to medium-high and cook, without stirring, swirling the pan so the caramel colors evenly. If sugar crystals form on the sides of the pan, brush with a wet pastry brush. Test the color of the caramel by drizzling a few drops onto a white plate. When the color is medium to dark amber, remove from the heat. Slowly and carefully—it will bubble up—add the cream.

Return the caramel to medium heat and cook for 3 minutes to thicken slightly, reducing the heat to medium-low if the caramel bubbles too much. Remove from the heat and cool for 15 minutes.

Place the tart shell on a baking sheet.

In a medium bowl, whisk together the vanilla, egg, and yolk. Slowly whisk into the caramel. Stir in the melted butter, followed by the nuts and nibs, if using. Pour the filling into the prepared tart shell. The filling will come to the top of the shell. (If the crust has shrunk during baking, it may not hold all the filling.)

Bake the tart for 15 minutes. Lower the oven temperature to 375°F and bake for an additional 15 minutes, or until the filling is set.

Let cool on a rack for about 10 minutes. While still warm, move the tart in the pan to loosen the edges where the caramel has stuck, but keep it in the pan. Let cool completely before removing the tart ring.

Serve each wedge of tart with a dollop of the cocoa whipped cream.

SERVES 10

ORANGE CHOCOLATE BAKLAVA

Chocolate and baklava aren't a traditional combination, but dark chocolate works surprisingly well with baklava's texture, adding a depth of flavor that makes this centuries-old dessert seem new. Fresh orange brightens the flavors of the almonds, walnuts, and dates and makes the crisp honey-soaked layers of phyllo dough taste less sweet.

FOR THE SYRUP:

Using a vegetable peeler, remove the zest from the orange in strips. Juice the orange.

In a medium saucepan, combine the zest, 3 tablespoons of the juice, the water, honey, both sugars, and the cinnamon stick and bring to a boil over medium-high heat, stirring to dissolve the sugar. Reduce the heat and let the syrup simmer gently for 45 minutes. As the syrup cooks, skim any foam that rises to the surface. Remove the pan from the heat, and discard the zest and cinnamon stick.

FOR THE FILLING:

In a food processor, pulse the almonds and walnuts until sandy in texture. Add the chocolate and pulse until finely chopped. Add the dates and pulse until the dates and chocolate are about the same size. Place in a small bowl, toss with the salt and cinnamon, and set aside.

Position a rack in the middle of the oven and preheat the oven to 350°F.

Near your work surface, set out the nut mixture, melted butter, a 9 by 13 by 2-inch baking pan, and a pastry brush. Unroll the sheets of phyllo and cover with a slightly damp towel to keep the layers from cracking.

When working with phyllo, don't let a tear throw you. Just piece a torn sheet back together and keep layering. Place 1 sheet of phyllo, with a long side facing you, on the work surface. Brush with a light coating of butter, and sprinkle the entire surface with a heaping ⅓ cup of the nut mixture. Repeat two more times to form three layers of phyllo, butter, and nuts. Carefully fold up the bottom edge and then roll up into a log. Trim the rough ends, cut the log in half, and place the two halves side by side at one end of the pan. Repeat with the remaining sheets and filling, making 2 more logs. Place these logs side by side across the pan, at a right angle to the first 2 logs. With a sharp paring knife, score the logs at 2-inch intervals. Bake for 45 minutes, or until golden brown. Transfer the pan to a cooling rack. Remove any excess butter with a turkey baster, and discard.

Reheat the syrup over medium heat. As soon as the logs are cool enough to handle, cut through the scored lines, then pour the warm syrup over the baklava. Using a turkey baster or a spoon, baste the pieces with the syrup that settles on the bottom of the pan, until almost all of the syrup has soaked in. Let cool.

Cover with plastic wrap or store in an airtight container at room temperature for up to 5 days.

MAKES 2 DOZEN PIECES

SYRUP

1 small orange

¾ cup water

1 cup plus 2 tablespoons honey

3 tablespoons granulated sugar

3 tablespoons light brown sugar

1 cinnamon stick

FILLING

1 cup lightly toasted, unblanched whole almonds (about 5 ounces)

1 cup lightly toasted walnuts (about 4 ounces)

6 ounces 70% bittersweet chocolate, coarsely chopped

4 ounces pitted dates (about 6 to 8), coarsely chopped

¼ teaspoon salt

1 teaspoon ground cinnamon

¾ cup clarified butter (see page 309), melted

9 sheets phyllo dough (about half of a 1-pound box), thawed

LEGENDS & LORE

The First Cacao in Europe

We know from recorded list and paintings that cacao beans were among the first gifts that Christopher Columbus brought from the New World to the Spanish court in 1502. Columbus knew the beans had value because he'd seen Mesoamericans scramble to find every bean when a basketful of cacao had overturned. Unfortunately, because Columbus had no idea what to do with the beans, they languished unused, and chocolate remained unheard of in Europe for another several decades. When Cortés brought cacao to Spain in 1529, he also brought the knowledge of how Montezuma's court had prepared the beans. Slowly but surely, chocolate's popularity spread throughout Spain.

Before the Spanish arrived in the New World, cacao was being cultivated and transplanted, but the influx of Spanish settlers and missionaries marks when cacao really began to move into new areas. Because cacao seeds can't live longer than two weeks, it's pretty clear that people in canoes were paddling cacao seedlings up and down the Amazon River and all along the coastlines of South and Central America. Merchants carried cacao along the Mayan trade routes, and settlers brought it from Mesoamerica to South America and the Caribbean. Seedlings were being carried across the ocean and finding fertile ground in Africa and Asia. The distinct strains of cacao began to merge.

CHOCOLATE GINGER
POTS DE CRÈME

CONTRIBUTED BY JOANNE WEIR

These silky pots de crème are flavored with fresh ginger, which adds a light, spicy tang to the chocolate's deeper tones.

To peel ginger easily, scrape the skin away with a teaspoon.

Place the ginger in a small saucepan, cover with 1 inch of water, and bring to a boil. Simmer for 2 minutes. Drain.

In a large saucepan, bring the cream, milk, ginger, and sugar to a simmer over medium-high heat, stirring occasionally to dissolve the sugar. (Keep a close watch on the pan; the cream can bubble up and over very quickly.) Remove from the heat, cover, and let stand for 2 hours to infuse the cream with the flavor of ginger.

Position a rack in the middle of the oven and preheat the oven to 325°F. Arrange eight 5- to 6-ounce ramekins (see page 25) in a large baking pan or roasting pan, making sure the ramekins don't touch each other or the edges of the pan.

Place both chocolates in a medium heatproof bowl and set over a pot of gently simmering water. Stir occasionally until the chocolate is melted and smooth. Remove from the heat.

Set a fine-mesh strainer over the top of the chocolate bowl. Reheat the milk and cream mixture over medium-high heat until it bubbles around the edges. Strain one-quarter of the hot milk and cream mixture onto the chocolate. Remove the strainer and whisk to combine. Return the strainer to the bowl, and slowly whisk in the remaining milk and cream mixture. Discard the ginger.

In a large bowl, whisk together the egg yolks. Whisking constantly, slowly add the chocolate mixture until well combined. Pour into a large measuring cup or a bowl with a spout.

Divide the custard among the ramekins, and wipe the rims clean. Break up any bubbles that have settled on the surface with a skewer or with a quick pass of a propane torch.

Pour enough very hot water into the pan to come 1 inch up the sides of the ramekins. Bake for 40 to 50 minutes, or until the edges of the custards are firm but the very centers are not completely set. Carefully remove from the oven, and let the ramekins remain in the water bath for 10 minutes.

Remove the ramekins and cool for 30 minutes, then cover and refrigerate for at least several hours or up to 3 days. To serve, top each pot de crème with a dollop of whipped cream. Serve cold or at room temperature.

SERVES 8

INGREDIENTS

⅓ cup thinly sliced peeled fresh ginger (about a 3-inch piece)

1½ cups heavy cream

1½ cups whole milk

¾ cup granulated sugar

2½ ounces 70% bittersweet chocolate, finely chopped

2½ ounces 62% semisweet chocolate, finely chopped

8 large egg yolks

Whipped Cream (page 315)

BLACK AND WHITE
CRÈME BRÛLÉE

CONTRIBUTED BY MICHEL RICHARD

Michel Richard adds an element of surprise to even the most classic of dishes. His version of crème brûlée pairs a smooth, cool layer of vanilla custard with a topping of silky dark chocolate mousse. The contrast is exceptional.

The dessert can be made the day before and refrigerated, but the caramelizing must be done just prior to serving. When caramelizing the topping, we prefer a propane torch—available in most hardware stores—to the smaller, more expensive, and less effective culinary torches.

CUSTARD

½ cup whole milk

2 cups heavy cream

½ cup granulated sugar

1 vanilla bean

9 large egg yolks, at room temperature

MOUSSE

2½ ounces 70% bittersweet chocolate, coarsely chopped

4 tablespoons (2 ounces) unsalted butter, cut into chunks

2 large eggs, separated, at room temperature

2 tablespoons granulated sugar

⅛ teaspoon cream of tartar

¼ cup dried and ground light brown sugar (see Note on the next page)

FOR THE CUSTARD:

In a heavy medium saucepan, combine the milk, cream, and sugar. Split the vanilla bean and scrape the seeds into the milk mixture (see Note on the next page). Add the pod and bring to a boil over medium heat. Remove from the heat and let steep for 30 minutes, or until the mixture cools to room temperature. Discard the vanilla pod or reserve for another use.

Place a rack in the center of the oven and preheat the oven to 300°F.

Lightly beat the egg yolks with a fork, then whisk into the milk mixture. Strain the custard through a fine-mesh strainer into a 2- to 3-quart shallow gratin dish.

Place the gratin dish in a large deep baking pan or a roasting pan. Pour enough very hot water into the pan to come three-quarters of the way up the gratin dish. Bake for 45 minutes. Check the custard by gently shaking the dish; the custard should be set but still move slightly. Test by inserting a knife into the custard; it should come out clean and almost dry. If necessary, cook the custard for 5 to 10 minutes longer, checking often.

Carefully remove the gratin dish from the water bath. Let cool to room temperature, then cover and refrigerate until cold, at least 4 hours or overnight.

FOR THE MOUSSE:

Melt the chocolate and butter in the top of a double boiler set over gently simmering water, stirring occasionally until smooth. Remove from the heat and let sit in a warm spot until tepid or barely warm. (If the chocolate is too hot when added to the yolks, the yolks could curdle; if the chocolate is too cool, flakes of chocolate may form in the yolks.)

The mousse is best made with a whisk or with a hand mixer; a stand mixer may not be able to whisk such a small quantity. In a medium bowl, whisk the egg yolks with 1 tablespoon of the sugar until a slowly dissolving ribbon forms when the whisk is lifted. Fold in the tepid chocolate. In a medium bowl, using a clean dry whisk or beaters, beat the egg whites with the cream of tartar until soft peaks form. Add the remaining 1 tablespoon sugar and continue beating until barely stiff peaks form. Gently fold half of the whites into the chocolate mixture, then fold in the remaining whites.

Spoon the chocolate mousse over the chilled custard, smoothing the top with a small offset spatula. Wipe the rim of the dish with a damp towel to remove any chocolate. Cover with plastic wrap and refrigerate for at least 6 hours, or, preferably, overnight.

Thirty minutes before serving, remove the crème brûlée from the refrigerator.

TO CARAMELIZE THE BRÛLÉE:

Sprinkle the sugar in an even layer over the top of the mousse. If using a torch, work from one end of the dish to the other. Adjust the level of the torch as necessary to regulate the heat, moving the flame over the surface to caramelize the sugar. If using a broiler, place a rack on the highest level and preheat the broiler. Broil until the sugar is melted and caramelized, about 2 minutes. Watch carefully, and move or turn the dish as necessary for even caramelization.

SERVES 6 TO 8

Notes: If your vanilla bean has dried out, place the whole bean in the cream mixture when bringing it up to a boil. Then remove the pod, split it lengthwise, and scrape the seeds into the milk. Return the pod to the mixture to steep.

Michel has found that dried and ground light brown sugar makes the best topping for crème brûlée. Spread the sugar in a baking dish and place in a 325°F oven until dry to the touch. (If you have older, dryer sugar, it may not be necessary to dry it in the oven.) Place the sugar in a small food processor or coffee grinder and grind until fine.

CHOCOLATE ZABAGLIONE TRIFLE

SPONGE CAKE

1¼ cups cake flour

2½ teaspoons baking powder

1 tablespoon finely ground espresso beans

Pinch of salt

5 large eggs, separated

1¼ cups granulated sugar

5 tablespoons boiling water

1 teaspoon pure vanilla extract

ZABAGLIONE CREAM

8 large egg yolks

½ cup granulated sugar

¾ cup sweet Marsala

Pinch of salt

2 ounces 62% semisweet chocolate, finely chopped

1½ cups heavy cream

¼ cup espresso or strong coffee, at room temperature

2 tablespoons sweet Marsala

4 ounces 62% semisweet chocolate, very finely chopped by hand or ground in a food processor

1 cup heavy cream

1 tablespoon granulated sugar

CONTRIBUTED BY EMILY LUCHETTI

A zabaglione is traditionally made with sweet Marsala, the Italian fortified wine that is Sicily's answer to sherry or Madeira. For a traditional presentation, make the trifle in a clear glass bowl that will show off the layers of coffee, mocha, and chocolate.

Emily's recipe produces a cake with a spongy texture that soaks up the liquid but still retains its shape.

FOR THE CAKE:

Position a rack in the middle of the oven and preheat the oven to 350°F. Line a 17 by 12 by 1-inch baking sheet (half sheet pan) with parchment paper. You may butter the pan lightly to anchor the paper if you like, but don't butter the top of the parchment.

Sift together the flour, baking powder, ground espresso, and salt into a medium bowl. Set aside.

In the bowl of a stand mixer fitted with the whisk attachment, combine the 5 egg yolks and sugar. Begin whipping on medium speed until combined then beat on high speed for 2 to 3 minutes, or until the mixture is thick and pale yellow. Stop to scrape the bottom and sides of the bowl as necessary. Reduce the speed to medium and slowly add the water and vanilla. Scrape the bowl. Return to high speed and whip for about 5 minutes, until the mixture is again thick and a slowly dissolving ribbon forms when the whisk is lifted.

Remove the bowl from the mixer and fold in the dry ingredients. Set aside.

In a clean mixer bowl with a clean whisk attachment, whip the 5 egg whites at medium-high speed until soft peaks form. Fold half of the whites into the batter, then fold in the remaining whites.

Spread the batter evenly in the prepared pan, pushing it into the corners.

Bake for 15 to 20 minutes, or until the cake springs back when lightly touched. Cool completely in the pan on a cooling rack.

FOR THE ZABAGLIONE CREAM:

In a medium heatproof bowl, whisk together the 8 yolks, sugar, Marsala, and salt. Set the bowl over a pot of gently boiling water and whisk the mixture constantly (use a pot holder or towel to hold the side of the bowl when it becomes hot from the steam). The zabaglione will bubble up, then subside after about 2 minutes and eventually reach the consistency of mayonnaise. Remove the bowl from the heat, and whisk in the chocolate until smooth. Continue whisking until the zabaglione is cool.

In a large bowl, whip the cream until soft peaks form. Fold in the cooled zabaglione. Refrigerate until ready to use.

TO ASSEMBLE THE TRIFLE:

Set out a 2½- to 3-quart trifle dish or other glass bowl. Run a knife around the edges of the cake to loosen it from the pan.

Mix together the espresso and Marsala in a small bowl or cup.

Reserve about 1 tablespoon of the chocolate for the top of the trifle. Spread about 1 cup of the zabaglione cream in the bottom of the bowl and sprinkle with the remaining chocolate. Cut cake pieces to fit on top of the cream in a single layer, and arrange them on the cream. Brush the cake with the espresso mixture. Cover the cake with the remaining zabaglione, and top with another layer of cake. Brush with the espresso mixture.

In a medium bowl, whip the cream and sugar until soft peaks form. Spread on top of the trifle and sprinkle with the reserved chocolate. Refrigerate for at least 2 hours or up to a day.

To serve, scoop through all of the layers.

SERVES 8 TO 10

LEGENDS & LORE

Gianduja Appears in Turin

Since the 1600s, the Italian town of Turin has been known for its chocolate. Legend has it that during the Napoleonic Wars, as cacao became scarce because of the blockade that kept ships from reaching Italy, confectioners stretched their chocolate supply by adding ground hazelnuts, which grew abundantly in the Piedmont region.

The mixture of dark chocolate, sugar, and hazelnut paste known as gianduja first appeared in the mid-1800s and was called *givu*—stub in Italian—because it was rolled into cylinders. In 1867, the treat appeared at Piedmont's carnival in the shape of a carnival mask, and was called *giandujotta,* which means small mask.

Gianduja is still very popular in Europe and has a growing number of fans in the States, perhaps because a paste made from finely ground fresh hazelnuts gives chocolate a creamy consistency even when no cream is added, and because people like the hazelnut flavor.

CHOCOLATE PEANUT BUTTER GIANDUJA

CONTRIBUTED BY NICOLE PLUE

Traditionally made with hazelnuts, this gianduja calls for peanut butter instead. Nicole first made this dessert while working at an Asian-themed restaurant, where she liked the flavor and texture peanuts added to savory Thai food. Experimenting with those same elements in a dessert led to this gianduja with a light, creamy chocolate peanut butter topping on a crunchy base.

Nicole's versatile gianduja can be cut and served in many different shapes as part of a dessert tray or on its own. This can stay in your freezer for several weeks.

Cut a 9 by 21-inch piece of parchment paper and line a 9 by 13 by 1- or 9 by 13 by 2-inch baking pan with the parchment, allowing it to extend evenly over the two short ends.

FOR THE CRUNCHY LAYER:

Combine the chocolate and peanut butter in the top of a double boiler set over gently simmering water, and stir occasionally until the chocolate has melted and the mixture is smooth. Remove from the heat and stir in the cookies, coating all the pieces with the chocolate mixture. Spread evenly in the bottom of the prepared baking pan. Set aside.

FOR THE CREAMY LAYER:

Place the chocolate in the bowl of a stand mixer and set it over a pot of gently simmering water. Stir occasionally until the chocolate has melted and is smooth. Remove from the heat and add the peanut butter. Fit the mixer with the whisk attachment, set the bowl on the mixer, and whisk to combine.

In a small saucepan, bring the milk and salt to a boil. Add half of the milk into the peanut butter mixture, and whisk until incorporated, then whisk in the remaining milk. Increase the speed to high and whip for 5 minutes, or until the mixture is creamy and cooled to room temperature.

In a clean bowl, whip the cream just until soft mounds form; do not overwhip. Fold the cream into the peanut butter mixture. Spread it over the crunchy layer in the pan. Cover the pan and freeze until set, at least 4 hours.

To serve, run a knife along the long sides of the dessert and lift it out of the pan using the parchment "handles." Cut into slices or other desired shapes. Dust with cocoa or sprinkle with chopped peanuts, place on serving plates, and let sit at room temperature for about 10 minutes to soften slightly.

SERVES 12 TO 14

CRUNCHY LAYER

2½ ounces 41% milk chocolate, coarsely chopped

¼ cup plus 2 tablespoons creamy peanut butter, at room temperature

1½ cups finely crushed, thinly rolled butter cookies, such as pirouette or pirouluxe

CREAMY LAYER

10 ounces 41% milk chocolate, coarsely chopped

½ cup creamy peanut butter, at room temperature

¾ cup whole milk

¼ teaspoon salt

1 cup heavy cream

Cocoa powder or chopped peanuts for garnish

Chocolate and Peanut Butter Panini

THIS GRILLED SANDWICH IS A SATISFYING AFTER-SCHOOL OR LATE-NIGHT SNACK for fans of peanut butter and chocolate. Start with 1/4-inch slices of white bread or egg bread. If you have a panini grill, preheat it.

Lightly brush one side of each bread slice with canola or any neutral oil. Place a bread slice on a cutting board oil side down and spread a thin layer of peanut butter. Sprinkle ground 62% semisweet chocolate over the peanut butter. (If you like, you can grate it using a Microplane as shown on page 219.) Top with a second slice of bread, oil side up. Sprinkle just a little granulated sugar on top, place in the panini grill, close the top, and cook until browned and crispy.

If you don't have a panini grill, use a griddle or a cast iron skillet instead, pressing the panini with a spatula and turning so each side gets brown and crispy.

SILKY CHOCOLATE PUDDING

Most people believe that a mousse is sophisticated, but that pudding is just cozy and casual. This recipe does away with that notion. When chocolate pudding is as intensely flavorful as this, with a refined texture, it can hold its own beside any mousse. Cooking the pudding in a double boiler and then straining it gives it a wonderful silkiness.

Combine the cornstarch, sugar, and salt in the top of a double boiler. Slowly whisk in the milk, scraping the bottom and sides with a heatproof spatula to incorporate the dry ingredients. Place over gently simmering water and stir occasionally, scraping the bottom and sides. Use a whisk as necessary should lumps begin to form. After 15 to 20 minutes, when the mixture begins to thicken and coats the back of the spoon, add the chocolate. Continue stirring for about 2 to 4 minutes, or until the pudding is smooth and thickened. Remove from the heat and stir in the vanilla.

Strain through a fine-mesh strainer into a serving bowl or strain the pudding into a large measuring cup with a spout and pour into individual serving dishes.

Some find the layer of "skin" that forms on the top of pudding after refrigerating to be the best part, while others can't bear the thought of it. If you're the type who dislikes a pudding skin, place plastic wrap on top of the pudding and smooth it gently against the surface; the wrap will keep a skin from forming. But if you want that dense, chewy layer to form, just pull plastic wrap tightly over the top of the serving dish(es) and don't allow it to touch the pudding.

Refrigerate for at least 30 minutes or up to 3 days.

MAKES 3½ CUPS; SERVES 4 TO 6

INGREDIENTS

¼ cup cornstarch

½ cup granulated sugar

⅛ teaspoon salt

3 cups whole milk

6 ounces 62% semisweet chocolate, coarsely chopped

1 teaspoon pure vanilla extract

Frozen Chocolate Mousse, page 170.

FROZEN CHOCOLATE MOUSSE

This dessert has the airiness of a mousse and the smooth, cold richness of a gelato. We like to serve it in individual portions in the style of a frozen soufflé, with the mousse extending over the top of the ramekins, but it can also be served in one large dish.

To serve the mousse in 5- to 6-ounce ramekins (see page 25), cut 6 strips of parchment or waxed paper about 4 inches wide and 1 inch longer than the circumference of the ramekins. Fold the strips lengthwise in half. Cut 6 long pieces of twine. Wrap each ramekin in a strip of paper, allowing the paper to extend about 1 inch over the top of the ramekin, and tie the collar securely with a piece of twine.

Place ¾ cup of the cream in a small saucepan and bring to a simmer. Turn off the heat, add the chocolate, and let stand for 2 minutes. Stir until the chocolate is melted.

In a medium bowl, whisk the egg yolks and sugar until thickened.

In a saucepan, bring the milk to a simmer over medium-low heat. As soon as it begins to simmer, add a few tablespoons of the warm milk to the yolk-sugar mixture, whisking constantly. Pour about half the warm milk into the bowl, while whisking, then return the mixture to the saucepan and stir constantly for about 8 to 10 minutes, or until the custard thickens and reaches 175°F.

Meanwhile, fill a large bowl with ice water. Strain the custard through a fine-mesh strainer into a large bowl set over the ice water. Stir until it is cool to the touch, then remove from the ice water.

In a large bowl, whip the remaining 1¾ cups cream until it forms very soft peaks. Stir the chocolate mixture if it has separated, and fold into the cooled egg mixture. Fold in the whipped cream.

Spoon the mousse into the prepared ramekins or into a serving bowl. If using the ramekins the mousse should extend about ½ inch over the rim of each ramekin. Place the ramekins on a tray and lay a piece of aluminum foil over the top. Freeze for at least 6 hours or up to 2 days.

About 5 to 10 minutes before serving, remove the mousse from the freezer. Remove the collars, and press the nibs or ground chocolate around the sides of the mousse.

SERVES 6

Note: Grind cacao nibs as you would grind chunks of chocolate. We use either a spice grinder or a coffee grinder, but a mini food processor works too.

INGREDIENTS

2½ cups heavy cream

4 ounces 99% unsweetened chocolate, coarsely chopped

6 large egg yolks

1¼ cups granulated sugar

1 cup whole milk

½ cup finely ground cacao nibs or 62% semisweet or 70% bittersweet chocolate

BAILEY'S MILK CHOCOLATE TRUFFLES

The flavor of Irish cream liqueur melds well with milk chocolate. You can adjust this recipe to taste, according to how subtle—or pronounced—a liqueur flavor you would like in these creamy truffles. We think ¼ cup of Bailey's Irish Cream with ½ cup heavy cream is well balanced, but the proportions can be increased or decreased to taste, as long as the total liquid is ¾ cup.

In a small saucepan, combine the Bailey's and cream and bring to a simmer over medium heat. Remove from the heat, add the chocolate, and let stand for 1 minute.

Stir until all of the chocolate is melted and the mixture is smooth. Pour into a small bowl, cover with plastic wrap, and refrigerate for about 2 hours, or until the ganache is firm enough to roll.

Place the nibs in a shallow bowl. Set out a serving platter or storage container.

Scoop out about 1 teaspoon of the ganache, roll it into a ball between your palms, roll it in the nibs, and place on the platter or in the storage container. Repeat with the remaining chocolate. If the ganache becomes too soft to work with, cover and return to the refrigerator for a few minutes.

The truffles can be stored in an airtight container in the refrigerator for up to 2 weeks or in the freezer for up to 3 months. Allow the truffles to come to room temperature before serving.

MAKES ABOUT 55 SMALL TRUFFLES

INGREDIENTS

¼ cup Bailey's Irish Cream liqueur

½ cup heavy cream

9 ounces 41% milk chocolate, finely chopped

¾ cup cacao nibs, crushed with a rolling pin

CHOCOLATE BISCOTTI

CONTRIBUTED BY SHERRY YARD

Biscotti, whose name means "twice baked," are easy to make. Sherry's recipe calls for chocolate and cocoa powder, producing deep, dark, tender biscotti. This recipe makes a generous amount, which means you can share without any sacrifice.

Sift together the flour, cocoa, baking powder, and salt, and set aside.

In the bowl of a stand mixer fitted with the paddle attachment, cream the butter and 1 cup of the sugar on medium speed for about 3 to 5 minutes, or until light and fluffy, stopping as necessary to scrape the sides and bottom of the bowl. Add the eggs one at a time, beating until each is incorporated. Add the vanilla and wine and beat for 1 to 2 minutes, or until fully incorporated.

With the mixer running on low speed, slowly add the flour mixture in a steady stream, mixing until fully incorporated. Remove the bowl from the mixer and fold in the chocolate.

Form the dough into a block, wrap in plastic wrap, and refrigerate for 30 minutes.

Position a rack in the middle of the oven and preheat the oven to 350°F. Line a baking sheet with a Silpat or parchment paper.

Combine the remaining ½ cup sugar, the coffee, and cinnamon in a small bowl, and set aside.

Lightly flour a board or work surface. Remove the dough from the refrigerator and divide in half. Shape each piece into a 2 by 12-inch log. Brush excess flour from the logs and board. Sprinkle about two-thirds of the cinnamon sugar onto the board and roll the logs in it, patting the sugar onto the surface. Place the logs 4 inches apart on the prepared pan. Sprinkle with the remaining cinnamon sugar.

Bake for 20 to 25 minutes, or until the logs are firm to the touch and a skewer inserted in the center comes out clean. Transfer the pan to a cooling rack and allow to cool for 30 minutes. Lower the oven temperature to 300°F and position the racks in the lower and upper third of the oven.

Brush any excess sugar from the baking sheet and line a second baking sheet with a Silpat or parchment paper. Using a serrated knife, slice the logs on the diagonal into biscotti that are about 3 inches long and ½ inch thick. Lay the biscotti on the prepared baking sheet.

Bake the biscotti for 15 to 20 minutes, rotating the pans halfway through baking. They should be toasted and somewhat dry but will not be as crisp as traditional biscotti. Remove from the pans and cool completely on a cooling rack.

The biscotti can be stored in an airtight container for up to 2 weeks.

MAKES ABOUT 40 COOKIES

INGREDIENTS

2½ cups all-purpose flour

½ cup unsweetened cocoa powder

1½ teaspoons baking powder

⅛ teaspoon salt

12 tablespoons (6 ounces) unsalted butter, slightly softened but still cool

1½ cups granulated sugar

2 large eggs

1 teaspoon pure vanilla extract

¼ cup dry white wine, such as Chardonnay

5 ounces 70% bittersweet chocolate, chopped into ½-inch chunks

1 tablespoon finely ground coffee beans

1 teaspoon ground cinnamon

TKOs

CONTRIBUTED BY THOMAS KELLER

These fantastic cookies are from Thomas's Bouchon Bakery. Dark chocolate on the outside, white chocolate on the inside, this version of a classic childhood treat is both reassuringly familiar and intensely flavorful. People sometimes line up just to carry out these sandwich cookies.

Don't make the dough until you're ready to roll out the cookies—it becomes difficult to work with when chilled. And it's best to use butter brought to room temperature, because if the butter is too cold, the dry ingredients will fly up out of the bowl during mixing.

The dough trimmings can be rerolled once to make more cookies, or they can be baked as pieces, cooled, and crushed, to use as a topping on Chocolate Sorbet (page 75) or other desserts. Or bake the whole recipe of dough (see instructions on the next page), crush, and use as the crust in Chocolate Chunk Cheesecake (page 136).

FILLING

½ cup heavy cream

8 ounces white chocolate, finely chopped

COOKIES

¾ cup granulated sugar

1½ cups plus 3 tablespoons all-purpose flour

¾ cup plus 1 tablespoon unsweetened cocoa powder

½ teaspoon baking soda

1½ teaspoons salt

15 tablespoons (7½ ounces) unsalted butter, cut into ¾-inch cubes, at room temperature

FOR THE FILLING:

In a small saucepan, bring the cream to a boil over medium heat. Remove from the heat and add the white chocolate; make sure all of the chocolate is covered by the cream. Let stand for 1 minute. Whisk to melt the chocolate.

Transfer the filling to a small bowl and let stand for about 6 hours, or until it has thickened enough to spread. Or, if you need to hurry the process, the filling can be carefully whisked over a bowl of ice water until thickened. If the filling hardens too much, it can be rewarmed in the microwave.

FOR THE COOKIES:

Position the racks in the lower and upper thirds of the oven and preheat the oven to 350°F. Line two baking sheets with Silpats or parchment paper.

In the bowl of a stand mixer fitted with the paddle attachment, combine the sugar, flour, cocoa powder, baking soda, and salt and mix on low speed. With the mixer running, add the butter a few pieces at a time. The mixture will have a sandy texture at first and then will begin to form pebble-size pieces. As soon as the dough starts to come together, stop the mixer.

Transfer the dough to a board and use the heel of your hand or a pastry scraper to shape the dough into a block about 5 by 7 inches. Cut the block into 2 pieces.

One at a time, roll each block of dough between two pieces of lightly floured parchment paper until ⅛ inch thick. Using a fluted cookie cutter, cut into 2-inch rounds. Place ½ to 1 inch apart on the prepared baking sheets.

Bake for 12 to 15 minutes, rotating the sheets halfway through the baking. Remove from the oven and cool on the sheets for 2 to 5 minutes (the cookies will be too soft to remove initially). Then transfer the cookies to a cooling rack and let cool completely.

The dough trimmings can be pushed together once and rerolled to make more cookies.

TO ASSEMBLE THE COOKIES:
Place half of the cookies upside down on a work surface. Whip the filling lightly with a whisk just to aerate it; it will lighten in color and fluff up. Do not overwhip, or the filling may begin to separate.

Transfer the filling to a pastry bag fitted with a ¼-inch plain tip or use a disposable pastry bag and cut an opening in the tip of the bag. Pipe about 1½ teaspoons of the filling in the center of each cookie. Top with another cookie, right side up. Gently, using your fingertips, press the cookies together until the filling comes just to the edges.

The cookies can be stored in an airtight container for up to 3 days.

MAKES ABOUT 3 DOZEN SANDWICH COOKIES

TO MAKE COOKIE CRUMBS:
Place a Silpat or a piece of parchment paper on the counter, place one block of the dough on top, and top with a piece of parchment paper. Roll the dough until ⅛ inch thick. Remove the top piece of parchment and transfer the Silpat (or parchment) to a baking sheet. Repeat with the remaining block of dough, and place on a second baking sheet. Bake for 15 minutes, or until the dough is completely dry, rotating the pans once halfway through baking. If the edges cook more quickly, carefully break them off, then continue to bake the remaining dough.

Let the sheets cool completely on a cooling rack. Break into large pieces, place in a food processor, and pulse to make very fine crumbs.

What Is White Chocolate?

Technically, white chocolate isn't chocolate at all. True chocolate must contain both cocoa butter and cacao particles. The nibs inside a cacao bean are made up of approximately fifty percent fat—cocoa butter—and fifty percent solid particles of cacao. These particles give chocolate its flavor and dark color. White chocolate contains no cacao solids, which is why it lacks chocolate's flavor as well as color. The best white chocolate is made using cocoa butter as its only fat. Cheaper white chocolates substitute vegetable oils for some or all of the cocoa butter.

We don't make white chocolate for a simple reason: both of us prefer dark chocolate. That doesn't mean we'll never make white chocolate. So many people have requested it that we're tempted to experiment to see how good we could make a white chocolate taste if we used cocoa butter from good cacao, great vanilla, and high-quality sugar.

When you buy white chocolate, read the label to be sure that it contains cocoa butter, not palm oil or cottonseed oil.

Chocolate Platter with Fruit and Nuts

WHEN DESSERT IS A CHOCOLATE TASTING, guests become involved creatively.

Set out one platter or several, and arrange chocolates ranging from milk to bittersweet. Serve with a variety of fresh and dried fruits and nuts.

Taste each chocolate with different flavors—a milk chocolate with cherries, a dark chocolate with almonds, a bittersweet with figs or apricots—to discover which flavor combinations work best.

You also can lightly grill fresh fruit, which intensifies its flavor. Frankie Whitman, Scharffen Berger's marketing director, serves chunks of 70% chocolate with grilled pineapple wedges. Cut off the skin, core the pineapple, and quarter it. Lay the wedges on a grill and turn each side to the heat for a minute or two.

As for wine, fruity wines with few harsh tannins go best with chocolate. Zinfandel and Syrah seem perfectly suited.

CHOCOLATE CHUNK COOKIES

CONTRIBUTED BY JOANNE CHANG

With her Flour Bakery + Café, Joanne Chang has created a little haven that's much loved by Bostonians. Because of the combination of all-purpose and high-gluten bread flour, these cookies have a tender, chewy center and crisp edges. If you make them using only all-purpose flour, the cookies will still be tasty, but they will be thinner, crisper, and less tender.

Position the racks in the lower and upper thirds of the oven and preheat the oven to 350°F. Line two baking sheets with Silpats or parchment paper.

Sift together both flours, the baking soda, and salt into a medium bowl. Set aside.

In the bowl of a stand mixer fitted with the paddle attachment, cream together the butter and both sugars on medium speed for about 5 minutes, or until pale, light, and fluffy. Scrape down the sides and bottom of the bowl as necessary. Beat in the eggs and vanilla until thoroughly combined. Scrape down the bowl. Reduce the speed to low, add the dry ingredients, and mix until the flour is completely blended, scraping the bowl as necessary.

Remove the bowl from the mixer and fold in the chocolate chunks until evenly distributed. (The dough can be refrigerated, well wrapped, for up to 1 week or frozen for up to 1 month.)

Drop the dough by heaping tablespoons, 2 inches apart, onto the prepared pans. Flatten each cookie slightly. Bake for 15 minutes, or until golden, rotating the pans halfway through baking transfer the cookies with a spatula to a cooling rack to cool completely.

The cookies can be stored in an airtight container for up to 3 days.

MAKES ABOUT 3 DOZEN COOKIES

INGREDIENTS

- 1¼ cups all-purpose flour
- 1 cup bread flour
- 1 teaspoon baking soda
- ½ teaspoon salt
- 16 tablespoons unsalted butter (8 ounces), at room temperature
- ¾ cup granulated sugar
- ¾ cup firmly packed light brown sugar
- 2 large eggs
- ½ teaspoon pure vanilla extract
- 9 ounces 70% bittersweet chocolate, chopped into chip-size chunks
- 2½ ounces 41% milk chocolate, chopped into chip-size chunks

ULTRA-THIN CHOCOLATE CHUNK COOKIES

CONTRIBUTED BY ALICE MEDRICH

Baked for our factory store by Deirdre Davis, Alice's thin, crisp, and buttery cookies fly out of the cookie jar. We literally can't bake enough of them. Their delicate flavor and texture make a good chocolate chunk taste even better.

INGREDIENTS

1¼ cups all-purpose flour

½ teaspoon baking soda

10 tablespoons (5 ounces) unsalted butter, melted

½ cup quick-cooking oats

½ cup granulated sugar

¼ cup lightly packed dark brown sugar

2 tablespoons plus 1 teaspoon light corn syrup

2 tablespoons whole milk

½ teaspoon salt

7 ounces 70% bittersweet chocolate, chopped into small chunks

Position the racks in the lower and upper thirds of the oven and preheat the oven to 300°F. Line two 17 by 12 by 1-inch (half sheet pan) baking sheets with aluminum foil.

In a bowl, stir together the flour and baking soda. Set aside.

In a large bowl, whisk together the melted butter and oats. Whisk in the granulated sugar, brown sugar, corn syrup, milk, and salt. Stir in the flour mixture until just incorporated. If the dough is warm from the butter, wait until it cools before stirring in the chocolate chunks.

Divide the dough into 15 equal pieces; arrange 5 cookies on each baking sheet, 2 on the top end, 1 in the center, and 2 on the bottom end, leaving equal space between the cookies and the sides of the pan. The cookies will spread considerably. Pressing with a piece of plastic wrap, flatten each one to a diameter of 3½ inches.

Bake for 25 to 30 minutes, or until the cookies are well browned and not at all shiny in the center, rotating the pans halfway through baking. Slide the cookies, on the foil, onto cooling racks and let cool completely before removing them from the foil. Repeat with the remaining pieces of dough, making sure the baking sheet is cool.

The cookies can be stored in an airtight container for up to 5 days.

MAKES 15 VERY THIN 5-INCH COOKIES

LEGENDS & LORE

Peters and Nestlé Mix Milk with Chocolate

Chocolate is mostly a fat, because of its high cocoa butter content, but milk is primarily water. Chocolate and milk weren't combined until 1873, when Swiss chemist Henri Nestlé found a way to condense milk by removing the water.

Two years later, when Nestlé employee Daniel Peters used Henri's techniques to mix chocolate with twenty percent milk solids, he and Nestlé got joint credit for inventing milk chocolate, which would become the most widely consumed form of cacao. The invention propelled Nestlé into its position as one of the world's ten biggest companies. Through the nineteenth century, the Swiss dominated chocolate manufacturing, producing the equivalent of up to 12,000 pounds per Swiss citizen per year, most of it for export.

If milk and chocolate taste as if they're made for each other, that's true on a molecular level as well. The fats and proteins of chocolate chemically combine well with the fats and proteins of milk.

PB&C Cookies

These soft cookies are so meltingly tender you'll be tempted to eat them right away, but don't attempt to remove them from the cooling rack until they've cooled completely. We prefer natural peanut butter with no added sugar for this cookie.

Position the racks in the lower and upper thirds of the oven and preheat the oven to 325°F. Line a 17 by 12 by 1-inch baking sheet (half sheet pan) with a Silpat or parchment paper.

In a small bowl, combine the flour, baking powder, and salt, and set aside.

In the bowl of a stand mixer fitted with the paddle attachment, combine the butter, brown sugar, and granulated sugar and mix on medium speed to blend, 1 to 2 minutes. Add the vanilla, egg, and peanut butter and mix for 2 to 3 minutes. Pour in the melted chocolate and mix until just combined. Stop the mixer, add the dry ingredients, and mix until just combined. Remove the bowl from the mixer and fold in the chocolate pieces.

Drop large mounds of dough, about 3 heaping tablespoons each, onto the prepared baking sheet, leaving about 2 inches between them. Bake for about 20 minutes, or until the cookies are lightly cracked on top, rotating the pans halfway through. Remove from the oven and cool on the sheets for 2 minutes, then transfer to a cooling rack to cool completely.

Store in an airtight container for 3 days.

MAKES 12 LARGE COOKIES

INGREDIENTS

1 cup all-purpose flour

½ teaspoon baking powder

½ teaspoon salt

8 tablespoons (4 ounces) unsalted butter, at room temperature

½ cup firmly packed dark brown sugar

⅓ cup granulated sugar

1 teaspoon pure vanilla extract

1 large egg, lightly beaten

½ cup chunky peanut butter, preferably natural

1 ounce 99% unsweetened chocolate, melted

6 ounces 62% semisweet chocolate, chopped into ¼-inch pieces

COCOA CABANAS

CONTRIBUTED BY FLO BRAKER

These dark, rich mini cupcake-like treats are at their very best the same day they're baked, but you can freeze them in an airtight container for a month. Flo believes these are prettier served without the muffin papers. To remove the paper easily from the sticky surfaces, freeze the cabanas for 30 minutes.

Position a rack in the lower third of the oven and preheat the oven to 350°F. Line 30 miniature muffin cups (1½ inches wide and ¾ inch deep) with miniature paper liners.

Sift the flour, cocoa powder, baking soda, and salt onto a sheet of waxed paper, and set aside.

In a small saucepan, melt the butter over low heat. Remove from the heat and stir in the sugar. Pour into a medium bowl and allow to cool slightly for about 5 minutes.

Add the eggs and vanilla to the butter mixture, stirring just until blended. Stir in the flour mixture, then the nuts.

Fill each paper-lined muffin cup two-thirds full. Bake for 13 minutes only; don't overbake. The top will be set, but the cabanas will still be somewhat soft. Cool in the pans on wire racks for 5 minutes to allow the cakes to firm a bit; then carefully remove the cakes to other racks to cool.

Sprinkle lightly with confectioners' sugar before serving.

MAKES 30 CABANAS

INGREDIENTS

½ cup all-purpose flour

½ cup plus 1 tablespoon unsweetened cocoa powder

¼ teaspoon baking soda

¼ teaspoon salt

8 tablespoons (4 ounces) unsalted butter

1 cup plus 2 tablespoons granulated sugar

2 large eggs

2 teaspoons pure vanilla extract

½ cup (2 ounces) finely chopped toasted pecans

About ¼ cup confectioners' sugar

LEGENDS & LORE

The Wedding of Maria Theresa and Louis XIV

Chocolate became popular in Spain shortly after Cortés brought cacao to the Spanish court in 1529, but the Spaniards kept chocolate a closely held secret until 1660. In that year, the Spanish princess Maria Theresa married Louis XIV, and she arrived in France with enormous wooden chests full of cacao and servants whose sole task was to grind the beans on a *metate*. Maria Theresa could be persuaded to leave her beloved country, but not without her chocolate.

Louis purportedly commented that his wife didn't need his company as long as she had her chocolate, her servants, and her dwarves, but eventually her chocolate—like Maria Theresa herself—grew on the Sun King. Records at Versailles include explicit instructions for how Louis liked his chocolate—stirred constantly in the pot with one egg yolk until rich and very thick. France never did receive the sizeable dowry that Spain had promised, but chocolate became a national treasure.

S'MORES

CONTRIBUTED BY STEPHEN DURFEE

That old campfire classic, s'mores (short for "some more, please"), becomes something new when made with great chocolate, homemade graham crackers, and homemade marshmallows, toasted over the coals after a summer BBQ. And if the craving hits when it is too cold and wet to go outside, the marshmallows can be toasted—very carefully—under the broiler.

It is easiest to use bars of milk chocolate that are about ¼-inch thick.

GRAHAM CRACKERS

1 cup all-purpose flour

¼ cup whole wheat pastry flour

¼ teaspoon baking soda

¼ teaspoon ground cinnamon

Pinch of salt

8 tablespoons (4 ounces) unsalted butter, at room temperature

2 tablespoons granulated sugar

2 tablespoons firmly packed brown sugar

2 teaspoons honey

Marshmallows (page 307), allowed to firm up for at least 2 hours

9 ounces 41% milk chocolate, broken or cut into pieces slightly smaller than the graham crackers

FOR THE GRAHAM CRACKERS:

Sift together both flours, the baking soda, cinnamon, and salt into a medium bowl. Stir to combine, and set aside.

In the bowl of a stand mixer fitted with the paddle attachment, beat together the butter, both sugars, and the honey on medium speed for 2 to 3 minutes, or until smooth and fluffy, stopping occasionally to scrape the sides and bottom of the bowl. Add the dry ingredients and mix on low speed to combine, then increase the speed to medium and mix until just combined.

Transfer the dough to a board and use the heel of your hand or a pastry scraper to press the dough together. Place a Silpat or a piece of parchment cut to fit a baking sheet on the work surface. Place the dough on top and cover with a second Silpat or piece of parchment paper. Roll the dough into a very thin rectangle approximately 10 by 14 inches.

Transfer the dough to a baking sheet and refrigerate about 30 minutes, or until firm.

Position a rack in the middle of the oven and preheat the oven to 350°F.

Remove the top Silpat or peel off the top sheet of parchment paper from the dough. Bake for 10 to 12 minutes, or until the top is slightly blistered and dry. Remove from the oven (leaving the oven on).

With a paring knife, carefully trim the rough edges of the dough (don't nick the Silpat). There is no need to remove the rough edge trimmings, or to separate the cut cookies, as long as the cut is all the way through the dough. Cut the rectangle into 3-inch squares. Return to the oven and bake for 4 to 5 minutes, or until golden brown.

Transfer the pan to a cooling rack and let the graham crackers cool completely in the pan. Once they are cool, remove the trimmings (they make great snacks) and then separate the individual crackers.

The graham crackers can be stored in an airtight container for up to 4 days.

TO FINISH THE MARSHMALLOWS:

Lift the marshmallow block from the pan and brush off the cornstarch mixture. Using scissors or a paring knife, cut the marshmallows into sixteen 2-inch squares. Roll each marshmallow in the remaining cornstarch mixture, tapping off any excess.

TO COMPLETE THE S'MORES:

If toasting the marshmallows over a fire, cut six marshmallows crosswise in half, creating 1 by 2-inch marshmallows. Reserve the remaining marshmallows for another use. Place the graham crackers on a tray and top with the chocolate.

Skewer the marshmallows one or two at a time, using two skewers to keep the marshmallows from turning around the skewers as they soften. Hold the marshmallows over the flame until toasted as desired, then place on top of a chocolate-topped graham. Serve immediately.

If toasting the marshmallows under the broiler, position an oven rack on the highest level. Preheat the oven to 350°F.

Cut six of the marshmallows in half horizontally to form thin 2-inch-square marshmallows. Reserve the remaining marshmallows for another use.

Place the crackers on a baking sheet and top with the chocolate. Place in the oven for 30 seconds to 1 minute, just to soften the chocolate. Remove from the oven and turn on the broiler. Top each chocolate graham with one marshmallow and return to the oven. Stay by the oven and, keeping a close watch on the marshmallows, toast just until it's the right color for your taste. Serve immediately.

MAKES 12 OPEN-FACED S'MORES

CHOCOLATE SMOOCHES

CONTRIBUTED BY MARY SUE MILLIKEN AND SUSAN FENIGER

When you bite into one of these treats while it's still warm, you get a luscious, gooey hit of melted chocolate. Whenever Mary Sue and Susan hit the road, they pack a few bars of great chocolate. Because most kitchens will have all the other ingredients for these smooches, they can whip them up just about anywhere.

INGREDIENTS

8 tablespoons (4 ounces) unsalted butter, at room temperature

¼ cup granulated sugar

Pinch of salt

1½ ounces 70% bittersweet chocolate, melted and cooled

1¼ cups all-purpose flour

9 ounces 70% bittersweet chocolate, cut into 18 small chunks (no larger than ½ inch) about the size of a hazelnut

Position the racks in the lower and upper thirds of the oven and preheat the oven to 350°F.

In the bowl of a stand mixer fitted with the paddle attachment, cream together the butter and sugar on medium speed for 3 to 5 minutes, or until light and fluffy, scraping down the sides of the bowl as necessary. Add the salt and melted chocolate and mix until combined. Stir in the flour by hand, mixing just until the dough comes together. Cover and chill the dough for 30 minutes.

Cut the dough into 18 pieces. Shape each piece into a small thick disk. Flatten each piece in the palm of your hand until it is wide enough to encase a piece of chocolate. Cup the sides slightly, place a piece of chocolate in the center, and bring the sides together, sealing in the chocolate. Arrange the smooches on two ungreased baking sheets, leaving at least 1 inch between them.

Bake for 12 minutes, or until the bottoms just begin to color around the edges, rotating the pans halfway through baking. Transfer the cookies to a cooling rack to cool completely.

Store the cookies in an airtight container for up to 3 days.

MAKES 18 COOKIES

BROWN BUTTER BLONDIES

Fans of milk chocolate sometimes feel slighted by all the attention we give to dark chocolate. This recipe, a wonderful combination of brown sugar, butter, and milk chocolate, really does justice to the flavors in our milk chocolate. We like these blondies better than any we've tasted—it's just coincidence that they're also the easiest to make.

Position a rack in the lower third of the oven and preheat the oven to 350°F.

Cut a 9 by 17-inch piece of parchment paper. Lightly butter the bottom of a 9 by 9 by 2-inch baking pan. Line it with the parchment, allowing it to extend evenly over the two short ends of the pan. Butter the parchment including the paper on the sides of the pan.

Place the brown sugar in a large bowl, and set aside.

In a small saucepan, melt the butter over low heat. Tilt the pan occasionally and watch the butter carefully. It will sizzle at first. After about 5 minutes, the solids will separate from the fat and turn a light brown color.

When the butter develops a toasty, nutty aroma, remove the pan from the heat and pour the butter over the brown sugar. Add the salt and stir. Don't worry if the mixture looks somewhat separated or oily at this point. Add the egg and vanilla. Beat until smooth. Add the flour and gently mix until just combined.

Pour the batter into the prepared pan. Bake for 10 to 15 minutes, or until the batter is shiny and a skewer inserted in the center of the pan comes out clean. Remove the pan from the oven and sprinkle the chocolate pieces evenly over the top of the blondies. Return to the oven for 30 seconds to 1 minute, just until the chocolate softens. Transfer the pan to a cooling rack, and quickly spread the chocolate in an even layer over the top. Sprinkle with the nuts.

Let cool for 10 minutes on a cooling rack. Remove the blondies from the pan, using the parchment paper "handles," and cool completely on the rack.

Cut the blondies into 1½ by 3-inch bars.

MAKES 18 BARS

INGREDIENTS

8 tablespoons (4 ounces) unsalted butter, cut into cubes, plus more for the baking dish

1 cup firmly packed light brown sugar

Pinch of salt

1 large egg, lightly beaten

½ teaspoon pure vanilla extract

1 cup all-purpose flour

6 ounces 41% milk chocolate, broken into 1-inch pieces

1 cup toasted pecans

Toasted Coconut Clusters

THIS EASY COMBINATION OF COCONUT AND CHOCOLATE LOOKS DECADENT but can be made in just minutes. This treat is fun to put together with kids and a nice addition when you're filling gift tins for holiday gifts. We prefer unsweetened shredded or flaked coconut but sweetened works as well.

To toast coconut, preheat the oven to 300°F. Spread 1 to 3 cups of coconut on an ungreased baking sheet. After 2 to 3 minutes, toss the coconut with a spatula or tongs. Toast another minute or two until coconut is a light golden brown. Coconut toasts very quickly, so remove the baking sheet from the oven as soon as you see the flakes begin to color.

Line a baking sheet with a Silpat or parchment paper. Melt either milk or dark chocolate (see page 22 for methods). Place the toasted coconut in a small bowl. If you like, you can add nuts or dried fruit to the coconut—raisins, diced apricots, cherries, or even mangoes—or keep the mixture simply coconut and chocolate.

Drizzle melted chocolate over the coconut, tossing with a spoon. Stop adding chocolate as soon as there's enough to coat the coconut. Drop tablespoons of the mixture onto the prepared baking sheet. Refrigerate until set.

Chocolate Caramels, page 196.

CHOCOLATE CARAMELS

CONTRIBUTED BY ERIC SHELTON

Similar to a Tootsie Roll in texture, these buttery, chocolaty caramels have a full-bodied, deeply satisfying flavor.

Cut a 9 by 17-inch piece of parchment paper. Lightly butter a 9 by 9 by 2-inch pan, and line it with the parchment paper, letting it extend evenly over two opposite sides.

Stir together the cream, sugar, corn syrup, and salt in a pot with a heavy bottom, and clip a candy thermometer to the side of the pot. Bring to a boil and then continue to cook until the mixture reaches 250°F. Remove the pot from the heat and let cool for 5 minutes.

Add the chocolate and stir with a heatproof spoon or spatula until the chocolate is melted and the mixture is smooth. Pour into the prepared pan and spread into an even layer with a small offset spatula.

Once the caramel has started to set, sprinkle with the nibs and press them in gently. Allow the caramels to cool at room temperature until firm, at least 2 hours.

Lift the caramel block from the pan, using the parchment paper "handles," and place on a cutting board. Dip a knife in hot water, dry, and cut the caramels into 1-inch squares, heating (and drying) the knife as necessary.

Store the caramels in an airtight container.

MAKES 81 CARAMELS

INGREDIENTS

Unsalted butter for the pan

1½ cups heavy cream

1½ cups granulated sugar

1 cup plus 2 tablespoons light corn syrup

1 teaspoon salt

9 ounces 62% semisweet chocolate, finely chopped

2 tablespoons cacao nibs, crushed with a rolling pin (optional)

CHOCOLATTE

This blend of espresso and chocolate is simple and irresistible. We drink this in winter and summer, either hot or over ice.

TO SERVE HOT:

Combine the cocoa powder and sugar in a small saucepan. Slowly whisk in the milk to make a smooth paste. Whisk in the half-and-half and place over medium heat. Continue to whisk, gradually raising the heat to medium-high, until frothy and steaming.

Pour ¼ cup of the espresso into each cup and ladle the chocolate mixture over the top.

TO SERVE COLD:

Combine the cocoa and sugar in a small bowl. Whisk in the hot espresso until the sugar dissolves. Stir in the milk and half-and-half.

Refrigerate for 30 minutes or up to 2 days.

Pour into tall glasses filled with ice.

SERVES 2

INGREDIENTS

2 tablespoons unsweetened cocoa powder

2 tablespoons granulated sugar

¼ cup whole milk

1 cup half-and-half

½ cup freshly brewed espresso

ROBERT'S EGG CREAM

The first time I had an egg cream, I was in my late teens. The (Jewish) grandmother of a friend (from New York) made one for me using a seltzer bottle that dispensed carbon dioxide from a lead cartridge. I loved the fact that it was chocolatey but still refreshing and not heavy, because it was mostly sparkling water.

To the surprise of everyone but native New Yorkers, egg creams contain neither egg nor cream—they are made with milk. My idiosyncratic version allows for cream (or milk or half-and-half), and is influenced by the fact that I grew up in Boston drinking ice cream sodas, which are a sort of an egg cream with ice cream.

When I was fifteen, I learned how to make ice cream sodas working as a soda jerk in the local drugstore. It was the first time I received a paycheck, although I'd had jobs in the neighborhood babysitting and mowing lawns. I worked breakfast and lunch on the weekends, making burgers and eggs on the grill as well as preparing sandwiches and as many fountain drinks and ice cream specialties as I could dream up.

When making an egg cream, it's best to use seltzer with a lot of fizz. You can make the chocolate mixture ahead, and keep it in your refrigerator for a week or two. Then, whenever you'd like an egg cream, spoon the syrup into a tall glass, add seltzer, and serve immediately.

INGREDIENTS
Chocolate Syrup (page 311)
Half-and-half
Seltzer water

TO MAKE EGG CREAMS:
For each egg cream, place 2 tablespoons of the chocolate syrup in the bottom of a tall glass. Add 2 tablespoons half-and-half, and stir to combine. Fill the glass with seltzer.

TO MAKE CHOCOLATE SODAS:
Make the egg cream following the steps above and then top with 2 scoops of your favorite ice cream.

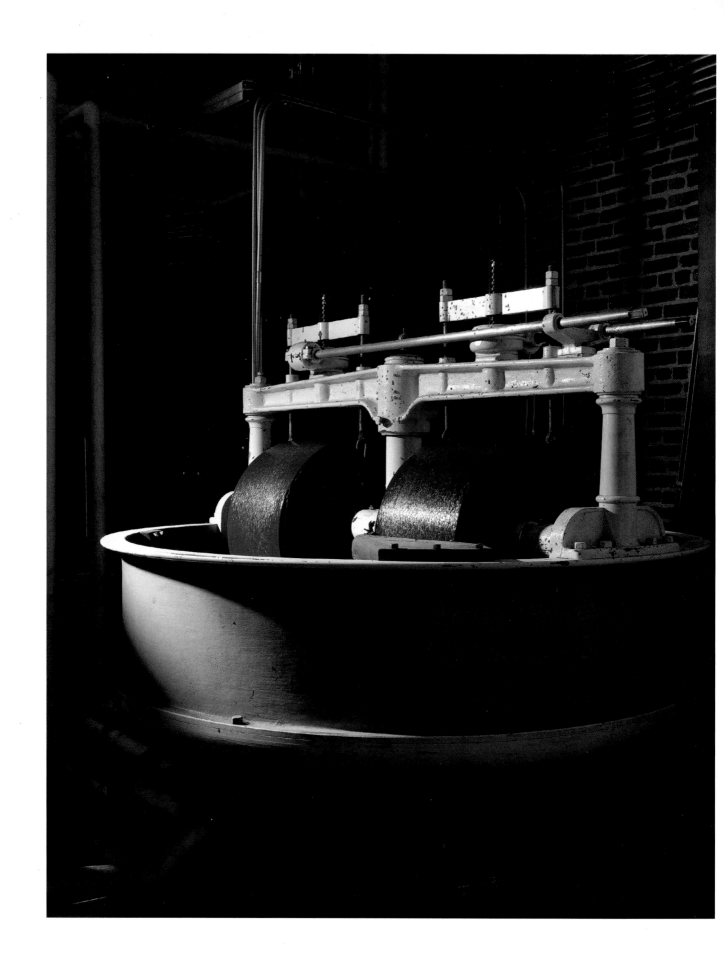

CHAPTER
5

HOW WE MAKE OUR CHOCOLATE

This chapter describes what happens to beans from the time they arrive at our factory until they leave as chocolate bars. Although we've made chocolate for almost ten years, seeing beans become dark, glossy chocolate still seems wondrous. People attach so many attributes to chocolate—chocolate relaxes them or makes them feel amorous. And yet, many chocolate lovers have no idea how cacao beans become chocolate, and thus miss out on one of its most interesting qualities—its powers of transformation. Just as touring a winery adds depth to the experience of tasting a wine, so does understanding chocolate making add to a chocolate's flavor.

The Bean Cleaner

Scooped up directly from the platforms where they've been dried and shoveled into burlap sacks, cacao beans often come accompanied by pebbles and tiny twigs. We pour the contents of each burlap sack into a mechanical bean cleaner, which separates the beans from all the non-bean material so that only cacao goes into the roaster.

The machine shakes the beans and uses suction to vacuum off light material such as dust and twigs. Anything heavier than a cacao bean falls into a bin, while the beans emerge on a conveyor belt. Because we create our chocolate by blending beans from various regions, the cleaned beans are kept separated by lot, poured into large white containers that are labeled with the name of the farm and the country where they grew.

The Roaster

Roasting is an important step in determining the final flavor of our chocolate. Only three or four people at Scharffen Berger are entrusted with roasting beans. We're extremely careful to avoid overroasting, which would obscure the inherent flavor characteristics.

Think about roasting cacao as you would toasting bread. As with toast, the beans have a long period of time when they're underdone, and then just a short window between optimally roasted and overheated. But if caught at just the right moment, well-roasted beans possess their full flavor and sweetness. What makes roasting tricky is that various types of beans have different roasting times. Because beans are different sizes, are fermented differently, and are dried for shorter or longer periods, and because they have different flavors from the beginning just based on their genes, the ideal roasting time for a bean from Ghana might be too long for a Venezuelan bean, even if both are the same type of cacao.

We use a fifty-year-old Sirocco roaster from Germany with a rotating chamber that keeps the beans from ever coming to rest in a hot spot. The person in charge of roasting pulls out a bean every thirty seconds or so during the last five minutes of roasting and tastes it. As soon as a bean tastes close to done, he turns off the roaster's heat source, a stream of air heated to about 300°F by natural gas. The beans will continue to roast for several minutes as they cool.

The Winnower

To winnow beans is to remove the outer husks or shells. Shelling cacao beans by hand is slow and painful, because the thin sharp shells leave tiny cuts in your fingertips. The winnower runs the roasted beans through metal rollers that gently crack the shells, then drops the cracked beans onto the top screen of a series of vibrating screens. The vibration jars the shells loose from the bean fragments—the nibs—that then either fall through the holes in the screen or collect in bins on one side of the machine. Shell fragments, which are lighter than nibs, rise through air-sucking vents positioned above each screen and are then jettisoned into a separate bin.

The Mélangeur

A solid granite disk five inches thick and six feet in diameter sits at the bottom of the mélangeur's metal tub. Two huge rollers, also granite, rest on this disk, held in place by a metal yoke. A motor turns the granite disk, and when we pour in three hundred pounds of nibs—the approximate amount of each batch— the rollers begin to turn, moved by the nibs sliding underneath them.

Before the rollers begin to turn, the dry nibs resemble small, dark chips of wood. But the friction between the granite disk, granite rollers, and the nibs generates heat, and as the nibs are ground, cocoa butter is released and melted by that heat. Soon the mass of nibs at the bottom of the mélangeur begins to look like melted chocolate as the solid particles of cacao in the nibs become suspended in the melted cocoa butter.

The full name for this machine, *mélangeur broyeur*, means mixer/grinder in French. Although few chocolate makers use this type of mélangeur, we prize this machine over all the others in our factory, in part because of its age. Built in Dresden, Germany, in the 1920s, it is a duplicate of mélangeurs dating back to the 1800s.

The Conche/Refiner

Many chocolate manufacturers use two machines in place of the one machine we use to both conch and refine our chocolate. The mélangeur begins the grinding process, then the conche/refiner finishes the grinding, refining the chocolate by further reducing the size of the solid cacao particles suspended in the cocoa butter. Conching simultaneously aerates the chocolate to rid it of unwanted volatiles, decreases viscosity, and creates smoothness by effectively coating the sugar and cacao particles with cacao butter so that the particles slide over each other more easily.

Our conche/refiner is a metal barrel with a central axle. Slender rods extending from this axle hold metal fins, or blades, which scrape against the inside of the barrel. Centrifugal force throws the chocolate against the barrel's walls, where it's trapped and scraped between the walls and blades. This scraping reduces the particle size of the cacao solids.

When we pour the cacao paste from the mélangeur into the conche/refiner, we also add pure cane sugar and whole vanilla beans, a blend of bourbon and Tahitian vanillas. The machine conches the mixture as it refines, aerating the chocolate while creating a smooth liquid by breaking the sugar and vanilla into tiny particles and coating every particle more evenly with cocoa butter.

Conching is sort of a buzz word among chocolate manufacturers. Many chocolatiers advertise the time they spend conching, as if conching time alone determined a chocolate's quality. Although a chocolate's flavor relies on more than conching, with the combination of the mélangeur and the conche/refiner, we're aiming to break down the cacao particles to a fairly distinct size.

We use a fineness-of-grind gauge, a tool created to measure the size of color particles in paint, to tell us the micron size of the cacao particles in each batch. By spooning some of the chocolate from the conche/refiner onto the gauge and then pulling the chocolate across, we can tell the size of the majority of particles.

Of course, particles don't break down at an even rate; in any particular batch, some particles will measure 40 microns while others measure 8 microns. We stop conching when most of the particles are between 30 and 35 microns, the point at which human beings can no longer distinguish individual particles on their tongue.

The Tempering Machine

Tempering is a way of solidifying liquid chocolate in a way that keeps the chocolate glossy, causes it to break with a distinct snap, and allows it to melt smoothly in your mouth. You can find straightforward instructions for tempering at home on page 92. Here we'll just explain how the tempering machine in our factory functions.

Temperature is a key aspect of tempering. Freshly made liquid chocolate enters the bowl of the tempering machine at 105°F. From there, the chocolate flows into a jacketed metal tube. The tube reduces the temperature inside to 85°F and then raises it to 91°F. These specific changes in temperature result in the formation of a particular type of cocoa butter crystal, an exceptionally stable crystal, that then multiplies throughout the chocolate. The presence of this stable crystal in the chocolate causes it to harden with a stable structure, one that also prevents the chocolate from blooming (see page 352) or melting at a lower temperature.

The Molding Machine

The chocolate then flows through a pipe from the tempering machine to the molding machine. This machine pumps out a premeasured amount of chocolate, set to correspond with the molds placed beneath it. The chocolate-filled molds then pass through a refrigerated tunnel. After twenty minutes in the tunnel, the chocolate has hardened into bars. The molds are inverted and the bars of chocolate continue on, carried by a white rubber conveyor belt to the end of the line, where they fall into waiting boxes.

We have to mention one part of the factory tour that can't be shared in a book: the aroma of chocolate. If the wind blows in the right direction, from a block away, you can smell a full-bodied, almost intoxicating scent that's a combination of cacao beans being roasted, nibs being crushed in the mélangeur, and warm chocolate cascading into molds. As people walk past the building, they'll sometimes lift their faces up and take a deep breath. A pan of brownies baking in the oven, as good as that can smell, is a poor, pale imitation of the aroma that surrounds you during chocolate making.

Cacao Nib Macaroons, page 237.

CHAPTER 6

A Hint of Chocolate

A HINT OF GOOD CHOCOLATE CAN BE
JUST THE RIGHT AMOUNT.

In the recipes in this chapter, chocolate enhances other flavors and adds depth to a few standards such as bread, muffins, scones, and waffles. Just a little chocolate can transform an ordinary recipe into something fresh, new, and enticing.

CHOCOLATE-MARBLED GINGERBREAD

CONTRIBUTED BY EMILY LUCHETTI

One nice thing about Emily Luchetti is that, while she's skilled at creating gorgeously extravagant desserts, she also has a sure hand with cozy, eat-in-your-kitchen desserts that are intensely flavorful. This very gingery gingerbread marbled with dark chocolate is a fine example. Ginger and chocolate is one of those inspired combinations, and this dense cake is just the kind of thing you want to have waiting as an afternoon snack.

Position a rack in the middle of the oven and preheat the oven to 350°F. Butter the bottom and sides of a 9 by 13 by 2-inch baking pan, and set aside.

In a small saucepan, bring the water to a boil. Remove from the heat and stir in the molasses and baking soda. Set aside to cool until lukewarm, about 10 minutes.

Sift together the flour, baking powder, salt, ginger, cinnamon, and cloves.

In the bowl of a stand mixer fitted with the paddle attachment, beat the butter and sugar on medium-high speed for about 2 minutes, or until light and fluffy. With the mixer running, add the egg and mix until combined, stopping to scrape down the sides of the bowl as necessary. On low speed, alternately add the dry ingredients and the molasses mixture.

Pour about one-third of the batter into a medium bowl. Add the chocolate and stir to combine.

Pour the plain batter into the prepared pan. Evenly space about 6 heaping spoonfuls of the chocolate batter on top of the plain batter. Pull a skewer through the batter to marble the chocolate and plain batters.

Bake for 30 to 35 minutes, or until a skewer inserted in the center comes out clean. Allow the gingerbread to cool completely in the pan on a cooling rack.

Cut into squares and top each with a scoop of ice cream, if desired.

SERVES 12

INGREDIENTS

8 tablespoons (4 ounces) unsalted butter, at room temperature, plus more for the pan

1½ cups water

1 cup unsulphured molasses

1 teaspoon baking soda

2½ cups all-purpose flour

1 tablespoon baking powder

½ teaspoon salt

2 teaspoons ground ginger

1¼ teaspoons ground cinnamon

Pinch of ground cloves

1 cup firmly packed light brown sugar

1 large egg

4 ounces 62% semisweet chocolate, melted

Ice cream (optional)

WHITE VELVET CAKE WITH MILK CHOCOLATE GANACHE

CONTRIBUTED BY ROSE LEVY BERANBAUM

No one knows cakes better than Rose Levy Beranbaum, who actually wrote her master's dissertation on whether or not sifting affects the quality of a butter cake. This soft and delicate butter cake happens to be John's mom's favorite. The milk chocolate ganache provides the ideal contrast without overwhelming the subtleties of the cake.

Be sure to use cake flour that doesn't contain leavening, *not* self-rising cake flour. If necessary, you can substitute 1¾ cups bleached all-purpose flour.

CAKE

Unsalted butter and flour for the pan

3 large egg whites

⅔ cup whole milk

1½ teaspoons pure vanilla extract

2 cups sifted cake flour

1 cup granulated sugar

2½ teaspoons plus ⅛ teaspoon baking powder

½ teaspoon salt

8 tablespoons (4 ounces) unsalted butter, at room temperature

GANACHE

15 ounces 41% milk chocolate, coarsely chopped

1 cup heavy cream

½ teaspoon pure vanilla extract

FOR THE CAKE:

Position a rack in the lower third of the oven and preheat the oven to 350°F. Lightly butter a 9-inch round cake pan. Line the bottom with parchment paper, then butter and flour the parchment.

In a medium bowl, mix the whites, about one-quarter of the milk, and the vanilla until just combined.

In the bowl of a stand mixer fitted with the paddle attachment, combine the flour, sugar, baking powder, and salt and mix on low speed for 30 seconds. Add the butter and the remaining milk and mix on low until the dry ingredients are evenly moistened. Increase the speed to medium and mix for 1½ minutes, or until the batter is light and fluffy, scraping the sides and bottom of the bowl as necessary.

With the mixer running, add the egg mixture in 3 batches, mixing for 20 seconds after each addition to incorporate the ingredients thoroughly. Scrape down the bowl as necessary.

Scrape the batter into the prepared pan, and smooth the top with a rubber or offset spatula. (The pan will be about half-full.) Bake for 35 to 40 minutes, or until golden brown. The cake should spring back when pressed lightly in the center and a skewer inserted in the center should come out clean. The cake will start to shrink from the sides of the pan only after it is removed from the oven.

Cool the cake in the pan on a cooling rack for 10 minutes. Lightly butter another cooling rack. Loosen the sides of the cake with a small spatula and invert onto the rack, then, to prevent splitting, reinvert the cake onto the first rack so the top is up. Cool completely. (At this point, the cake can be stored in an airtight container or resealable plastic bag for 1 day at room temperature, refrigerated for 3 days, or frozen for up to 2 months.)

FOR THE GANACHE:

Place the chocolate in the bowl of a food processor and process until very finely ground.

In a small saucepan, or in a heatproof glass measuring cup in the microwave, bring the cream to a boil. Immediately, with the processor running, pour the cream through the feed tube onto the chocolate. Process until smooth, about 15 seconds, stopping to scrape the sides of the bowl once or twice. Add the vanilla and pulse a few times to incorporate.

Transfer to a bowl and allow the ganache to stand for several hours, until it reaches frosting consistency. To speed the process, the ganache can be refrigerated; stir gently from time to time for even cooling and setting.

To assemble, using a serrated knife, slice the cake into two layers. Place the bottom layer cut side up on a serving plate. Spread about ¾ cup of the ganache over the top. Top with the second layer, cut side down. Spread the remaining frosting over the top and sides of the cake.

SERVES 6

LAYERED CREPE TORTE

A traditional Hungarian *Palacsintatorta,* this torte is a dozen delicate crepes stacked with layers of jam, ground nuts, and chocolate. You can make crepes a day or even weeks ahead and then freeze them or assemble and freeze the whole dessert ahead of time.

FOR THE BATTER:
Place the eggs in a large bowl, add about one-third of the flour, and whisk to combine. Whisk in the remaining flour, the sugar, and salt. Carefully whisk in about one-quarter of the milk (it will tend to splatter), then gradually whisk in the remaining milk. Whisk in 1 tablespoon butter. Let sit at room temperature for 30 minutes to 1 hour, or cover and refrigerate for up to 1 day.

TO COOK THE CREPES:
Heat an 8-inch nonstick skillet over medium-high heat. Brush on a coating of butter and let it sizzle. Lift the pan from the heat and ladle in 1 ounce (2 tablespoons) of the batter. Shake and rotate the pan to spread the batter in an even layer. Return the skillet to the heat. Fill in any holes in the crepe with a bit more batter. Cook the crepe for about 1 minute, or until the bottom is set and golden brown. Lift an edge of the crepe with a heatproof spatula and quickly flip the crepe. (If you do this with your hands, be careful not to burn yourself.) Cook the second side for about 5 seconds to set and lightly brown. Slide the crepe onto a plate, and cook the remaining crepes, stacking them on the plate. Use immediately or, to freeze the crepes, place a piece of waxed paper between each crepe, then wrap the stack tightly in plastic wrap.

TO ASSEMBLE THE TORTE:
Remove the lid from the jar of jam, place the jar in the microwave, and microwave for 1 minute. Stir and continue to heat until the jam is melted or heat the jam in a saucepan over medium heat until softened. Strain the jam into a small bowl.

Preheat the oven to 325°F. Lightly butter a 9- or 10-inch pie plate or deep ovenproof serving dish. Tear off a piece of aluminum foil large enough to cover the dish and butter it on one side.

In a small bowl, mix together the chocolate, pecans and sugar. Place a crepe in the center of the pie plate. Spread a scant tablespoon of jam over the crepe and sprinkle with about 1 tablespoon of the chocolate mixture. Top with another crepe and continue to stack and fill the crepes until all of them are used, leaving the top one plain. (At this point, the torte can be wrapped tightly and refrigerated for 1 day or frozen for up to 1 month. Defrost before baking.)

Cover the torte with the aluminum foil (buttered side down) and place in the oven. Bake for 20 to 30 minutes, or until heated throughout. The filling will bubble around the edges. Remove from the oven and let sit for 5 minutes.

Cut into wedges and serve with the chocolate sauce.

SERVES 8

CREPE (MAKES ABOUT 20)

3 large eggs

1 cup all-purpose flour

1 tablespoon granulated sugar

½ teaspoon salt

3 cups whole milk

1 tablespoon (½ ounce) unsalted butter, melted plus more for the pans and foil

One 18-ounce jar apricot jam

4 ounces (½ cup) finely ground 62% semisweet chocolate

½ cup ground pecans

¼ cup granulated sugar

1 cup John's Simple Chocolate Sauce (page 310)

Banana Caramel Cake

We tasted many recipes combining chocolate and bananas before choosing this one, which is basically a chocolate and banana cake with caramel poured over just as it comes from the oven. Don't give in to the temptation to add extra bananas to the mix, or the cake will acquire a gummy texture. The creamy bananas and the caramel layer keep this flavorful cake moist for days.

Position a rack in the middle of the oven and preheat the oven to 350°F. Butter and flour a 12-cup (10-inch) nonstick Bundt pan.

In a medium bowl, combine the flour, cinnamon, nutmeg, cloves, salt, and baking soda.

In the bowl of a stand mixer fitted with the paddle attachment, combine the eggs, oil, granulated sugar, vanilla, and almond extract. Mix on medium speed until thoroughly combined, stopping to scrape the sides of the bowl as necessary. Mix in the dry ingredients, about ½ cup at a time, stopping to scrape the bowl as necessary.

Remove the bowl from the mixer and fold in the pecans and the chocolate. Carefully fold in the bananas; do not overmix.

Pour into the prepared pan. Bake for 50 minutes to 1 hour, or until a skewer inserted in the center of the cake comes out clean.

Meanwhile, about 5 minutes before the cake is done, combine the brown sugar, milk, and butter in a small saucepan and bring to a boil over medium heat, swirling the pan occasionally as the butter and sugar melt. Once it is amber in color, remove from the heat.

Remove the cake from the oven and immediately, using a long skewer, poke holes all over the surface of the cake. Pour the hot caramel over the top, poking more holes and pushing the cake slightly away from the sides of the pan as necessary to allow the caramel to soak into the cake's top and sides. Place on a cooling rack to cool slightly.

When the cake has cooled, but is still warm to the touch, unmold onto a serving platter.

Serve warm or at room temperature.

SERVES 12

CAKE

Unsalted butter and flour for the pan

3 cups sifted all-purpose flour

½ teaspoon ground cinnamon

¼ teaspoon freshly grated nutmeg

¼ teaspoon ground cloves

1 teaspoon salt

1 teaspoon baking soda

3 large eggs, lightly beaten

1¼ cups canola oil

2 cups granulated sugar

1 teaspoon pure vanilla extract

½ teaspoon pure almond extract

½ cup coarsely chopped toasted pecans

3 ounces 62% semisweet chocolate, chopped into chip-size chunks

1½ cups diced (¼-inch) ripe bananas (about 2 bananas)

CARAMEL

½ cup firmly packed light brown sugar

2 tablespoons whole milk

4 tablespoons (2 ounces) unsalted butter, cut into chunks

Bread and Chocolate

CHEF JACQUES PÉPIN SAYS, "The chocolate that Robert and John make is my type of chocolate—deep, strong, good dark chocolate. As a boy, I had chocolate like this with the French bread called *ficelle*, which was only an inch and a half in diameter, thinner even than a baguette, so it was very crisp. My brother, a friend, and I would share a long bar, carefully dividing the tablets evenly between us. The dark chocolate and the thin, crisp bread together was like my little madeleine.

"This combination has become more sophisticated, or snobbish, if you like. Now we have *pain au chocolate,* or a croissant filled with a ribbon of chocolate, but when I was a boy, these things did not exist. Putting a dark chocolate on thin, crisp bread still works very well when you have good chocolate."

Another option, ideal for mornings, is to grate dark chocolate over warm toast. A friend of John's called soon after we began making chocolate to tell us that our 70% had become part of his morning routine. Using a Microplane grater, he grates the chocolate over his honey-wheatberry bread and has this with his first latte.

This tastes very luxurious for such a simple breakfast. We love it on brioche too.

PULL-APART KUCHEN

Also known as monkey bread, this version of kuchen lets you roll balls of dough in ground pecans and semisweet chocolate. When the kuchen is hot out of the oven, it takes some restraint to wait for it to cool long enough to avoid burning your fingers.

FOR THE DOUGH:

In a small bowl, combine the water and yeast and stir to dissolve. Let stand for 10 minutes or until foamy.

Place the yolks in the bowl of a stand mixer fitted with the paddle attachment. In a small saucepan, heat the butter and milk over medium-low heat until the butter has melted. With the mixer running on low speed, carefully pour the butter mixture into the yolks, and mix until combined. Let stand until just warm to the touch.

With the mixer on low speed, add the salt, sugar, and yeast mixture, mixing until just combined. Stop the mixer and add 2 cups of the flour, then mix on low speed until just incorporated. There will still be some lumps. Add the remaining 2 cups flour and mix for 30 seconds. Increase the speed to medium and continue to mix until the dough is smooth, about 5 minutes; it will still be sticky.

Lightly butter a large bowl. Using a plastic dough scraper, transfer the dough to the bowl. Turn to coat the dough with butter. Cover with a kitchen towel or plastic wrap and let rise in a warm place for 1 to 1½ hours, or until doubled in size.

FOR THE TOPPING:

Place the pecans, chocolate, and sugar in a food processor and pulse until the mixture has a sandy consistency. Set aside. Butter and sugar a 12-cup (10-inch) Bundt pan.

Pour the melted butter into a small bowl. Pull off small pieces of the dough, and roll into balls about the size of a golf ball. Roll in the butter, then in the nut and chocolate mixture to coat, and place in the prepared pan. Line the bottom of the pan and then stack more coated balls on top until all of the dough is used. Arrange the balls (and make smaller balls if necessary) so that the top layer is fairly even. Cover with a kitchen towel or plastic wrap and let rise in a warm spot for about 1 hour, or until doubled in size. Reserve any remaining melted butter.

Position a rack in the middle of the oven and preheat the oven to 350°F. Brush the top of the kuchen with any remaining melted butter. Bake for 45 to 50 minutes, or until the top is dark brown and a skewer inserted in the center comes out clean. The melted chocolate and sugar will be hot, so be careful.

Let the kuchen stand for 3 to 5 minutes, then turn out onto a cooling rack and let cool for 15 minutes. Serve warm.

SERVES 8

DOUGH

¼ cup warm water (110° to 115°F)

2½ teaspoons active dry yeast

3 large egg yolks, lightly beaten

8 tablespoons (4 ounces) unsalted butter

1 cup whole milk

¼ teaspoon salt

⅓ cup granulated sugar

4 cups all-purpose flour

TOPPING

¾ cup coarsely chopped toasted pecans (about 2½ ounces)

¾ cup coarsely chopped 62% semisweet chocolate (about 4 ounces)

½ cup granulated sugar

8 tablespoons (4 ounces) unsalted butter, melted

Butter and sugar for the pan

CHOCOLATE CHUNK CHALLAH

CONTRIBUTED BY SHARON LEBEWOHL

It's hard to tell which is more appealing—this pretty braided loaf's glossy surface studded with chunks of dark chocolate, or the aroma of bread and chocolate that fills the room while it bakes. Since challah is traditional for the Sabbath, Sharon likes to serve this for the Sabbath meal, but it also makes a great bread pudding or French toast. Feel free to add toasted nuts and dried fruit along with the chocolate.

When measuring the honey for this recipe, use the same measuring spoon you used for the oil. The oil will coat the spoon, allowing the honey to slide right off.

INGREDIENTS

1½ cups room-temperature water

½ cup plus 1 tablespoon granulated sugar, plus more for sprinkling the loaves

2½ teaspoons active dry yeast

4½ to 5½ cups all-purpose flour

¼ cup plus 2 tablespoons canola oil, plus more for the bowl and baking sheets

2 tablespoons honey

3 large eggs

4 ounces 62% semisweet chocolate, chopped into chip-size chunks

In a small bowl, combine ¼ cup of the water, 1 tablespoon of the sugar, and the yeast and stir until the yeast has dissolved (see Note on next page). Set aside for 10 to 15 minutes, or until the yeast begins to foam. (If it does not foam, discard the yeast and start again with new yeast.)

In the bowl of a stand mixer fitted with the paddle attachment, combine 1½ cups of the flour, the remaining ½ cup sugar, the oil, honey, 2 eggs, and the remaining 1¼ cups water. Mix on low to medium-low until all of the ingredients are incorporated, stopping to scrape the bottom and sides as necessary.

Switch to the dough hook. Add the yeast mixture and 3 cups of the flour, and knead on the lowest speed, scraping the sides and the bottom of the bowl as necessary, until a smooth, elastic dough forms. (If the dough seems too sticky, add up to 1 additional cup of flour. The amount of flour needed will vary depending on the eggs and the moisture in the room, but use as little as possible; too much flour will cause the dough to be tough.) Let the dough rest for 10 minutes.

Place the dough on a lightly floured board, and shape into a rectangle approximately 7 by 10 inches. Press the chocolate chunks into the top of the dough and fold the dough in half over the chips. Seal the edges and tuck them slightly under the dough. Let rest for 10 minutes.

Lightly oil a large bowl. Folding the edges inward and under, form the dough into a ball and place in the bowl. Turn the dough, coating lightly with oil on both sides, and then turn the smooth side up. Cover the bowl with a kitchen towel and let rise until doubled in size, about 45 minutes to 1 hour.

Lightly oil two baking sheets or line with Silpats.

Turn the dough out onto a lightly floured board and punch down to deflate. Divide the dough into 6 equal pieces. Roll each piece into a rope about 14 inches long. Pinch 3 ropes together at one end and braid them, then pinch the other ends together. Tuck both ends under slightly, and transfer to one of the baking sheets. Repeat with the remaining 3 ropes to make a second loaf, and place on the other pan.

In a small bowl, whisk the remaining egg. Brush the top of each loaf with the egg glaze, being careful not to let egg run under the loaves, where it could burn during baking. Brush with the egg every 15 minutes during the rising time. Let rise until doubled in size, about 45 minutes to 1 hour. Just before baking, brush the tops a final time and dust with sugar.

Position the racks in the upper and lower thirds of the oven and preheat the oven to 350°F.

Place the loaves in the oven and bake for about 45 minutes, or until well browned, rotating the pans halfway through baking. If the top of the challah browns too quickly, cover loosely with a sheet of aluminum foil. Cool the loaves on a cooling rack.

MAKES 2 LOAVES

Note: Most recipes using yeast call for warm water that is approximately 110° to 115°F. Using water that's any warmer will kill the yeast. You can avoid this risk by using room-temperature water to which a bit of sugar has been added. This foolproof method takes just a little longer, but the yeast will usually foam within 10 to 15 minutes.

CHOCOLATE CHUNK MUFFINS

CONTRIBUTED BY JOANNE CHANG

Try using chunks of chocolate bigger than the standard chips for these muffins. The large chunks, which stay intact when baked, give every bite just the right proportion of chocolate to muffin.

Although crème fraîche is available in many markets, it is simple to make your own (see page 309). Mix this batter by hand; it's easy to do, and helps prevent overmixing, which would make the muffins tough.

Position a rack in the middle of the oven and preheat the oven to 350°F.

Butter and flour 12 muffin cups (¾-cup capacity) or line with paper muffin liners.

In a small bowl, whisk together the butter, eggs, and crème fraîche.

In a large bowl, combine the flour, baking powder, baking soda, salt, and sugar. Add the butter-egg mixture and stir with a wooden spoon or rubber spatula just until combined. Fold in the chocolate chunks.

Divide the batter among the muffin cups. Bake for 20 to 25 minutes, or until the muffins spring back slightly when pressed in the center.

Let cool in the pan for 10 minutes, then transfer to a cooling rack and let cool completely.

The muffins can be stored in an airtight container for 1 day. After that, they begin to dry out and toughen.

MAKES 12 MUFFINS

INGREDIENTS

Butter and flour for the muffin cups (or paper liners)

8 tablespoons (4 ounces) unsalted butter, melted and cooled

2 large eggs

¾ cup crème fraîche, homemade (page 309) or store-bought

2 cups all-purpose flour

1½ teaspoons baking powder

¼ teaspoon baking soda

½ teaspoon salt

1 cup granulated sugar

3 ounces 62% semisweet chocolate, cut into chunks

CHOCOLATE CHUNK SCONES

CONTRIBUTED BY JOANNE CHANG

We like scones that aren't overly sweet. For us, Joanne Chang's scones have the ideal proportions of sugar and semisweet chocolate, with a perfect crumb and texture. You can keep the unbaked scones on hand in your freezer—they go from freezer to oven without any need for defrosting.

INGREDIENTS

½ cup plus 2 tablespoons buttermilk

½ cup crème fraîche, homemade (page 309) or store-bought

1 large egg

3¼ cups all-purpose flour

⅓ cup granulated sugar

1½ teaspoons baking powder

½ teaspoon baking soda

½ teaspoon salt

3½ ounces 62% semisweet chocolate, chopped into chip-size chunks

8 tablespoons (4 ounces) unsalted butter, cut into ½-inch chunks and chilled

1 tablespoon sparkling or other coarse sugar

Position a rack in the middle of the oven and preheat the oven to 350°F. Line a baking sheet (half sheet pan) with a Silpat or parchment paper.

In a small bowl, combine ½ cup of the buttermilk, the crème fraîche, and egg. Set aside.

In the bowl of a stand mixer fitted with the paddle attachment, combine the flour, sugar, baking powder, baking soda, salt, and chocolate and mix on low speed to blend. Add the butter and mix on medium-low speed for 2 to 3 minutes, or until most of the butter pieces are about the size of small pebbles. If there are any larger pieces at this point, break them up with your fingers.

Add the buttermilk mixture and mix until just combined, about 1 minute. Turn the dough out onto a lightly floured board and bring together by hand. Roll the dough out to a square about 11 inches across and ½ inch thick.

To cut the dough into 12 even triangles, first cut the square in half, then cut each half into 3 even rectangles. Finally, cut each of the rectangles in half on the diagonal. (The scones can be made up to this point and frozen. There's no need to defrost the dough before baking.)

Place the scones on the prepared pan being sure they do not touch, and brush the tops with the remaining 2 tablespoons buttermilk. Sprinkle with sparkling sugar. Bake for about 24 minutes, or until golden.

Transfer the scones to a cooling rack and cool completely.

MAKES 12 SCONES

MASCARPONE-STUFFED FRENCH TOAST

CONTRIBUTED BY JASON HAMMEL AND AMALEA TSHILDS

This upgraded version of French toast is sandwiched with a creamy mixture of mascarpone and chocolate. If you like, you can assemble the sandwiches a day ahead of time and then dip and cook the French toast just before serving. The addictive Candied Almonds add a layer of crunch.

Combine the mascarpone, cream, and sugar in a small bowl. Add the melted chocolate, and mix until incorporated. Spread about 2 tablespoons of the mixture on one slice of brioche, and top with another slice. Repeat with the remaining slices, making 6 sandwiches.

In a shallow bowl, whisk together the eggs and half-and-half.

Preheat a nonstick griddle or large skillet over medium heat. Add 1 tablespoon butter. Dip each sandwich in the egg and half-and-half, turning to soak both sides. Let any excess drip back in the bowl. Place the sandwich on the griddle. Repeat with only as many sandwiches as fit comfortably in the griddle, and cook for about 2 to 3 minutes per side, or until golden. Transfer to a platter and cover to keep warm. Add more butter to the pan as necessary and cook the remaining sandwiches.

Slice each sandwich in half on the diagonal, and serve 3 halves per person. Sprinkle with the candied almonds and, using a Microplane, grate chocolate over the top. Serve with maple syrup.

SERVES 4

INGREDIENTS

4 ounces (½ cup) mascarpone, at room temperature

1 tablespoon heavy cream

1 tablespoon granulated sugar

½ to 1 ounce 62% semisweet chocolate (to taste), melted and cooled

Twelve ¼- to ⅜-inch slices day-old brioche

3 large eggs

1½ cups half-and-half

1 to 2 tablespoons (½ to 1 ounce) unsalted butter

Candied Almonds (page 314)

62% semisweet chocolate for grating

Maple syrup, warmed

CACAO NIB WAFFLES

CONTRIBUTED BY NANCY OAKES AND PAM MAZZOLA

At San Francisco's Boulevard Restaurant, tender waffles studded with dark, crunchy cacao nibs serve as the base for buttery foie gras. The earthy quality of the nibs means these waffles work well with savory foods, but we tend to eat them for breakfast served right out of the waffle iron with citrus sugar and a pitcher of warm maple syrup.

The number of servings will vary depending on your waffle maker. A classic waffle iron will make 8 to 10 thin waffles.

Place the nibs and coffee in a small bowl and let sit for 1 hour.

In a large bowl, mix the flour, cloves, cinnamon, ginger, baking soda, and salt. Set aside.

In the bowl of a stand mixer fitted with the paddle attachment, beat the butter and brown sugar until smooth. Add the eggs one at a time, beating until each egg is incorporated before adding the next one.

Strain the nibs and reserve the coffee. Blend the nibs and molasses into the egg mixture. The mixture may look curdled at this point. With the mixer running on low speed, add the dry ingredients, stopping to scrape the sides of the bowl as necessary. The batter will be thicker than traditional waffle batter, but if it looks and feels too thick to ladle, add the reserved coffee 1 tablespoon at a time as necessary.

Preheat the oven to 250°F. Heat the waffle iron, and spray with the cooking spray.

Ladle the batter onto the waffle maker, and cook according to the manufacturer's instructions. Keep the cooked waffles warm in the oven.

Serve the waffles with butter, maple syrup, and citrus sugar, if desired.

MAKES 8 TO 10 CLASSIC WAFFLES

INGREDIENTS

¼ cup plus 2 tablespoons cacao nibs, lightly crushed with a rolling pin

1 cup hot freshly brewed coffee

2 cups all-purpose flour

¼ teaspoon ground cloves

¼ teaspoon ground cinnamon

¼ teaspoon ground ginger

½ teaspoon baking soda

½ teaspoon salt

9 tablespoons (4½ ounces) unsalted butter, at room temperature, plus more for serving

1 cup firmly packed light brown sugar

2 large eggs, at room temperature

½ cup unsulphured molasses

Nonstick cooking spray

Maple syrup, warmed

Citrus Sugar (page 306, optional)

Oatmeal with Nibs

OUR PHOTOGRAPHER, DEBORAH JONES, CAME UP WITH this great combination. Because nibs don't contain any added sugar, this might be the healthiest way to eat chocolate. The nibs add crunch, flecks of color, lots of flavor, and a hint of the exotic to oatmeal, definitely starting the morning on a good note.

Cook your oatmeal and sweeten it as you would normally. Sprinkle nibs over the oatmeal and serve with warm milk. If you like, add dried cherries or raisins, slices of banana, chunks of mango, or your favorite fruit.

BROWN SUGAR MERINGUE BARS

These taste like soft chocolate chip cookies, but they're topped with a light meringue that turns golden brown in the oven. They are best eaten the same day they are baked.

INGREDIENTS

1 cup sifted all-purpose flour

¼ cup granulated sugar

½ teaspoon baking powder

⅛ teaspoon baking soda

¼ teaspoon salt

1 large egg white

8 tablespoons (4 ounces) unsalted butter, cut into 1-inch cubes, at room temperature

1½ teaspoons water

1 teaspoon pure vanilla extract

3 ounces 62% semisweet chocolate, chopped into chip-size chunks

1 large egg, separated

½ cup firmly packed light brown sugar

Position a rack in the center of the oven and preheat the oven to 350°F.

Cut an 8 by 14-inch piece of parchment paper and line an 8 by 8 by 2-inch baking pan with the paper, letting it extend evenly over two opposite sides of the pan.

Combine the flour, sugar, baking powder, baking soda, and salt. Set aside.

Place the egg yolk in the bowl of a stand mixer and beat lightly with a fork. Place the bowl on the mixer, fitted with the paddle attachment.

Add the dry ingredients to the yolk and mix on low speed until combined. Add the butter, water, and vanilla and mix on medium speed until combined.

Spread the dough evenly in the prepared pan. Sprinkle with the chocolate chunks, and press them lightly into the dough.

In a clean bowl, using a handheld mixer or by hand, whip the reserved whites until foamy. Add the brown sugar and continue to whip until stiff peaks form. Spread the meringue over the top of the dough.

Bake for 30 to 35 minutes, until the meringue is golden brown and set. Allow the bars to cool completely in the pan on a cooling rack.

Cut into 2 by 2-inch bars.

MAKES 16 BARS

POLVORONES

CONTRIBUTED BY RICK BAYLESS

An authentic Mexican *bizcochito* with a pronounced cinnamon flavor, this cookie's tenderness is due to Rick's use of lard. Lard in a dessert may sound unusual, but many bakers swear that it makes the most tender piecrusts.

Rick says, "People stop in their tracks when they hear the word *lard*. But lard has less than half the cholesterol and about one-third less saturated fat than butter. It's easy to digest and delicious, so please keep an open mind and try it. You can find fresh-rendered lard from a Mexican or other ethnic butcher. Avoid the pale blond bricks of lard sold in standard groceries."

Sift together the flour, baking soda, and cinnamon. Set aside.

In the bowl of a stand mixer fitted with the paddle attachment, beat together the butter, lard, and sugar on medium speed for 3 to 5 minutes, or until light and fluffy, stopping to scrape down the sides of the bowl as necessary. With the mixer running, add the yolks one at a time, making sure the first is incorporated before adding the second. Stop the mixer, add the dry ingredients, and mix on low speed until just combined. Mix in the orange juice, then the nibs.

Turn the dough out onto a lightly floured work surface and divide it in half. Roll each half into a 1½-inch-wide log 10 to 12 inches in length. Wrap the dough in plastic wrap and chill for at least 2 hours or overnight. (The logs can be frozen for up to 1 month.)

Position the racks in the lower and upper thirds of the oven and preheat the oven to 325°F. Line two baking sheets with Silpats or parchment paper.

Cut the dough into ¼-inch slices, and place 1½ to 2 inches apart on the prepared sheets.

Bake for 15 minutes, or until golden, rotating the pans halfway through baking. Transfer the cookies to a cooling rack to cool completely.

The cookies can be stored in an airtight container for up to 1 week.

MAKES ABOUT 6 DOZEN COOKIES

INGREDIENTS

- 2 cups flour, preferably a low-gluten all-purpose
- 1 teaspoon baking soda
- 1 tablespoon ground cinnamon, preferably freshly ground Mexican cinnamon (*canela*)
- 8 tablespoons (4 ounces) unsalted butter, at room temperature
- 4 ounces fresh lard
- ¼ cup plus 1 tablespoon turbinado or granulated sugar
- 2 large egg yolks
- 1 tablespoon freshly squeezed orange juice
- ¼ cup plus 1 tablespoon cacao nibs, crushed with a rolling pin

CACAO NIB MACAROONS

Add cacao nibs to classic macaroons and you'll get a nice chewy texture as well as an intriguing depth of flavor. You can form the macaroons neatly by using a pastry bag (see page 25). If you don't have a pastry bag and tip, use a resealable 1-quart plastic bag and cut ½ inch off one bottom corner.

Position a rack in the middle of the oven and preheat the oven to 400°F. Line two baking sheets with parchment paper.

Place the nibs in a small bowl. Split the vanilla bean lengthwise in half with a paring knife, and scrape the seeds into the bowl with the nibs. Grind half the mixture in a coffee or spice grinder, pulsing the machine and scraping the sides as necessary, until finely ground. Transfer the mixture to a small bowl. Repeat with the remaining nibs and vanilla.

Grind the sugar and add it to the bowl of ground nibs. Toss the ingredients together with your fingers or the tines of a fork, then sift through a medium strainer into a medium bowl.

Using a handheld mixer or by hand, in a medium bowl, beat the egg whites with the cream of tartar until they hold stiff peaks. Fold in the nib and sugar mixture until just incorporated. Do not overmix.

Transfer the mixture to a pastry bag fitted with a ½-inch tip or use a disposable pastry bag and cut an opening in the tip of the bag. With one hand, hold the pastry bag perpendicular to the baking sheet, with the tip ¼ inch above the parchment. Holding the pastry tip with the other hand, apply even pressure to the end of the pastry bag, while slowly pulling the bag up from the baking sheet to pipe a 1-inch round macaroon. Once the macaroon is formed, lift up the bag in a circular motion to release the top of the macaroon. Continue piping the macaroons, leaving 1½ inches between them. Let the cookies sit at room temperature for 10 minutes to form a skin.

Bake for 10 minutes, or until the cookies begin to darken at the edges. Remove from the oven and let the cookies firm slightly on the parchment, then slide the parchment liners with the macaroons onto cooling racks.

When they are cool, remove the macaroons from the parchment. If they stick to the parchment, lift the parchment and slightly moisten the paper under each macaroon with a damp towel to release it.

The macaroons can be stored in an airtight container for several days.

MAKES ABOUT 3 DOZEN COOKIES

INGREDIENTS

½ cup cacao nibs

1 vanilla bean

¾ cup granulated sugar

2 large egg whites

¼ teaspoon cream of tartar

APRICOT HAZELNUT SQUARES

Ground hazelnuts, cacao nibs, and apricot jam give these cookies a wonderful fruit-and-nut flavor and a texture reminiscent of a Linzertorte. They're ideal for picnics but on very hot days, you may prefer to skip dipping them in chocolate.

TO MAKE THE COOKIES:

Combine the hazelnuts, nibs, flour, cinnamon, and cocoa powder in a medium bowl, and set aside.

In the bowl of a stand mixer, fitted with the paddle attachment, combine the butter, zest, and lemon juice and mix on medium speed. Add the sugar and mix on low speed for 30 seconds to blend, then increase the speed to medium and beat until fluffy, 2 to 3 minutes. Add the dry ingredients and mix on low speed, stopping to scrape down the sides of the bowl, until just incorporated, 2 to 3 minutes.

Form the dough into a 7-inch square, wrap in plastic wrap, and refrigerate for 30 minutes.

Meanwhile, remove the lid from the jar of jam, place the jar in the microwave, and microwave for 1 minute. Stir and continue to heat until the jam is melted and hot. Or place the jam in a small saucepan and heat over medium heat until softened. Strain the jam into a small bowl and set the fruit aside for another use.

Position the racks in the lower and upper thirds of the oven and preheat the oven to 350°F. Line two baking sheets with Silpats or parchment paper.

Cut the dough in half. Roll each piece between two pieces of parchment paper or plastic wrap until ³⁄₁₆ inch thick. Cut out cookies with a 1½- to 2-inch square cutter or a knife and place on the prepared sheets about ½ inch apart.

Bake for 18 to 20 minutes, rotating the sheets halfway through baking. Slide the Silpats or parchment with the cookies onto cooling racks to cool completely.

Place half the cookies upside down on a work surface. Top each with about 1 teaspoon of jam. Place the remaining cookies right side up over the filling, and push down gently to sandwich the cookies.

TO COAT THE COOKIES IN CHOCOLATE:

Line a baking sheet with parchment paper.

Dip half of each cookie in the chocolate and place on the baking sheet to harden.

The cookies can be stored in an airtight container for up to 3 days.

MAKES ABOUT 20 SANDWICH COOKIES

INGREDIENTS

¾ cup finely ground hazelnuts

¼ cup finely crushed cacao nibs

1½ cups all-purpose flour

¼ teaspoon ground cinnamon

½ teaspoon unsweetened cocoa powder

12 tablespoons (6 ounces) unsalted butter, at room temperature

1 teaspoon finely grated lemon zest

½ teaspoon freshly squeezed lemon juice

¾ cup confectioners' sugar

One 8- to 10-ounce jar apricot jam, at room temperature

6 ounces 70% bittersweet chocolate, tempered (see page 92)

Lace Cookies, page 242.

LACE COOKIES

These thin, crisp old-fashioned cookies really play up the flavor of the chocolate filling. Lovers of dark chocolate may want to try filling these cookies with 82% chocolate, but you can use any chocolate you like.

Position the racks in the lower and upper thirds of the oven and preheat the oven to 375°F. Line two baking sheets with Silpats or parchment paper.

In a medium bowl, combine the flour, sugar, cinnamon, baking powder, salt, and oats. Set aside.

In a large bowl, combine the butter, cream, corn syrup, vanilla, and rum. Stir until smooth. Slowly add the dry ingredients, stirring to combine.

Drop about ¾ of a teaspoon of the batter onto the prepared baking sheets. Make the cookies as close in size as possible. Place only 12 cookies on each baking sheet (four rows of three), as they will spread considerably.

Bake the cookies for 8 to 10 minutes, rotating once halfway through baking. Remove from the oven and let stand on the sheets for 1 to 2 minutes. If any of the cookies have run together, cut them apart, then transfer the cookies to cooling racks to cool completely.

Choose 2 cookies that are similar in shape. Drizzle the bottom of one cookie with melted chocolate and spread with a small offset spatula. Sandwich with the second cookie. Repeat with remaining cookies.

The cookies can be stored in an airtight container for up to 2 days.

MAKES ABOUT 20 SANDWICH COOKIES

INGREDIENTS

½ cup sifted all-purpose flour

½ cup granulated sugar

½ teaspoon ground cinnamon

¼ teaspoon baking powder

Pinch of salt

½ cup old-fashioned or quick-cooking oats (not instant)

⅓ cup (generous 2½ ounces) unsalted butter, melted

2 tablespoons heavy cream

2 tablespoons light corn syrup

1 teaspoon pure vanilla extract

1 teaspoon dark rum

2 ounces 82% extra dark chocolate, melted and still warm

MINI MADELEINES

CONTRIBUTED BY CAROLE BLOOM

Miniature almond madeleines are perfect for dipping into Chocolate Orange Fondue (page 61). They're also a nice "side" cookie, to place on the plate next to a bowl of ice cream, fruit, or sorbet, or on the saucer of a cup of tea.

Finely grind the almonds in a small food processor or in a coffee or spice grinder. Transfer to a small bowl. Finely grind the nibs, add to the almonds, and set aside.

In the bowl of a stand mixer fitted with the whisk attachment, combine the eggs and salt and whip on medium-high speed until foamy. Gradually add the sugar and continue to whip until the mixture is very thick and pale and forms a slowly dissolving ribbon when the whisk is lifted. Add the vanilla and blend well. Remove the bowl from the mixer.

Sift together the flour and baking powder, and fold into the egg mixture one-third at a time, blending thoroughly after each addition. Fold in the melted butter one-third at a time, blending thoroughly after each addition. Fold in the zest and almond mixture. Cover the bowl tightly with plastic wrap and let stand at room temperature for 1 hour.

Position a rack in the center of the oven and preheat the oven to 400°F. Spray two mini madeleine pans (15 to 20 molds each), preferably nonstick, with cooking spray. (If using silicone-lined pans, it is not necessary to spray.) Place the pans on a baking sheet.

Fit a pastry bag with a ½-inch plain tip or use a disposable pastry bag and cut an opening in the tip of the bag. Fill with the batter, and pipe it into the madeleine molds.

Bake for 10 to 13 minutes, or until the madeleines are golden brown and spring back when touched lightly. Remove from the oven and immediately turn out onto cooling racks; if necessary, gently shake the pans to remove the madeleines.

Store the madeleines in a baking pan between layers of parchment or waxed paper, tightly covered with aluminum foil, or in a large airtight container at room temperature for up to 2 days.

MAKES 40 MINI MADELEINES

INGREDIENTS

3 tablespoons toasted sliced almonds

1 tablespoon cacao nibs, crushed with a rolling pin

2 large eggs

⅛ teaspoon salt

½ cup granulated sugar

½ teaspoon pure vanilla extract

⅔ cup all-purpose flour

⅛ teaspoon baking powder

4 tablespoons (2 ounces) unsalted butter, melted and cooled

½ teaspoon finely grated lemon zest

Nonstick cooking spray

COCOA CARAMEL PANNA COTTA

CONTRIBUTED BY MICHAEL CHIARELLO

Michael Chiarello, known for his knack of transforming a classic into something new, reinvented his signature panna cotta by adding caramel and cocoa. These cool, silky confections are so delicately beautiful you hate to mar the glossy surface with a spoon.

Prepare these a day or two ahead, if possible. They can be made in traditional panna cotta molds or in other small decorative molds, like those used for Bavarians. They are charming served alone or with a custard sauce and a bowl of fresh cherries or figs.

Arrange eight 4-ounce molds (see page 25) in a baking dish, for easy transfer in and out of the refrigerator.

Combine the gelatin and 2 tablespoons of the cold water in a small bowl. Set aside to soften.

Combine the sugar and the remaining 2 tablespoons water in a medium saucepan, bring to a simmer over medium heat, and cook, without stirring, for 5 to 6 minutes, swirling the saucepan occasionally to cook the caramel evenly. Test the color of the caramel by drizzling a few drops onto a white plate. If sugar crystals form on the sides of the pan, brush with a wet pastry brush. When the color is medium to dark amber, remove the pan from the heat.

Stir the cocoa into the caramel until it has dissolved. Carefully pour in the cream. Some of the caramel may seize, but it will dissolve again as it is heated. Stir, being sure to incorporate any bits of caramel that may be clinging to the bottom of the pan, until all of the caramel has dissolved. Remove from the heat, and stir in the gelatin until dissolved.

Set a fine-mesh strainer over a large liquid measuring cup or a bowl with a spout, and strain the caramel mixture.

Divide the mixture evenly among the molds. Refrigerate until completely chilled and set, at least 4 hours or, preferably, overnight.

To unmold the panna cotta, fill a bowl with very hot tap water. Dip a mold into the water, then lift from the water, dry the bottom with a towel, and invert onto a serving plate. If it does not slide out, redip in the water. Continue with the remaining panna cotta. Be sure to replace the hot water in the bowl as it cools.

Serve plain, or with custard sauce or a bowl of cherries or figs.

SERVES 8

Note: Superfine sugar is available in most grocery stores. Granulated sugar ground in the food processor can be used as a substitute.

INGREDIENTS

- 2½ teaspoons gelatin
- ¼ cup cold water
- ½ cup superfine sugar (see Note)
- 2 tablespoons unsweetened cocoa powder
- 3 cups heavy cream, warmed
- Custard Sauce (page 313) or fresh cherries or figs (optional)

MINT-BASIL CHOCOLATE CHUNK ICE CREAM

CONTRIBUTED BY ELIZABETH FALKNER

When we began selling our chocolate, Elizabeth Falkner was the first chef to enthusiastically embrace what we were trying to do. Elizabeth's excitement over dessert making extends to using ingredients that we would never have imagined—for example, adding fresh basil and spinach to that old standard, mint chocolate chip ice cream. Try this vibrant green minty ice cream made with chunks of dark chocolate, and you'll find that the old variety of mint chocolate chip suddenly seems lackluster.

For fans of cilantro, Elizabeth suggests adding a few fresh cilantro leaves along with the mint and basil for an extra piquant kick.

In a small saucepan, combine the milk and sugar and bring to a boil over medium heat, stirring until the sugar has dissolved. Transfer to a bowl, cover with plastic wrap, and refrigerate. (The milk syrup should be chilled before it is added to the blanched spinach because if it is warm, the syrup can cook the spinach further and change the color from pale green to khaki.)

In a clean small saucepan, combine the cream, mint, and basil and bring to a simmer over medium-low to medium heat. Remove from the heat, cover, and allow the herbs to steep in the cream for 30 minutes.

Bring a medium saucepan of water to a boil. Fill a medium bowl with ice water. Drop the spinach leaves into the boiling water and blanch for 30 seconds. Using a slotted spoon or tongs, transfer the leaves to the ice water, then remove the leaves from the water and dry on a kitchen towel. Wring out any excess water. Coarsely chop the spinach.

Line a fine-mesh strainer with dampened cheesecloth and place over a medium bowl.

Place the spinach and half of the milk mixture in a blender and blend well. With the blender running, slowly add the remaining milk. Strain the milk mixture into the bowl. Lift up the cheesecloth and carefully wring out any remaining liquid through the strainer into the bowl. Then pour the cream mixture through the strainer into the bowl, and stir to combine. Cover with plastic wrap and refrigerate for at least 2 hours or overnight.

Place a metal bowl in the freezer to chill. Pour the ice cream base in an ice cream maker and freeze following the manufacturer's instructions. Transfer the ice cream to the chilled metal bowl and fold in the chocolate. For a firmer ice cream, place in the freezer for 1 to 2 hours before serving.

Serve alone or with the hot fudge sauce.

MAKES ABOUT 1 QUART

INGREDIENTS

2 cups whole milk

1 cup granulated sugar

2 cups heavy cream

40 large peppermint or spearmint leaves

12 large basil leaves

A generous handful of spinach leaves

6 ounces 62% semisweet chocolate, finely chopped

Hot Fudge Sauce (page 311, optional)

Pepper Mill Nibs

CONTRIBUTED BY STEPHANIE HERSH

AT A PARTY, STEPHANIE WATCHED ONE OF THE GUESTS passing around a new and very fancy pepper grinder. Stephanie, who had been cooking with nibs, had the idea of filling the grinder with nibs.

This works very well when you want a subtle taste of chocolate. Use a clean pepper grinder, and grind right at the table. Mill the nibs over a slice of melon, a bowl of strawberries sprinkled with balsamic vinegar, fresh raspberries, or even over vegetables or soups—anything you like.

PUMPKIN SEED NIB BRITTLE

CONTRIBUTED BY ARNON OREN

At Café Cacao, the restaurant in our factory, we like to crumble this unusual brittle over a composed salad of endive, roasted beets, and goat cheese. It's terrific with any type of hot cereal too. Just grind it into "nib brittle dust" and sprinkle over the top. This crisp brittle is at its best the same day it's made.

Coarsely chop the nibs and strain through a small strainer. Removing the dustier pieces will make a clearer brittle.

Toast the pumpkin seeds in a small skillet over medium heat, shaking often, until they begin to pop, 2 to 3 minutes. Remove the seeds from the skillet, and set aside.

Line a baking sheet with a Silpat or brush it with butter.

In a medium saucepan, combine the sugar, water, and cream of tartar and bring to a simmer over medium heat, stirring until the sugar dissolves. Lower the heat to medium low, cover, and let simmer for 2 to 3 minutes. Remove the pan lid and brush any sugar crystals from the sides of the pan with a wet pastry brush. Continue simmering for 3 to 5 minutes, or until the syrup begins to color. Watch closely, because the caramel can quickly burn. Test the color of the caramel by drizzling a few drops on a white plate. When the color is medium to dark amber, remove the pan from the heat and stir in the nibs, pumpkin seeds, and cayenne, if using. Working quickly, pour the mixture onto the prepared pan and spread as thin as possible with a heatproof spatula or wooden spoon.

Allow the brittle to cool completely, then break into small pieces. Store in an airtight container for up to 4 days.

MAKES ABOUT 1½ CUPS

INGREDIENTS

¼ cup cacao nibs

¼ cup hulled raw pumpkin seeds

½ cup granulated sugar

¼ cup water

⅛ teaspoon cream of tartar

Pinch of cayenne pepper (optional)

ALMOND ROCA

This recipe can be doubled without any extra effort. Just make sure you use a large enough pot. Break this roca into big irregular pieces and pack them into gift tins, or store in your freezer. Fair warning—even frozen, the roca is pretty hard to resist.

Lightly butter a 17 by 12 by 1-inch baking sheet (half sheet pan), and line with parchment paper to cover the bottom and all sides. (The butter will anchor the parchment to the pan.)

Melt the butter in a large pot over medium-high heat. Add the sugar, water, lemon juice, and corn syrup and and bring the mixture to a gentle boil, stirring to dissolve the sugar. Once the mixture boils, stop stirring. Brush down any sugar crystals clinging to the sides of the pot with a pastry brush dipped in water.

Clip a candy thermometer to the side of the pot and cook for 15 minutes, or until the mixture reaches 300°F. If the mixture threatens to boil over, lower the heat as necessary. (If the liquid is too shallow to measure the temperature, tilt the pot to get an accurate reading.) Resist the temptation to stir; if the caramel is not coloring evenly, swirl the pan from time to time.

Remove the pot from the heat and stir in 2 cups of the almonds. Quickly spread the caramel in an even layer on the prepared baking sheet. Let cool completely.

Spread the chocolate over the top of the caramel, then sprinkle with the remaining 1½ cups almonds. Let the chocolate harden at room temperature or in the refrigerator.

Break the roca into irregular pieces. Store in an airtight container at room temperature or freeze for longer storage.

MAKES ABOUT 3½ POUNDS

INGREDIENTS

1 pound unsalted butter, cut into chunks, plus more for the pan

3 cups granulated sugar

¼ cup plus 2 tablespoons water

½ teaspoon freshly squeezed lemon juice

2 tablespoons light corn syrup

3½ cups coarsely chopped toasted slivered almonds

9 ounces 41% milk chocolate, melted

LEGENDS & LORE

Milton Hershey and Chocolate

In 1893, when Milton Snavely Hershey first saw German chocolate-making machinery at the Chicago Columbian Exposition, he was the owner of the Lancaster Caramel Company, the nation's leading manufacturer of caramels. His success with caramels had come after two failed attempts to establish his own candy business, first in Philadelphia and later in New York City. Following the failed New York venture, Hershey had returned home, penniless, to Lancaster, Pennsylvania, but he got back on his feet and began making caramels in 1886. His company did well because Hershey used fresh milk in his caramels, a technique he'd learned from a Denver, Colorado, candy maker, and also because his own two failed businesses had taught him how to make a company work.

When Hershey came upon the chocolate-making equipment at the exposition, he bought the entire exhibit and had the equipment shipped to Lancaster. He began making chocolate coatings for his caramels, and within a year, the Hershey Chocolate Company was born, a subsidiary of the caramel company. In 1900, Hershey sold off the caramel company but kept ownership of the chocolate company.

He moved his rapidly growing chocolate business to Derry Church, Pennsylvania, the small town where he was born, in part because the area was mostly dairy farms, able to provide all the fresh milk he needed for his chocolate. He also envisioned building a model town for the workers of the new factory, which opened in 1905. A year later, the town was christened Hershey when the U.S. Postal Service gave permission for a new post office.

Hershey and his wife, Kitty, began a school for poor orphaned boys in 1909 when they realized they wouldn't be able to have children. Kitty died in 1915, and three years later Hershey placed his fortune, then valued at $60 million, in trust for his school. The Milton Hershey School still exists, although it's no longer an orphanage. The school, which every year gives 1,400 disadvantaged boys and girls an education, food, clothing, and health care, owns 30 percent of the total equity outstanding and 78 percent of the combined voting power of The Hershey Company's two classes of common stock.

COCOA NUTS

Susie Heller created these addictive treats. These nuts are coated with a soft meringue and then baked. The resulting shell isn't hard like rock candy, but it isn't soft either. It's crisp and, in thicker spots, it's almost airy.

These nuts make a unique gift when packed into tins or in cellophane bags tied with ribbon.

Position a rack in the middle of the oven and preheat the oven to 325°F.

Spread the nuts on a 17 by 12 by 1-inch baking sheet (half sheet pan) and toast for 10 minutes. Remove the nuts from the baking sheet, and set aside.

Scatter the butter pieces over the baking sheet and place in the oven to melt. Remove from the oven as soon as they're melted.

In the bowl of a stand mixer fitted with the whisk attachment, whip the egg whites on medium speed until they just start to hold a shape. With the mixer running, gradually add the sugar, then continue to whip for 2 minutes. The mixture will be very sticky and shiny, much thinner than a typical meringue.

Remove the bowl from the mixer. Sift the cocoa on top of the whites and fold in, then fold in the nuts.

Lay the coated nuts on top of the melted butter on the baking sheet, and gently spread them out. (Not all of the butter will be covered by nuts.) Bake for 10 minutes. Remove the pan from the oven and use a metal spatula to break up the nut mixture and turn the pieces in the butter. Return to the oven for another 10 minutes, then break up the nuts and turn them again. Return to the oven for a final 10 minutes. When done, the butter should be absorbed, the coating will be dry, and the nuts will be coated in a crispy meringue. Place the pan on a cooling rack and let cool completely.

Break up any clumps of nuts, and store in an airtight container for up to 1 week.

MAKES ABOUT 6 CUPS

INGREDIENTS

2 cups pecan halves

1 cup walnut halves

8 tablespoons (4 ounces) unsalted butter, cut into cubes

2 large egg whites

1 cup granulated sugar

1 tablespoon unsweetened cocoa powder

CHOCOLATE BANANA MILKSHAKE

Chocolate and bananas taste terrific together, especially in a sentimental favorite like the chocolate banana milkshake. Traditionally, the chocolate syrup is poured right into the blender and combined with vanilla ice cream, chunks of banana, and milk. We think it's a little more interesting to stripe the chocolate syrup in thick lines down the inside of the glass before the shake is poured in. Use a squirt bottle to make the stripes and with a long-handled spoon lightly touching the glass, stir to marble the stripes and the shake. If you want to add a little extra chocolate syrup into the blender with the banana, go right ahead, but the contrast between the cream-colored shake and the dark chocolate stripes won't be as great.

Break the banana into 3 to 4 pieces and place in a blender with the ice cream and milk. Blend until thoroughly combined.

Squeeze thick lines of chocolate syrup in stripes down the insides of two large glasses. Pour in the milkshake. Run a spoon lightly against the stripes of chocolate to marble the syrup.

SERVES 2

INGREDIENTS

1 ripe banana

8 scoops (about 1 pint) vanilla ice cream

1½ cups whole milk

About ¼ cup Chocolate Syrup (page 311)

ALTHOUGH THESE SAVORY RECIPES CALL FOR
ONLY A HINT OF CHOCOLATE, THEY'RE IN A CATEGORY
ALL THEIR OWN.

Other countries use chocolate's dark richness in savory dishes—moles, chilies, and stews—but, for most Americans, chocolate without sugar is a new idea. We've taken advantage of the crunchy, dark flavor of nibs throughout this section. You'll be surprised by how much nibs contribute to a green salad or a simple round of goat cheese.

ROASTED SQUASH WITH NIB VINAIGRETTE

CONTRIBUTED BY ARNON OREN

Café Cacao, the restaurant in our factory, surprises some visitors. Many expect a coffee bar that serves nothing but chocolate cake and cookies. While we do serve many kinds of desserts, Berkeley residents come more for the savory foods made with cacao nibs.

Arnon Oren, our first executive chef, created this fresh, memorable dish. Combining roasted squash with pancetta and crunchy cacao nibs brings out the depth and sweetness of the squash, making it taste almost creamy. Prosciutto or any salty cured meat works well in this recipe.

INGREDIENTS

One 4-pound butternut squash, peeled, cut in half lengthwise and seeded

½ cup plus 2 tablespoons extra virgin olive oil

Salt and freshly ground black pepper

1 tablespoon balsamic vinegar

1½ teaspoons cacao nibs, coarsely chopped

1 shallot, finely minced

3 ounces thinly sliced pancetta

Position the racks in the lower and upper third of the oven and preheat the oven to 450°F. Line two baking sheets with Silpats or parchment paper.

Trim the ends of the squash and cut off the neck portions from the bulbs. Place the 4 pieces of squash cut side down on a board, and cut into ¼-inch slices. Toss with 2 tablespoons of the olive oil and sprinkle lightly with salt and pepper.

Lay the slices on the prepared baking sheets and roast for about 20 minutes, until golden brown and soft. Rotate the baking sheets halfway through cooking.

Meanwhile, prepare the vinaigrette and cook the pancetta.

TO MAKE THE VINAIGRETTE:

Combine the remaining ½ cup olive oil, the vinegar, nibs, and shallot in a small bowl. Season with salt and pepper.

In a large skillet, cook the pancetta over medium heat until crisp, 10 to 15 minutes, turning to brown evenly. Drain on paper towels. When it is cool, chop or crumble into small pieces.

Place the squash in a large bowl, add about ¼ cup of the vinaigrette, and toss gently to coat. Arrange the slices on individual plates or a large platter. Drizzle with the remaining vinaigrette and top with the pancetta. Serve warm.

SERVES 6

Goat Cheese with Nibs

FOR AN INTRIGUING APPETIZER, crush cacao nibs with a rolling pin and mix them into goat cheese. Use 1/2 to 1 teaspoon of nibs for every ounce of goat cheese. For a hint of sweetness, add 1/4 teaspoon of honey, granulated sugar, or ginger preserves for every ounce of cheese.

Because the flavors will continue to emerge over time, it's best to combine all ingredients, cover, and refrigerate for at least an hour or overnight. Before serving, spoon into a small decorative bowl or form small disks or balls from the cheese mixture and dust them lightly with cocoa powder.

Spinach and Walnut Salad with Pears and Nib Vinaigrette, page 268.

SPINACH AND WALNUT SALAD WITH PEARS AND NIB VINAIGRETTE

CONTRIBUTED BY ARNON OREN

A Café Cacao favorite, this salad combines juicy pears, fresh spinach, and our unique nib vinaigrette. You can top almost any salad or a simple plate of greens with this same combination of walnuts and nibs for added texture and flavor.

Place the shallots and the vinegar in a small bowl and let sit for 15 minutes.

Add the nibs to the vinegar, and slowly whisk in the olive oil.

Place the spinach, pears, and walnuts in a large bowl. Add ¼ cup of the vinaigrette and toss. Add additional dressing as necessary to lightly coat the greens, and serve. (Reserve any remaining vinaigrette for another use.) Season to taste with salt and pepper.

SERVES 4

INGREDIENTS

2 shallots, minced

2 tablespoons balsamic vinegar

1½ teaspoons coarsely chopped cacao nibs

½ cup extra virgin olive oil

8 ounces spinach leaves (about 10 cups), any large stems removed, washed, and dried

2 ripe pears, peeled, cored, and thinly sliced

½ cup coarsely chopped toasted walnuts

Salt and freshly ground black pepper

BBQ Sauce

Dry mustard, yellow mustard, and cayenne pepper give this sauce a definite kick, while an ounce of 70% dark chocolate gives it a smooth finish. Serve this alongside meat that's been prepared with John's Cocoa Rub (page 274) or use it as a basting sauce.

In a medium bowl, whisk together the tomato paste and yellow mustard until smooth. Add the water, vinegar, corn syrup, lemon juice, and both sugars. Whisk until combined, and set aside.

In a medium saucepan, place the olive oil over medium heat. Add the onion and sauté for 1 minute. Add the garlic and cook until softened, about 2 minutes. Stir in the chili powder, dry mustard, paprika, and cayenne and stir for 1 minute, or until the spices are fragrant. Add the tomato paste mixture, stir to combine, and bring to a boil. Lower the heat and simmer for 30 minutes, stirring occasionally.

Remove from the heat, stir in the chocolate, and season with salt and pepper.

MAKES 2 CUPS

INGREDIENTS

3 tablespoons tomato paste

3 tablespoons yellow mustard

1½ cups water

½ cup apple cider vinegar

2 tablespoons dark corn syrup

1 tablespoon freshly squeezed lemon juice

1 tablespoon granulated sugar

1 tablespoon firmly packed light brown sugar

1 tablespoon extra virgin olive oil

½ cup finely chopped onion

1 tablespoon finely chopped garlic

1 tablespoon chili powder

1½ teaspoons dry mustard

1½ teaspoons paprika

1 teaspoon cayenne pepper

1 ounce 70% bittersweet chocolate, finely chopped

½ teaspoon salt

½ teaspoon freshly ground black pepper

Tortilla Soup, page 272.

TORTILLA SOUP

CONTRIBUTED BY ELIZABETH FALKNER

INGREDIENTS

1 dried chipotle chile (or 1 canned chipotle, wiped dry and minced)

1 ear of corn, husked, kernels cut from cob, and cob reserved, or 1 cup drained canned hominy or posole

1 large chile, such as Anaheim, or 4 smaller chiles, such as serrano

2 tablespoons extra virgin olive oil

1 medium onion, skin on, cut into ¼-inch pieces

2 medium carrots, peeled and cut into ¼-inch pieces

1 stalk celery, cut into ¼-inch pieces

3 cloves garlic, smashed but not peeled

¼ teaspoon chili powder or ground cumin

¼ teaspoon ground coriander

½ teaspoon annatto seeds

¼ teaspoon dried epazote or Mexican oregano

One 14½-ounce can crushed tomatoes

1 tablespoon tomato paste

4 cups chicken, beef, or vegetable stock

1 cup water

1 to 2 ounces 70% bittersweet chocolate, coarsely chopped

Salt and freshly ground black pepper

1 avocado

1 lime, cut into wedges

Coarse sea salt

¼ to ⅓ cup cilantro leaves

Tortilla chips, lightly crushed

Annatto seeds, epazote, and chipotle chiles (found in Mexican or specialty markets), along with chocolate, give this soup its traditional spicy flavors. If you can't find dried chiles, you can substitute canned, but be sure to wipe away any adobo sauce with a paper towel.

Add just one ounce of chocolate initially and taste the soup before you begin adding more a little at a time, tasting after each addition. If you make the soup in advance, don't add the chocolate until just before serving, because the flavor of the chocolate can overwhelm some of the other flavors if it is added in advance.

If using a dried chipotle, bring a small pan of water to a boil. Place the dried chipotle in a bowl and cover with the boiling water. Let stand for 20 minutes, or until softened.

Drain and dry the chile. Remove and discard the stem and seeds, and mince the chile. Set aside.

If using corn, slice the kernels from the cob, reserve the cob, and set aside the kernels.

Meanwhile, place a rack on the highest level and preheat the broiler. Place the fresh chile(s) on a small baking sheet and place under the broiler. Turn occasionally to char the skin on all sides. Remove from the oven, place in a small bowl, and cover with plastic wrap. Let the chile(s) steam until cool enough to work with.

Peel the roasted chile(s) and discard the stem(s) and seeds. Coarsely chop, and set aside.

In a medium pot, heat the olive oil over medium heat. Add the onion, carrots, celery, and garlic and cook, stirring occasionally, for 5 to 10 minutes, until the onion is translucent.

Stir in the chili powder or cumin, coriander, annatto seeds, and epazote or oregano, coating the vegetables with the spices. Add the tomatoes, tomato paste, chipotle, stock, and water, and bring to a boil. Lower the heat, add the corncob, if using, and simmer for 30 minutes.

Strain the soup through a fine-mesh fresh strainer into a bowl, wipe out the pot, and pour the liquid back into the pot. Discard the vegetables and herbs. Add the chocolate to taste, and stir over low to medium-low heat until it's melted. Add the corn kernels or the hominy or posole and the roasted chile and cook for about 5 minutes, or until hot. Season to taste with salt and pepper.

Just before serving, cut the avocado into large chunks. Place some avocado in the center of each soup bowl. Squeeze the lime juice over the top and sprinkle lightly with sea salt. Ladle the soup around the avocado. Top with the cilantro and tortilla chips.

SERVES 4

THREE-BEAN CHILI

This great vegetarian chili is easy enough to be made on a busy weeknight. Stir in the cocoa powder when you add the other herbs, and you'll notice the chili take on a richer color and aroma.

Bring a medium saucepan half full of water to a boil. Fill a large bowl with ice water. Add the carrots to the boiling water and blanch for about 2 minutes, or until tender. Drain the carrots in a strainer and plunge the strainer into the ice water. Remove from the water, drain, and dry on a kitchen towel. Set aside.

In a large stockpot, heat the oil over medium heat. Add the garlic and cook for about 1 minute, or until light golden. Add the cocoa powder, chili powder, basil, oregano, cumin, and pepper. Stir in the tomatoes and their liquid, water, mustard, and tomato paste. Add the beans and bring to a boil. Lower the heat, cover, and simmer for 10 minutes.

Stir in the carrots, corn, and zucchini. Cover and simmer for an additional 10 minutes. Season to taste with salt and pepper.

To serve, ladle into bowls and set out a selection of toppings.

SERVES 6

INGREDIENTS

1 cup diced (¼-inch) carrots

1 tablespoon extra virgin olive oil or canola oil

3 cloves garlic, minced

2 tablespoons unsweetened cocoa powder

1 tablespoon chili powder

1 teaspoon dried basil, crushed

1 teaspoon dried oregano, crushed

½ teaspoon ground cumin

½ teaspoon freshly ground black pepper, or to taste

One 28-ounce can tomatoes, chopped, with their liquid

1 cup water

1 tablespoon Dijon mustard

One 6-ounce can tomato paste

One 15-ounce can red kidney beans, drained and rinsed

One 15-ounce can Great Northern or cannellini beans, drained and rinsed

One 15-ounce can garbanzo beans (chickpeas), drained and rinsed

1 cup corn kernels, preferably fresh

1 cup diced (¼-inch) zucchini

Salt

OPTIONAL TOPPINGS

Hot sauce

Grated Parmesan cheese

Green chiles, coarsely chopped

Scallions, thinly sliced white and light green portions

Sour cream

John's Cocoa Rub

I LIKE A SIMPLE ROASTED CHICKEN that's been coated with a spice rub just before cooking. One rainy afternoon, I had just lugged in a big box of unsweetened cocoa and I thought I'd mix a bit of it with salt to see how that would taste on a roasted bird. The results were really great, even better than I'd hoped for. The flavor of the chicken was fantastic—more complex than you'd expect from an easy rub that combines just unsweetened cocoa and salt. The heat and the juices from the bird bring out all kinds of savory flavors in the cocoa and give the poultry a nice flavorful crust.

Best of all, this is really easy. Mix two parts of unsweetened cocoa powder (natural, not Dutch-processed cocoa) with one part salt. Rub the mixture liberally over every part of the bird, and roast it either in the oven or over a grill. I have used this on lamb, pork, and vegetables as well as every sort of poultry, with great results.

CHILE-MARINATED FLANK STEAK

CONTRIBUTED BY ARNON OREN

An authentic Mexican mole calls for more than two dozen spices, added in a particular order. This marinade, based on the flavors of those spices, adds a wonderful savoriness and spiciness to beef. The thin slices of flank steak are wonderful on their own, with a basket full of warm tortillas, or served on top of a green salad.

Start this recipe the night before you intend to serve to allow it to marinate overnight. To retain the steak's juiciness, be sure to let the meat rest before slicing, and remove the steak from the heat while it is still a bit rare, as it will continue to cook as it rests.

INGREDIENTS

2 garlic cloves, coarsely chopped

1 cup extra virgin olive oil

½ cup cilantro leaves, rinsed and patted dry

½ cup ancho chile paste (see Note)

½ cup unsweetened cocoa powder

Juice of 2 limes

Salt and freshly ground black pepper

One 2-pound flank steak

Lime wedges for serving

With a mortar and pestle, or the back of a chef's knife, pound or mash the garlic to a paste.

Pour the olive oil into a blender, add the cilantro, and blend on high speed to puree. Add the garlic, ancho paste, cocoa powder, and lime juice and blend to combine. The marinade will be thick. Season to taste with salt and pepper.

Trim any fat from the flank steak and pat dry with paper towels. Place in a baking dish and season lightly on both sides with salt and pepper. Cover one side of the meat with half of the marinade. Flip over and cover the other side with the remaining marinade. Cover with plastic wrap and refrigerate for 24 hours.

Thirty minutes before grilling, remove the steak from the refrigerator. Wipe off the excess marinade.

Prepare a fire in a charcoal grill or preheat a gas grill to medium-high.

Sear the meat on both sides, turning once, over medium-high heat. Then move the meat to indirect heat to avoid burning the marinade, and grill, turning once until rare to medium-rare. Transfer to a platter and let rest for 15 minutes.

Thinly slice the meat against the grain. Serve with lime wedges.

SERVES 4 AS A MAIN COURSE OR 6 TO 8 AS PART OF A SALAD

Note: Ancho chile paste is available in Mexican markets and specialty food stores, or you can make your own. Pour hot water over dried ancho chiles to cover, and let soak for 20 minutes, or until the chiles are softened. Drain and puree in a food processor to make a paste. Eight ounces of dried anchos will make about 2 cups of paste.

BAKED BEANS

Although they're not actually baked, these beans have the rich, savory flavor of traditional baked beans. The unsweetened chocolate adds a subtle note. If you didn't know there was chocolate in the recipe, you might not be able to identify it—but you would notice a richer flavor. If you have a favorite recipe for baked beans, try adding chocolate during the last minutes of cooking.

Be sure to begin soaking the beans the night before you plan to cook them.

Place the beans in a large bowl, cover with cold water, and let soak overnight.

In a large stockpot, sauté the bacon over medium heat until browned. Add the onions and cook for about 5 minutes, until softened and lightly browned. Add the molasses, brown sugar, ketchup, mustard, and water and bring to a boil.

Drain the beans, add to the stockpot, and bring back to a boil. Reduce the heat to a simmer and cook for 4½ to 5 hours, or until the beans are tender.

Remove the beans from the heat, stir in the chocolate, and season to taste with salt and pepper.

MAKES 6 CUPS

INGREDIENTS

1 pound dried navy beans, rinsed and picked over

8 ounces bacon, cut into ¼-inch dice

1 cup finely diced yellow onions

¼ cup plus 3 tablespoons unsulphured molasses

¼ cup plus 3 tablespoons firmly packed brown sugar

1⅔ cups ketchup

1 tablespoon plus 2 teaspoons yellow mustard

13 cups water

1 ounce 99% unsweetened chocolate, coarsely chopped

Salt and freshly ground black pepper

CHAPTER

7

CACAO

Seeing your first cacao tree is an experience. Even if you've looked at dozens of photographs and you *know* that the pods grow right from the trunk as well as on the branches, it's an odd sight. Because the tree's trunk and branches are relatively slender and the pods are big, the whole picture seems so unlikely. Pods may grow on the trunk as low as a foot or two above the ground. Standing in front of the tree, you only have to reach your hand forward to touch a pod—you don't even have to lift your arm.

Called *cauliflory,* cacao's trait of growing fruit right on the trunk is very rare, and part of the tree's unique survival strategy. A cacao tree has no mechanism for releasing its pods. Even a pod that is past ripe stays attached to the tree until an animal gnaws through the stem or a human with a machete brings it down. In order to distribute its seeds, the tree needs to attract animals so they take a closer look, and it does this very well.

Cacao pods advertise their presence through their size, bright colors, and something more—a quality that makes you want to reach out and take hold of one. From the bumpy, deeply ridged yellow-green pods of amelonado cacao to the sunny yellow, smooth-skinned oval pods of calabacillo cacao to the cream-colored pods tinged with pink that grow on rare criollo trees, every pod, no matter its shape or size, seems ready to drop into your hands. You want to grab it—and the tree needs you, or a monkey or a rodent, to do just that.

An Understory Tree

Standing in front of a cacao tree, you get a sense of how the earliest Americans must have reacted to this fruit. Cacao is an understory tree, which means that in a high-limbed rain forest, it's short—under forty feet high generally, with most cacao trees closer to twenty feet. It's a sure bet that early Americans who wandered through these forests thousands of years ago would have noticed these pods. After watching a parrot or a monkey gnaw through the pod to get to the sweet pulp inside, they would have investigated a potential source of food. They would have pulled out a pulp-covered seed and examined it. Sweet with the flavors of melon and citrus, the pulp alone would have given people reason enough to seek out the tree.

Like the sight of pods on the trunk, the first look inside the pod can be surprising. You can't see the seeds, because each one is encased in its own little capsule of pulp. This isn't a delicate membrane like the translucent pulp around a pomegranate seed—it is serious pulp, thick and milk-colored. The scientific word for the consistency of the pulp is *mucilaginous,* and even if you don't know the word, you get the idea.

Appearances aside, the pulp tastes incredibly cool and sweet. The flavors of pulp vary from farm to farm, so you can taste white nectarine in some, grapefruit in others, and melon, bananas, or oranges in others. If you bite into a seed, though, the sensations in your mouth are completely different—an astringent flavor fills your mouth.

The Bitter Seeds

Cacao seeds are packed with polyphenols, or tannins, which make them so bitter animals spit them out at first bite. This is another part of the tree's seed distribution plan. The same polyphenols that keep the seeds from being chewed and eaten also protect the tree from various viruses, bacteria, and fungi. The polyphenols give the seeds the ability to withstand many of the hazards in the rainy, tepid places where cacao grows.

A Vulnerable Crop

To grow cacao requires dedication and a willingness to take risks. Cacao trees grow exclusively between twenty degrees north and twenty degrees south of the equator, and they won't survive a dry period of more than a few months. Strong winds and hurricanes are a constant threat, and even under the best of circumstances, pests and disease reduce cacao's yield by an average of thirty percent annually.

A young cacao tree has to be five or six years old before it will bear fruit. Twice a year, mature trees burst forth with small blooms, cream-colored flowers that look like miniature orchids with spiky, waxy petals around a maroon center. Thousands of these flowers may cover the mossy patches on the tree's trunk and limbs in the fall and spring, but fewer than five percent will become pods. Flowering continues sporadically throughout the year, and it's common to see flowers and pods on the same branch.

Each tree bears about twenty-four to thirty viable pods a year—a dozen or so pods at each of the twice yearly harvests, with only a few pods appearing between harvests. Each pod holds about forty seeds, so each tree produces approximately a thousand beans per year. It takes five hundred beans to produce one pound of bittersweet chocolate, which means that during a good year, without any hurricanes, pest infestation, disease, or other natural disasters, one tree provides seeds for only two pounds of chocolate. By comparison, a mature apple tree produces about 840 pounds of edible fruit each year.

The low yield tempts farmers to plant trees more densely. Cacao trees can be planted as little as about three yards apart, but dense planting exhausts the soil and makes the spread of disease from one tree to another more likely.

Cultivating Cacao

Before cultivation, cacao grew wild in the low-lying rain forests of Central and South America. Evidence of cultivation goes back at least to 600 B.C., and successive cultures in Central America have used cacao over centuries for ceremonies, as a type of currency, and as food.

When Spain, France, and England began colonizing these regions, the colonists attempted to grow cacao on large plantations. These attempts failed almost universally because of disease, rapid exhaustion of the soil, political upheaval, and lack of skilled labor. Even today, eighty percent of all cacao is grown on

small, often family-run farms of between eight and fifteen acres. The remaining twenty percent grows on plantations, and most of these are smaller than a hundred acres.

Harvesting the pods demands laborers with some skill. Pods must be removed from the tree one at a time by cutting the thick, woody stem with a machete or another sharp tool. Some farmers then strike open the pods and scoop the pulp-coated seeds into a sack, leaving the empty pods beneath the trees. Carrying the pulpy seeds—called *babas*—instead of the heavier pods makes sense when you have to trek down a steep hillside covered with slippery leaves while lugging a heavy bag of fruit. Other farmers bring in the whole pods and allow the seeds to ferment inside the shell for several days before cutting the pods open.

LEGENDS & LORE

Cacao at the Beginning of the World

Just as Christianity has a creation story that revolves around an apple tree, the Mayan culture had a creation story involving the cacao tree. In a lecture given at the University of Pennsylvania, Michael Grofe ties a story in the *Popol Vuh* to cacao's importance to the Mayans. The *Popul Vuh* is the sacred book of the Quiché people, detailing their traditions, religious beliefs, and history. The book was written much earlier but transcribed by a Quiché Mayan shortly after the arrival of the Spanish in the New World. In the *Popul Vuh*, One Hunahpu and Seven Hunahpu are ball-playing twins killed by the lords of death in the underworld, Xibalba. One Hunahpu returns, his head appearing in the trunk of a tree that looks in ancient renderings like cacao. The citizens of Xibalba are ordered to stay away from this tree, but they can't resist it. After an immaculate conception involving One Hunahpu (in the cacao tree) and Xquic (her name can be translated alternately as Lady Blood and Blood Moon), the sun, the moon, and the earth all take their place in the cosmos.

If the pulp-coated seeds are to be fermented, they are poured into bins, dumped into pits in the ground, or shaped into piles and covered with banana leaves. As the yeasts and bacteria naturally present in the environment convert the sugar in the pulp to alcohol and subsequently to lactic and acetic acid, the fermentation process kills the seeds, breaking down their internal structures and allowing compounds that had been separated to combine. The merging of these compounds gives chocolate its flavor. Unfermented cacao beans are highly astringent and have little or none of the flavors we associate with chocolate.

A Closer Look at Fermentation

Many cacao farmers don't ferment because they don't know how. It isn't a matter of simply forming a pile of beans and waiting. You must also know how long a particular type of bean should be left to ferment and how often to turn the beans, and then be able to tell when fermentation is complete.

An understanding of the basic steps helps clarify the process. First, there must be an adequate amount of seeds and pulp to form a critical mass. Strictly speaking, it isn't the seeds that ferment, but rather the pulp around them. If there aren't enough seeds and pulp to generate the conditions necessary for fermentation—the right temperature, the right amount of oxygen, the right acidity—the pulp won't ferment.

In the simplest terms, fermentation begins when wild yeasts and bacteria eat the sugar in the pulp and excrete alcohol. This conversion of sugar to alcohol raises the temperature in the pile of beans and changes the pH balance. These changes kill the seeds and break down the cell walls inside each seed. Molecules that had been separated from each other by the seed's cell walls mingle and form new compounds—compounds with a far greater complexity of flavors.

You can tell by cutting a bean open whether or not it's been fermented. As shown on page 327, well-fermented beans have a dry-looking, fissured surface that crumbles easily, while unfermented beans look hard and have a subtle sheen—a glossy surface that we describe as slatey. We use a tool called a guillotine that slices through random samplings of beans from one harvest to give us a rough idea of how much of that harvest is fermented. If a batch of beans contains more than fifteen percent unfermented beans, that will negatively affect the flavor of chocolate made from those beans.

Fermentation of cacao differs from that of wine, beer, or cheese in that the yeasts and bacteria required aren't introduced. They are wild yeasts present in the environment and bacteria that appear naturally in a heap of pulpy cacao seeds—rather than yeasts that are deliberately isolated and brought in by humans—and they represent a range of types. However, recent experiments with inoculums may change how cacao beans are fermented in the future.

Astringency is the drying sensation caused in the mouth by chewing grape skins or tasting an underripe persimmon. Fermentation transforms the beans, reducing the polyphenols responsible for astringency. Given this fact, you might assume that all cacao is fermented. In fact, a far greater percentage of cacao is either unfermented or poorly fermented. If properly fermented cacao tastes so much better, why does so much of the world's cacao go to market unfermented?

Fermentation requires effort and time, which to a farmer means increased costs. In the past century, the world's biggest producers of chocolate have valued consistency and quantity over how well their beans were fermented. This can be explained in part by the fact that mass-produced chocolate often contains less than fifty percent cacao, with sugar and milk making up the balance. If you make a product that contains as much sugar as it does cacao, astringency isn't a big concern. And, if a buyer is willing to accept unfermented beans, farmers see no point in spending the extra time and money to ferment—especially the farmers who own the small family-run farms that produce the majority of cacao. These farmers need the money that comes in when they sell their cacao; they often can't afford to wait another week.

The other impediment to adequate fermentation is lack of knowledge. Many farmers, even those who have grown cacao for years, have never fermented their beans. Because fermentation requires actually tending the mass of beans—not just letting the pile sit, but monitoring aeration and temperature—there are some specific skills involved. Ideally, people who know how to ferment cacao in a specific area will help

nearby farmers who are unfamiliar with fermentation. When fermentation is done well, generally it's by communities who have passed down their methods and knowledge of fermentation. Where there is no local tradition of fermenting, or if abrupt changes occur in the variety of cacao grown, problems arise. In Ecuador, for example, thirty years ago a government-sponsored program introduced a more productive, more disease-resistant strain of cacao—a strain, unfortunately, with less flavor than the cacao previously grown there. So a region that once had a reputation for producing well-fermented beans with complex flavors now produces cacao that is poorly fermented and has little flavor.

Because harvesting cacao is labor-intensive, and because the beans account for such a large proportion of a small farm's income, farmers are reluctant to experiment with fermentation.

In order to procure well-fermented beans, bean buyers (and we include chocolate manufacturers in this group) have to communicate with the people who grow the beans, explain what a well-fermented bean looks like, and compensate the farmers fairly for the time and effort involved in fermenting. Only then does it make economic sense for the farmer to go to the trouble.

The First Taste of Cacao

Archaeologists don't agree on what first led humans to cultivate cacao. Clearly, the first taste of cacao would have been the pulp, which early Amazonians may have sucked from the seeds as long as ten thousand years ago. But once people began looking at the beans as food, did they roast and grind the beans and make a drink similar to our modern-day hot chocolate from them? Or were the seeds secondary to the process of turning the pulpy mass into the fermented drink called *cacao chicha*—a sort of chocolate beer? How people first prepared cacao beans is really part of a larger discussion on the origins of cacao. Anthropologists—and even chocolate makers who founded a company together—can disagree on cacao's history.

JOHN

In his wonderful book *The Chocolate Tree,* Allen Young says that although the genus *Theobroma* has been around for millions of years, *Theobroma cacao* is much newer, on the scene for only ten to fifteen thousand years. His thought is that ancient people in Amazonia may have selectively crossed two species, *Theobroma pentagona* and *Theobroma leiocarpa,* to produce cacao, cultivating it not for the seeds but for the pulp. In the humid climates of South America, drying the beans might have been problematic, and they would have tended to mold easily. When cacao was cultivated later, in Mesoamerica and Mexico, which had a dryer climate, drying the beans for chocolate would have been easier.

I believe, along with Sophie and Michael Coe, the authors of *The True History of Chocolate,* that early Mesoamericans would have treated cacao beans as they treated corn. We know that the Aztecs had more than two thousand recipes for corn. The people who preceded the Aztecs—the Mayans and, before them, the Olmec—spent much of their daylight hours searching for and preparing food, and corn was a big part of their diet. It makes sense that they would also experiment with cacao beans as a source of food, and it seems logical that they would have treated cacao beans as they did corn kernels—toasting the beans on a parching stone until dry, shelling them, and then grinding them on a metate. Corn made up the largest percentage of their diet, and they spent a lot of time preparing corn. Fermentation of the beans might have come about naturally when baskets came along (baskets meant storage capabilities), allowing piles of pulp-coated beans to rest undisturbed long enough for fermentation to occur.

The Coes make a good argument that because the inhabitants of South America used cacao's pulp only to make a fermented drink and occasionally nibbled the beans, most likely cacao did not originate in South America, but rather in Mesoamerica.

ROBERT

The Coe and Coe argument does sound convincing. But Professor Rosemary Joyce, professor of archaeology at the University of California, Berkeley, and her colleague John S. Henderson, professor of anthropology at Cornell, believe that a kind of chocolate beer called *cacao chicha* was the true motive for natives of South America to cultivate cacao. Those who believe that chocolate making originated in Mesomerica have to explain how the beans came to be fermented. The standard theory is it happened by accident—beans that had fermented were thrown onto a fire accidentally, and the rich smell of chocolate alerted early Mesoamericans that the seeds might be good to eat. The argument of Rosemary Joyce and John Henderson doesn't have to make that leap of imagination, because the cacao beans would be fermented just by virtue of sitting in the pulp while it became beer.

The point that the many recipes for corn must indicate similar preparations for cacao is a good one—*if* the corn recipes existed when cacao was first being fermented. Joyce points to evidence that corn was not all that important until 300 to 500 B.C. in those areas where scientists have tested for it. She says, "The bone chemistry work that assesses how much corn was eaten by these early people pretty consistently shows that corn was not the central seed it would become later. It was the primary seed for the Aztecs and the Classic Mayans, but it wasn't for the Formative Mesoamericans. At this writing no actual experimental results support corn as the main food source."

The major support for the Joyce-Henderson model is the shape of the vessels found in archaeological digs. "The vessel forms in which we have early [cacao] residue," they write, "are narrow-necked bottles, appropriate for alcoholic beverages but not for frothing cacao."

Once you accept the idea that ancient people were experimenting with cuisine—specifically, with alcohol—it makes sense to think they would have used anything tasty, including cacao pulp, to vary their beers. It doesn't seem as if it was an accident, and they were undoubtedly—according to residue tests on those narrow-necked vessels—putting the pulp into containers to ferment, and not into piles.

LEGENDS & LORE

The First Hot Chocolate

The first chocolate "drinks" were really more like a soupy oatmeal, a kind of corn gruel to which ground cacao was added for flavor. As the stimulating properties of cacao became more appreciated, the cacao proportion of the gruel grew larger. This was the start of the day for many people, the meal they'd consume before heading out to hunt for food.

Those early concoctions weren't warm. The drink was made with cold water, mixed by pouring it back and forth between two cups, often from a height of several feet. Over years, the cacao "processing" was refined. Heating the water allowed the oil in the cacao to emulsify, for a smoother drink. The ingredients added to the mixture ranged from achiote and flower petals to spices and honey to a wide variety of chile peppers, varying from region to region and with the seasons.

The Three Types of Cacao

The names of the three main types of cacao—criollo, forastero, and trinitario—no longer correspond to pure genetic strains. Purity disappeared many hundreds of years ago as a result of the cacao tree's penchant for spontaneous cross-pollination. And deliberate hybridization has occurred on numerous occasions in the four hundred-plus years of cacao's history as a cash crop. Thus the relationship between variety and flavor is so variable as to be almost useless. This is especially true of criollo.

CRIOLLO

When Cortés invaded Mexico, criollo was the predominant cacao in Central America and the northern regions of South America. Because of its low productivity and its susceptibility to disease, both of which motivated farmers to replace criollo with more productive varieties, criollo now constitutes only about 0.1 percent of the world's crop. And, when someone does present you with criollo, there's no telling whether it will have the mild fruitiness that makes criollo so prized. The only way to know for sure is to taste.

FORASTERO

Forastero, by far the most common of the three varieties, is believed to be indigenous to the northern Amazon River Basin, in what is now Brazil. As a result of its resistance to disease and its high productivity, forastero represents almost ninety percent of the world crop. A "pure" forastero would tend to have earthy,

relatively simple flavors with moderate acidity. It is often referred to as "bulk" cacao, meaning forastero beans form a solid base with a reliable but not overly complex range of flavors. Depending on the timeliness with which it is harvested and the degree of care taken in fermenting and drying the beans, forastero can either add extremely desirable elements to a blend or add little more than color.

TRINITARIO

A spontaneous hybrid of criollo and forastero, trinitario may be the most difficult to define in terms of flavor, a result of the fact that the ratios of criollo and forastero within any given trinitario pod can vary widely. Flavor notes range from spicy to earthy to fruity to highly acidic. Even trinitario beans that resemble criollo, suggesting a high percentage of criollo genes, often exhibit little of its characteristic taste profile.

Although several countries maintain living gene banks of cacao strains, no one consistent attempt has been made to create certifiable bean types on a commercial basis. Thus, when a label states that the cacao variety of a particular bar of chocolate is criollo or trinitario, it is difficult, if not impossible, to calculate the significance of that claim. Manufacturers rarely boast about using forastero cacao, but most of the chocolate consumers eat comes from that bean. And that isn't necessarily bad. The ultimate danger in the careless use of labels, aside from the confusion it creates, is that genetic diversity may disappear before anyone realizes that its existence is at risk. When diversity departs, flavor goes with it.

JOHN

It's easy to get caught up in cacao's types and origins and lump the three types of beans into a sort of flavor pyramid: criollo at the top of the pyramid, because it's rare and it offers the mildest, fruitiest flavors; forastero the bottom, because it accounts for ninety percent of all cacao grown and because it's the sturdy workhorse of all beans, with a flavor that's earthy but rarely exciting; and trinitario in the middle, a melding of the two. This idea has a historical basis, but cacao has undergone such changes in the past few centuries that it doesn't always make sense to choose beans—or dismiss them—based on type.

A Closer Look at Cacao Genetics

To get an idea of how cacao confuses people, cut open a trinitario pod, choose ten seeds at random, and slice them in half. Chances are the seeds will be a variety of colors, ranging from dark purple to pale pink. This range reflects centuries of crossbreeding between cacao strains. Imagine being the biologist whose job it is to track down all the varieties of cacao that produced this pod's multicolored beans.

CACAO'S TRAVELS

Cacao's movement in the past half millennium has contributed to the confusion. When Spain and other European countries took an interest in cacao, people began transporting plants around the world to different colonies. A seedling from Mesoamerica might have traveled to the Caribbean and fostered a seedling there that went on to Asia, where that strain of cacao crossed with another variety that had made similar hops around the equator. The fact that few records exist about where the various cacao strains were gathered and where they landed results in a big headache for scientists who are trying to untangle cacao's breeding lines.

Records are lacking, too, on breeding selection among cacao farmers. Until recently, work within cacao breeding took place separately within the various countries that grow it, and new derivations or hybrids were given different names across borders.

CACAO'S PROMISCUITY

Cacao's promiscuity adds to the problem. If you think of a cacao tree as a pregnant alley cat, you could imagine searching for its lineage as comparable to trying to figure out that cat's kittens' other parent and grandparents. And cacao's genealogy is more complicated than that of an alley cat, because the genes that determine specific traits are not necessarily what they appear to be. In other words, a pod might look like criollo and the seeds inside might taste like criollo, yet a DNA test could reveal the pod is more forastero than criollo. Unless you pollinate by hand and cover the blossoms with netting, it's difficult to be sure of a pod's parents.

This means that breeding programs—efforts to create, for example, cacao hybrids that resist disease and yield bigger harvests—are hit-and-miss. If you're fuzzy on the genetic lineage of the parental stock, crossbreeding results will have some surprises—and you may be surprised even when you think you know a cacao pod's lineage. Because a young cacao tree won't produce fruit for five or six years, a decade can go by before scientists see the results of crossbreeding.

DNA testing has made the biologist's job a little easier. Still, it's clear that you can't determine a bean's flavor by its origin or the shape or color of its pod. You have to taste the beans.

CACAO'S MANY MERGINGS

The first records of criollo and forastero merging came from Trinidad. In 1727, a blight swept across the country, jumping from plantation to plantation and wiping out the criollo pods. When the trees still did not produce pods after a few years, new stocks of forastero trees were imported. The forastero and the old criollo trees resulted in a hybrid that plantation owners found hardier than the delicate criollo and better tasting than the sturdy forastero. They named this new hybrid trinitario.

If this hybridization had occurred in just one isolated area, we'd have a clearer sense of cacao's origins, but hybridization began taking place everywhere. Over centuries, cacao was bred across all kinds of geographic and varietal boundaries, and from this movement and cacao's promiscuity came a whole new complex of varieties—in other words, numerous subspecies of trinitario as well as criollo and forastero.

All of this means we have to taste the beans we buy. We don't dismiss any beans based on their origins, and we've been pleasantly surprised more than once by beans with a modest pedigree. It also means we have to keep actively searching for sources of cacao that both of us really like.

ROBERT

We are constantly looking for new sources of cacao because of the many things that can go wrong. Cacao is vulnerable to all kinds of natural catastrophes. In 2004, for example, cacao trees throughout the Caribbean produced few pods because an autumn hurricane stripped the flowers from the trees. Regions that normally brought in hundreds of tons of cacao brought in fewer than twenty tons that year. Farms in the Dominican Republic were especially hard hit by the winds, and several of those farms supply us with cacao. But if we have a variety of cacao sources in different regions, we can continue making chocolate even when one or two of those regions produce less cacao than usual.

THE THREAT OF DISEASE

Diseases that strike cacao trees are an even bigger concern than the threat of hurricanes. Monilia pod rot has hit many farms in Ecuador, Colombia, and Costa Rica, and because small farms often lack the resources to replant, farms hit by the disease may simply be abandoned. Black pod rot, another fungal disease, attacks pods when they're still months from being mature. Witches'-broom, caused by a fungus called *Crinipellis perniciosus,* devastated the Bahía region of Brazil in 1989, causing all new growth on the cacao trees to shrivel and blacken and preventing pods from forming. It wiped out one of the most vital cacao growing regions in the world, and because of that one disease, Brazil, which had exported more than $100 million worth of cacao to the United States every year for decades, now imports cacao for its own use.

Bahía was vulnerable to witches'-broom because of its *monoculture* of cacao, which just means that humans planted the same stock of cacao over wide areas of land. Cacao was first planted in Bahía in the 1700s, but in the early 1900s, because of rising cacao prices, Bahían farmers planted huge new areas with cacao, always the same stock of cacao, which soon flourished across the region. Because there was so little genetic variance, the trees were more vulnerable to disease. When witches'-broom hit, it swept rapidly from farm to farm.

Everybody who works with chocolate worries about the diseases that threaten cacao. Gene banks now exist in many countries, dedicated to protecting and conserving rare strains of cacao while providing a place for scientists and agronomists to study it. New technologies offer hope of protecting cacao's future and preventing further genetic erosion. Biologists such as Allen Herre (page 337) are finding ways to protect plants

against diseases, and with DNA analysis and genome mapping, scientists may discover specific traits in various cacao strains that can help ward off diseases.

. . . .

Organic Because of Economics

Most cacao—as much as eighty percent worldwide—comes from small farms. Because small-scale farmers don't have the resources to buy chemicals such as fertilizers, fungicides, or pesticides, their cacao is organic by economic necessity. Even though much of the cacao we buy from small farms isn't certified organic, it is organic. But because we blend beans, some of which come from regions where organic certification isn't a priority, we can't place an organic label on our bars even when they're made primarily from organic beans.

. . . .

The Forest Garden

When you first visit a typical chocolate farm, you can't help but be struck by the house that opens up to the forest around it. Usually cacao farmers plant fruit trees—banana, citrus, zapote, papaya, macadamia

nut, and mango—to provide shade for the sun-sensitive cacao trees. (Cacao thrives with an understory and overstory of other trees.) It takes a while to realize that in addition to growing cacao for sale, the farmers are raising their own forest garden. As you walk between the trees, usually you're accompanied by a friendly chicken or two. Casaba, yams, breadfruit, and sometimes even vanilla can all be found just a few feet from the kitchen door. These farmers have created a self-sustaining system that produces great cacao while at the same time surrounding themselves with an enviable array of fruits.

Cacao's Need For the Biting Midge

In his book *The Chocolate Tree,* Allen Young explains that the biting midge is cacao's primary pollinator. A tiny fly—it's about the size of a dust speck—from the dipteran family Ceratopogonidae, a biting midge can leave an irritating welt on your skin. Midges are one reason cacao farms aren't on the typical tourist itinerary.

These midges need a specific environment to reproduce. The thick mulch beneath cacao plantings provides this environment. Even during hot seasons, when the top layer of leaves is so dry it crackles as you step on it, there is still a moist layer beneath where the midges can thrive.

Biting midges are susceptible to chemicals, but most growers have found that the use of fungicides and pesticides is counterproductive, because fewer midges means less "fruit set" or fewer pods on each cacao tree. (For more about the dangers of fungicides, see page 337.)

The Meaning of the Percent Sign

The percentage listed on a bar of chocolate indicates what fraction of the bar, by weight, comes from the cacao bean. Most of that amount is ground cacao beans, but in many cases it also includes a little added cocoa butter. A one-ounce chocolate bar marked 75% contains three-quarters of an ounce of cacao, or unsweetened chocolate. The higher the percentage, the more chocolate—as opposed to other ingredients—you get in each bite.

Sugar is by far the largest proportion of the remaining ingredients, which means the percentage can also tell you how sweet the chocolate is likely to be. Although vanilla and soy lecithin are often present in chocolate, together they will add up to less than one percent of the total. This means that in that same one-ounce 75% bar, sugar accounts for almost twenty-five percent. You can calculate the approximate percentage of sugar in a chocolate bar by subtracting the cacao percentage from 100.

The terms *cacao solids* and *cocoa butter* can often be a source of confusion when discussing cacao percentage. A cacao bean is made up of about fifty-four percent pure fat, in the form of cacao butter, which has no taste, and forty-six percent cacao solids, which give the chocolate its flavor as well as its color. The percentage on the chocolate tells you the amount of cacao—both cocoa butter and cacao solids—is present in the bar. To figure out the percentage of cocoa solids, just calculate forty-six percent of the cacao percentage.

Why We Also Make Single-Origin Chocolates

A single-origin chocolate is made from beans grown by one source. We began chocolate making with the idea that a blend of beans gives you a fuller, more intense experience. Chocolate has a wide range of flavor notes, and you get to hit more of those notes in one bite of chocolate if you use a variety of beans that have different characters. So, for example, if you pick one bean from Ghana that has an exceptional low note, add a different bean from Venezuela with a great fruity quality, and throw in some beans from Madagascar that give the chocolate a long, lingering finish, the final result lets you taste all of these flavors.

If we agree that blended chocolate tastes better than single-origin chocolate, why do we make our limited-edition bars? Our limited-edition chocolate has come about when we've stumbled across some absolutely phenomenal beans, a single variety with the complexity and flavor to justify a bar made from just one type of bean.

Our first chance to make a single-origin bar came about when a small sack of rare porcelana beans arrived with our regular shipment from Venezuela. We checked with the growers, who had packed those beans into the wrong shipment. When we got news that we could keep the beans, we tasted them, decided they were too good to blend with anything else, and created a bar around those beans. To our surprise, the Porcelana bar made a splash. We made very little of this chocolate, but it sold out much faster than we expected.

Our second limited edition bar, called Cuyagua, was made from beans grown in a secluded valley near Venezuela's central Carribbean coast along with single-plantation trinitario beans from La Concepción. The central coast beans had nutty, dairy notes while the La Concepción beans had intense dark fruit notes.

Our third limited edition bar, El Carmen, was made using select trinitario beans from an old Venezuelan plantation. This smooth yet potent chocolate has the pronounced lingering flavor of dried cherries and raisins—a flavor that made Caracas beans famous all over the world during colonial times.

Right now we're working on a bar called Kumasi Sambirano. This blends exceptional beans from Ghana with rich, impressively fermented beans from Madagascar. For years, we'd hoped to spotlight some of the particularly fine beans that come from Africa, and with this bar we finally can.

CHAPTER 8

Basics and Add-ons

CITRUS SUGAR

This colorful sugar adds bright flavor to our Cacao Nib Waffles (page 231) or other desserts. We prefer orange zest for the waffles, but try lime or lemon zest as well. Use a Microplane grater to get fine, even zest.

Spread the zest on a plate and place in the microwave on high for 30 seconds to 1 minute, or until it is dry to the touch. Let cool.

Combine the zest and sugar in a coffee grinder, spice grinder, or a mini chopper and pulse until the sugar takes on the color of the zest.

Store in an airtight container for up to 2 weeks.

MAKES ABOUT ¼ CUP

INGREDIENTS

2 tablespoons finely grated citrus zest

¼ cup granulated sugar

MARSHMALLOWS

CONTRIBUTED BY STEPHEN DURFEE

Marshmallows are one of those foods that we're so used to buying we don't think about making them. But once you've tasted the homemade version, store-bought marshmallows seem about as appealing as a store-bought chocolate cake. Stephen's recipe for marshmallows is both straightforward and fun, and his marshmallows are the heart of our favorite Fudge (page 98) and S'mores (page 188), as well as a terrific dipper for Chocolate Orange Fondue (page 61).

Sift together the confectioners' sugar and cornstarch into a small bowl.

Spray the sides of an 8 by 8 by 2-inch baking pan with nonstick spray. Sprinkle about ⅓ cup of the cornstarch mixture over the bottom of the pan, and set aside.

In the bowl of a stand mixer, combine ¼ cup of the cold water and the gelatin, and stir gently with a small rubber spatula or wooden spoon. Set aside.

In a medium heavy-bottomed pot, stir together the sugar, corn syrup, the remaining ½ cup water, and the salt. Clip a candy thermometer to the side of the pot. Bring to a boil over medium to medium-high heat, brushing the sides of the pot as necessary with a pastry brush dipped in water. Continue to cook until the temperature reaches 236°F.

Meanwhile, fill a medium bowl with ice water. Remove the pan from the heat and dip the bottom in ice water for 5 seconds to lower the syrup temperature to 210°F.

When the syrup has reached 210°F, pour it into the gelatin and stir to combine. Place the bowl on the mixer fitted with the whisk attachment, and whisk at medium-high to high speed for 5 to 7 minutes, or until thick and fluffy. Add the vanilla and whip for another 30 seconds.

Spray a rubber spatula with nonstick cooking spray. Scrape the mixture into the prepared pan, being sure to spread it into the corners. Cover with about half of the remaining cornstarch mixture, and allow the marshmallows to sit until firm, about 2 hours.

CUTTING THE MARSHMALLOWS:

Once the marshmallow is firm, invert the pan, removing the marshmallow in one large piece from the pan. Brush off the cornstarch mixture. For S'more marshmallows, see page 188. For standard marshmallows and fondue marshmallows, using scissors or a paring knife, cut into 1-inch squares.

Roll the marshmallows in the remaining cornstarch mixture.

The marshmallows are best served the day they are made, but they keep well in an airtight container for up to 3 days.

MAKES 32 TO 64 MARSHMALLOWS

INGREDIENTS

¾ cup confectioners' sugar

¾ cup cornstarch

Nonstick cooking spray

¾ cup cold water

Two ¼-ounce envelopes gelatin (1 tablespoon plus 2 teaspoons)

1½ cups granulated sugar

½ cup light corn syrup

¼ teaspoon salt

1 tablespoon pure vanilla extract

HONEYCOMB

CONTRIBUTED BY NICOLE PLUE

The tiny air holes that run through these crunchy candies take in chocolate when these are used as a dip for Chocolate Orange Fondue (page 61). We also like to pack them in tins as part of a selection of homemade cookies and candies.

Be sure to use a large pot. The amount of caramel in the pot will seem small at first, but adding the baking soda causes the mixture to froth and bubble considerably.

INGREDIENTS

1¾ cups granulated sugar

2 tablespoons plus 1 teaspoon honey

¼ cup plus 2 tablespoons glucose (see Note)

¼ cup water

1 tablespoon baking soda

Line a 17 by 12 by 1-inch baking sheet (half sheet pan) with a Silpat.

In a large pot, stir together the sugar, honey, glucose, and water and cook over medium heat, stirring from time to time until the sugar has melted. If any sugar crystals cling to the sides of the pot, brush them down with a pastry brush dipped in water. Watch the caramel, because the color will change quickly. Tilt the pot to see the depth of color. After about 15 minutes, the liquid will be a deep, rich amber in color and will just begin to smoke.

Immediately remove the pot from the heat and carefully whisk in the baking soda. The mixture will bubble up quite a bit. Pour onto the prepared baking sheet. Don't be tempted to spread the mixture out: the varying thickness adds to the honeycomb effect.

Let cool completely, then break into pieces and store in an airtight container for up to 3 weeks.

MAKES ABOUT 1 POUND

Note: Most stores that carry cake decorating supplies will carry glucose.

CRÈME FRAÎCHE

Crème fraîche can be difficult to find and expensive, but you can make it at home quite easily. If you do have a little crème fraîche on hand, use it instead of the buttermilk to make yourself a larger batch.

INGREDIENTS
1 quart (4 cups) heavy cream
2 tablespoons buttermilk

Stir together the cream and buttermilk in a medium bowl or storage container. Leave at room temperature, uncovered, overnight, to thicken.

Stir the thickened crème fraîche, cover, and refrigerate.

Store in the refrigerator for up to 1 week.

MAKES 4 CUPS

CLARIFIED BUTTER

Clarifying butter means cooking it over low heat until the white milk solids separate from the clear yellow butter. Removing the milk solids from the butter allows you to cook at higher temperatures without scorching the butter. Be sure to use unsalted butter.

INGREDIENTS
16 tablespoons (8 ounces) unsalted butter, cut into chunks

Place the butter in a small saucepan and melt over low heat; do not stir. Once the butter has melted completely, skim off the foam that has risen to the top and discard. Carefully pour the clear yellow liquid, the clarified butter, into a container, leaving the white milky layer in the bottom of the pan. Discard the milky layer.

Cover and refrigerate for 1 week or freeze for longer storage.

MAKES ABOUT 3/4 CUP

JOHN'S SIMPLE CHOCOLATE SAUCE

When people ask me for this recipe and I tell them how to make it, they'll often say, "You just add sugar and *water?*" Yes, water, if you want to really emphasize the flavor of the chocolate. If you want the sauce to have more body, use milk. I keep this on hand to drizzle over ice cream, fruit, or a slice of cake. It can be stored in the refrigerator for two weeks and reheated as needed.

Place the chocolate and water or milk in a small heavy saucepan over low heat and stir constantly for about 1 minute, until the chocolate begins to melt. Add the sugar and continue stirring for 3 to 4 minutes, or until the sugar has dissolved and the sauce is smooth. Add additional water or milk 1 tablespoon at a time to desired consistency.

Serve warm or at room temperature.

Store in the refrigerator for up to 2 weeks.

MAKES ABOUT 1 CUP

INGREDIENTS

6 ounces 70% bittersweet chocolate, coarsely chopped

¼ cup water or low-fat milk, plus more as needed

2 tablespoons granulated sugar

HOT FUDGE SAUCE

Of all possible sundae toppings, hot fudge sauce has to be the favorite. This recipe makes a sauce that's rich, thick, and creamy—everything you want from hot fudge.

INGREDIENTS

1 cup granulated sugar

½ cup unsweetened cocoa powder

5 ounces 72% bittersweet chocolate, chopped

8 tablespoons (4 ounces) unsalted butter, cut into chunks

1 cup half-and-half

In a medium bowl, whisk together the sugar and cocoa powder.

In the top of a double boiler, melt the chocolate and butter over simmering water.

Meanwhile, place the half-and-half in a small saucepan over medium heat. As soon as steam begins to rise from the half-and-half, whisk in the cocoa mixture and continue cooking, whisking, until the sugar and cocoa are dissolved. Do not allow the mixture to boil; adjust the heat as necessary to keep it at a very low simmer.

When the chocolate and butter have melted, stir until smooth, then stir into the cocoa mixture. Whisk the sauce for 2 to 3 minutes until slightly thickened. Pour into a container and let cool.

Store, covered, in the refrigerator. Rewarm portions in a double boiler or in the microwave.

MAKES ABOUT 2½ CUPS

CHOCOLATE SYRUP

Keep this syrup on hand in your refrigerator, and you'll have the base for chocolate milk (see below), Robert's Egg Cream (page 199), or a Chocolate Banana Milkshake (page 259).

INGREDIENTS

¼ cup plus 2 tablespoons unsweetened cocoa powder

½ cup granulated sugar

¼ cup plus 2 tablespoons hot water

Combine the cocoa and sugar in a small bowl. Add 2 tablespoons of the hot water and stir until smooth; add another 1 to 2 tablespoons water if necessary. When the cocoa mixture is completely smooth, add the remaining hot water. Whisk until the sugar and cocoa have completely dissolved.

Transfer to a small storage container and refrigerate until ready to use.

Store in the refrigerator for up to 1 month.

MAKES ABOUT ¾ CUP

TO MAKE CHOCOLATE MILK:
Add 1 tablespoon of the syrup to 1 cup cold milk, and stir well.

Dulce de Leche

This idea comes from the Chilean grandmother of one of our recipe testers, Mariela de la Cerda. Mariela says that her grandmother always had several dulce de leche cans at the ready. Dulce de leche is cooked directly in the can and is submerged in water: Take care to keep the can submerged during cooking.

The dulce de leche will be very thick when it's done. It's ready to be used as a sauce right out of the can, or you can whip it with a mixer for a lighter consistency.

Remove the label from the can. Place the can on its side in a medium saucepan and cover completely with water. Bring the water just to a boil. Keep at a low boil, adding more water as necessary to keep the can covered with at least an inch of water, turning the can from time to time, for 4 hours. Take care to keep the can covered with water as there's a very slim chance the can could explode if the water boils away.

Carefully remove the can from the water. The dulce de leche can be cooled in the can and stored at room temperature or used right away. If opening the can while it is still warm, open it slowly, because the dulce de leche may spurt slightly.

MAKES ABOUT 1¾ CUPS

INGREDIENTS

One 14-ounce can sweetened condensed milk

CUSTARD SAUCE

Pale, creamy custard sauce provides just the right counterpoint to dark chocolate, both visually and as a contrast in flavor. You can add Grand Marnier, or the liqueur of your choice, to taste.

Place a fine-mesh strainer over a medium bowl, and set aside.

In another medium bowl, whisk the yolks lightly.

In a medium heavy saucepan, place the half-and-half over medium heat just until a slightly wrinkled skin begins to form on the surface. Remove from the heat. Add a few tablespoons of half-and-half to the yolks, whisking constantly. Add one-third of the half-and-half to the yolks, while whisking, and then pour the mixture back into the pan. Whisk in the sugar and salt. Cook over low heat, stirring constantly, until the mixture is thick enough to coat the back of the spoon. Strain through the fine-mesh strainer into the bowl.

Cool slightly, then add the vanilla and the liqueur, if using. Cool completely, cover, and refrigerate.

The sauce can be stored in the refrigerator for up to 3 days.

MAKES ABOUT 1¾ CUPS

INGREDIENTS

4 large egg yolks

1¾ cups half-and-half

⅓ cup granulated sugar

Pinch of salt

½ teaspoon pure vanilla extract

1 to 2 tablespoons Grand Marnier or other liqueur (optional)

MACERATED BERRIES

Just a slight amount of lemon juice and sugar brings out the juiciness in berries and brightens their flavor. Macerated berries can dress up any plain dark chocolate dessert, but they especially enliven dense flourless cakes, tarts, and Chocolate Sorbet (page 75).

INGREDIENTS

1 cup whole, sliced, or cut berries

2 tablespoons granulated sugar, or to taste

1 teaspoon freshly squeezed lemon juice

Place the berries in a bowl and toss with the sugar and lemon juice. Allow to sit at room temperature for 30 minutes, gently stirring the berries from time to time.

Cover and refrigerate until ready to use. These are best eaten within a day.

MAKES 1 CUP

CANDIED ALMONDS

CONTRIBUTED BY JASON HAMMEL AND AMALEA TSHILDS

Jason and Amalea scatter these candied almonds over their Mascarpone-Stuffed French Toast (page 229), but the almonds are also a nice addition to a bowl of ice cream, cupcakes, or a slice of cake.

INGREDIENTS

1 cup sliced blanched almonds

¼ cup granulated sugar

Combine the almonds and sugar in a heavy-bottomed medium skillet or sauté pan and cook over medium-low to medium heat, stirring constantly with a wooden spoon or heat-resistant spatula. The sugar will melt and then caramelize as the nuts are toasted. When the caramel is golden brown, scrape the nuts onto a plate to harden and cool completely.

Break into pieces, and store in an airtight container.

MAKES A GENEROUS 1 CUP

WHIPPED CREAM

A cold bowl and whisk will give you much better results when you whip
cream. Chill the bowl, the whisk or whisk attachment, and the cream until very cold.

Place the cream in a chilled metal bowl or mixer bowl. With a whisk, or the whisk attachment,
whip the cream until slightly frothy. Sprinkle in the sugar and continue to whip until soft
peaks form. Use immediately, or refrigerate for up to 1 hour.

MAKES 2 CUPS

TO MAKE COCOA WHIPPED CREAM:

Combine the sugar with 1 tablespoon plus 1 teaspoon unsweetened cocoa powder before
adding it to the cream.

CHAPTER
9

THE FUTURE OF CACAO

ROBERT

Much of my knowledge of what makes chocolate taste good comes from making it. From the beginning, I judged the quality of the bean samples we received by cutting three hundred randomly selected beans and noting the number of poorly fermented beans versus those that were well fermented. Unroasted, the fermented beans often had hints of fruity or earthy flavors that predicted a positive contribution to the chocolate, while those that were poorly fermented were highly astringent, with virtually no flavor. In testing for doneness during the early batches I roasted, I noticed that even prolonged exposure to heat could not bring out desirable attributes in poorly fermented beans. The higher the percentage of poorly fermented beans in any given lot, the more likely it was for the chocolate to lack flavor and complexity. I thought then that fermentation was probably the single most important factor in creating chocolate with the range of flavors that led to eating pleasure.

Yet when we bought beans from brokers on the open market, there was no way to create a dialogue with the farmers to affect the quality of fermentation. Bean procurement would always be a question of choosing among samples that were available, rather than tailoring the beans to our specific needs. To truly have control over quality would obviously require more direct communication with farmers.

The earliest efforts to alter the fermentation levels of the beans we received occurred through a Venezuelan company we worked with for the first few years of Scharffen Berger, but at that time it was more a question of agents in the field selecting lots at our request than our suggesting changes to the farmers themselves. The first real opportunity I had to affect the quality of beans from a specific farmer took place when we began to work with a single relatively large grower in Costa Rica. The first sample he sent had a larger-than-acceptable percentage of underfermented beans, and the lot had undergone a five-day fermentation—his normal procedure. I suggested he send me samples of beans fermented for five, six, and seven days of fermentation. It was almost immediately clear that those fermented for seven days were the most flavorful. The change in technique was particularly important in this case because we were planning to use his cacao for a single-origin bar for the Milwaukee County Museum to help promote their efforts in ecosystem preservation in Costa Rica.

Several years later, after I received an e-mail from a representative of the Kallari Association, a cooperative of farmers in the Amazonian region of Ecuador, I asked for a sample from their crop. The farmers suspected they were growing a now-rather-rare variety of cacao limited to Ecuador called nacional. Nacional is a type of forastero, although without genetic testing there was no way to prove this. Nacional is an indigenous variety, in danger of being supplanted by a hardier but less flavorful type. Well-fermented nacional beans have a soft, floral character rarely found among other varieties. Unfortunately, the beans were so poorly fermented, it was impossible to determine their quality. Several conversations and e-mails regarding the basics of fermentation followed, leading to a gradual improvement in the fermentation of the beans, and their taste.

These two experiences, in Costa Rica and Ecuador, represent the very different challenges we will face in the future as we, along with other producers, try to produce chocolate that depends above all on the flavor of cacao beans from which it is made.

Ecuador

ROBERT

When the Kallari Association contacted me in 2003 to ask for advice on how the farmers could get higher prices for their cacao, I had the chance to work with Judy Logback, and she opened a door for working with farmers who were most in need of help. Judy is an environmental biologist who divides her time between Quito and the Amazon, seeking ways to bring income to the people who live along the Napo River. Judy impressed me because she seems to be motivated by a sincere desire to help, and she's devoted to the people in a region that is both very poor and at risk for deforestation. Judy helped found the Kallari Association to fight the poverty as well as the clearing of trees. Members of the cooperative grow cacao on small remote plots of land spread over more than fifty square miles. Roads are limited and electronic communication is virtually nonexistent. When this group had sold cacao in the past, it had been to itinerant buyers offering low prices with little regard for the degree of fermentation.

During this same time, I was working with the Terra Madre project, a forum created by the Slow Food organization that connected individuals working toward sustainable agriculture. Anya Fernald asked if I knew of cacao producers who might fit Terra Madre's requirements, and Kallari came to mind.

When a group of Kallari farmers presented their chocolate to the 2004 Terra Madre Conference in Turin, Italy, they wore traditional dress—kilts woven from the fibers of plantain and bromeliad, necklaces, armbands, and headbands all made from Amazon seeds and fibers. They attracted more attention than anyone else at the conference, and their chocolate sold more quickly than any other chocolate there.

By analyzing Kallari's fermentation steps, I was able to note the basic elements of a successful fermentation program. Farmers needed a standardized record-keeping system, simple instruments to measure variables such as weight, temperature, and pH, rudimentary shelters where temperature and aeration of the fermenting cacao could be controlled, adequate structures for drying the beans, and, most important, training for the farmers to help them respond to the many variables, such as temperature, humidity, bean size and chemical composition. In the end, the farmer must be able to recognize the difference between a well-fermented bean and one that is over- or under-fermented, and passing along this knowledge isn't always easy.

Working with the Kallari Association motivated us to widen our search for cacao to include groups of small farmers, to help with fermentation where we could, and whenever possible to buy from the farmers directly, so they could earn as much money as possible for their cacao.

The Dominican Republic

JOHN

The simplest way to buy cacao beans is to have brokers send you samples, make small batches from those sample beans, taste, and then place your bean order. Bypassing the brokers and working directly with the people who grow cacao is one of the best things we do, but it's a lot more challenging than buying from brokers. It can take days to reach the areas where cacao grows—a long plane ride is just the start of the journey. There are cultural differences and language barriers, and you have to start taking anti-malarial drugs weeks before any trips to cacao country. On the other hand, the benefits of working directly with farmers are fantastic. First, we can make a difference in very poor communities by paying premium prices for their cacao. We still use brokers for our bulk beans, but our goal is to pay the dollars we spend on cacao directly to the farmer as often as possible.

Second, we can apply cacao's ability to thrive under a rain forest to aid conservation efforts. Hardwood trees don't have to be cut down in order for people to grow cacao, which means cacao growers can play a part in keeping rain forests from shrinking and even contribute to extending the jaguar corridors and floral bird cover for migrating birds in Central and South America.

Third, we can locate some really amazing species of cacao in out-of-the-way forest gardens (see page 301). If we can explain to the person farming the cacao how we need the beans to be fermented, we can increase the amount and variety of cacao that's available to us.

If the best part of my job is walking through a forest garden with the person who tends the land, then the worst part of my job is telling a small-scale farmer that we can't buy his beans. Our sample success rate is still low—as I write this, we still buy only one sample out of every ten we get. Much of the time this is due to poor fermentation, but sometimes we find beans that we believe will taste great if the farmer ferments his crop and this ends up not being the case. Yet sometimes a farmer will do everything right and—just because of his cacao's genetics—the beans won't have the flavor we need for our chocolate.

When a bean broker sends you samples, you're tasting beans that aren't connected to someone you know. You can reject the usual nine batches out of ten, and the process is painless. When you've worked with the farmers, when they've gone to the trouble to ferment exactly the way you've asked them to, and their beans still aren't flavorful, rejecting those beans isn't simple. From a business standpoint, you can afford to buy only the beans you'll use, but you find yourself in a position of wanting to help a farmer whose beans you can't buy.

This was one of the reasons I hired Brad Kintzer. Brad studied botany in Vermont and wrote his thesis on sugar maples, but when he first saw cacao in a botanical garden, he was fascinated. He talked his way into a course on tropical plants so he could go with the class to Central America. While his classmates were scouting out orchids, Brad was talking to cacao farmers and climbing over fences to get a closer look at the pods. Brad worked for a small chocolate maker after graduating and then returned to Mexico, hitchhiking with a pack on his back. He taught himself Spanish by talking to people he met on the road.

Brad came to Scharffen Berger for an interview just as Robert and I were planning a few trips to meet small-scale farmers. Brad understood cacao and fermentation, he was fluent in Spanish, and clearly travel didn't worry him. He was just the person to help us stay in contact with the small-scale farmers we were meeting.

ROBERT

On a trip we took in 2005, we arranged to visit three cacao growers in the Dominican Republic: Jo Locandro, Héctor José Rizek Sued, and a group of farmers working with a nonprofit called the Loma Quita Espuela Foundation.

Jo Locandro cultivates cacao on a farm overlooking the Los Haitises rain forest preserve. Raised both in New York and Rio de Janeiro, Jo wanted a career that would take him back and forth between the States and South America. In the 1970s, he began working as a tropical commodities futures trader, specializing in coffee, cacao, sugar, and orange juice. These days many investment firms have large tropical commodities departments, staffed with teams of brokers, but thirty years ago, few futures brokers specialized in tropical commodities.

When Jo met his wife, Lulys, whose family had farmed in the Dominican Republic for generations, he began coming to the family's cacao farm as often as he could.

Jo pointed out cacao pods on the trees as we drove along the dirt road that cut through the farm. In

2004, an autumn hurricane had swept away most of the cacao blossoms. The farm produced a total of two hundred bags of beans—about twelve tons—when they'd expected closer to one hundred tons. Jo hoped this harvest would be especially extra large to compensate.

As someone who moves between trading cacao and growing it, Jo sees cacao as both crop and commodity. "Volume was always the most exciting thing for me," he said. "To a trader, a few tons are nothing. That's a blip. But when I'm here, I see all the work that goes into a hundred bags of beans. I see what the costs are to the farmer and what the beans sell for. To be a farmer in the Dominican Republic is very hard. Local prices often aren't enough to cover production costs. Large-scale farms can export what they grow, but the guys who own small farms here don't always have that option."

Jo believed that this would change. "Before Starbucks," he said, "coffee was just a commodity. Volume was what mattered, and people didn't think about bean quality. Once coffee drinkers understood the difference a good bean made in flavor, prices changed to reflect quality. This will happen with cacao too."

Is Chocolate Good for You?

Unfortunately, we can't yet state conclusively that chocolate is good for you. Some laboratory experiments suggest that antioxidants and other substances in cacao might be useful in treating aspects of cardiovascular disease and various cancers; however, every study also cautions that there is no evidence that either chocolate or these extracted substances prolong life or prevent disease.

First, let's consider what we mean by chocolate. It's very likely that any healthful benefits of a chocolate bar that is fifty percent sugar will be outweighed by the risk attached to its high calorie content—and the potential weight gain from eating that chocolate.

Second, even when the chocolate has a higher percentage of cacao than sugar, there are many variables that affect antioxidant levels. The levels vary depending on bean origin, degree of fermentation, roasting temperature, and the presence, if any, of added alkali. Quantifying the effect these variables have on antioxidant levels for a given amount of chocolate would be almost impossible because the concentration of the variables themselves can change in unpredictable ways. When considering the antioxidants in cacao beans, we can't view them the same way we think about, say, grapes in wine. Origins and even varieties of cacao beans are far more diverse genetically than, for example, grapes identified as Chardonnay or Cabernet Sauvignon. Because an-

tioxidant levels can vary among individual beans from a particular origin and because we don't usually know the exact mixture of beans from a given harvest, even average antioxidant levels will differ from harvest to harvest.

And then there's the matter of dosage. Studies on chocolate's antioxidants are so preliminary that nobody has even tried to pin down what amount might be beneficial.

In short, given how widely antioxidant amounts can vary in dark chocolate, the significance these might have on health remains unclear. It is possible that research will uncover health benefits, and that forms of cacao—other than the chocolate bar—may come to be considered a nutritious food rather than just a decadent treat. Consider cacao nibs. Nibs, which are just now finding a following in this country and Europe, provide the same antioxidants found in dark chocolate without any added sugar, and they have an intense, interesting flavor. In light of all the chocolate that has been consumed around the world for centuries, it's funny to think of an incarnation of cacao that is just now being "discovered." Nibs give rise to the idea that, decades from now, we may very well see cacao used in ways that we haven't yet dreamed of.

JOHN

Héctor José Rizek Sued is the vice president of Nazario Rizek, the largest cacao exporter in the Dominican Republic. Héctor José has a clear goal for his company: he wants to produce the best cacao in the world.

Nazario Rizek isn't just the name of the company; it's also the name of Héctor José's grandfather. Nazario first came to the Dominican Republic in 1905 from Nazareth. At a gathering of immigrants from the same town, Nazario met his future wife, Badía. He reportedly told Badía's parents that he would wait until she was old enough to marry him. But Badía's parents, José Jabaly and Carmen Abdo, alarmed when their oldest daughters began falling in love with Dominicans, made plans to return to the Middle East with all eight daughters. The family went (and Héctor José's cousins still live in the Middle East today) but Badía remained and married Nazario.

Beginning with only a small farm that he bought at the age of nineteen, Héctor Jose's father slowly amassed a cacao empire, buying one piece of property at a time. When Héctor José began working for Nazario Rizek, he hired cacao scientists, professionals, and researchers and even built a small but up-to-date laboratory in the center of one of the Rizek cacao farms. A visit to the Rizek facility fascinates me because it's so different from most of the cacao farms we visit. The Rizeks' farms are high-end, with high-tech materials and research facilities. As we walked from the fermentation area to the lab, we stayed on a paved path—the first paving I'd seen on a cacao farm—but we still walked beneath mango and zapote trees. It is a forest garden, but better groomed and on a much larger scale.

All of this effort and expense, the technology and the attention that the Rizeks have given their farms, appears to have paid off. Although cacao fluctuates from season to season and the flavor of the seeds depends on many factors, from what I tasted on that trip, I think the Rizeks have achieved their goal of growing the world's finest cacao. The earthy, dark, rich flavor in their cacao is wonderful when blended with fruitier, more acidic cacao, but it's also a delight just on its own. The Rizeks provide cacao to two of our competitors, Cluizel and Valrhona, but they have planted a few hectares of criollo just for us, and we can't wait to taste those beans.

ROBERT

When we reached the Nazario Rizek offices in San Francisco de Macorís, Héctor José greeted us warmly. Héctor José looked cool and crisp—his khaki pants had a sharp crease. After spending the morning hiking through a cacao farm, we looked less crisp and smelled faintly of insect repellent. When we walked into Héctor José's office and the heavy wooden door swung closed, the sense of being in a modern office environment evaporated. The brocade-upholstered armchair across from us held a pillow embroidered in English with the words "Men, Coffee, Chocolate—The richer the better!"

Héctor José opened a tall chest of drawers across from his desk. Each drawer was packed with chocolate, and he began to pull out samples, most of them single-origin chocolate, all made by different chocolate companies, from cacao plantations around the world. We unwrapped the samples one at a time, and tasted. There was a bar of chocolate from Ecuador with strong but muddy flavors and not much of a high note. There was a chocolate from Madagascar with really good fruit notes and a long finish. We tasted chocolate made from rare Venezuelan porcelana beans. Instead of a bar, this chocolate was shaped into petals, with each piece part of a large flower held in place by petal-shaped indentations in a heavy plastic tray. This chocolate was smooth with a very good flavor, but it lacked the long finish I had expected.

Héctor José leaned forward in his chair, listening intently and with obvious pleasure to our comments about each chocolate. On an earlier trip, he had taken us to visit the patriarch of the company, his father. Héctor Senior is still a formidable presence at Nazario Rizek. Though he is shorter than his son and has a round grandfatherly face, Héctor Senior's bearing demands a certain formality; even though both Héctors repeatedly gestured for us to sit, both John and I remained standing until Héctor Senior had taken his seat.

The fact that the Nazario Rizek company owns many farms puts the Rizeks in a unique position. They have the resources to experiment, to test various fermentation techniques—such as determining how long cacao seeds should remain in the pod before the pod is cut open—and to try new ideas. The Rizeks tested in-pod fermentation very methodically, leaving some cacao pods unopened for one day, others for two days, others for three days, before continuing the fermentation process in bins. After many experiments, Héctor José found that there was a set period of time during which in-pod fermentation set up the process so the final product was more evenly fermented. Keeping beans in the pod beyond this period resulted in cacao that didn't taste as good. The fact that the Rizeks could test this theory, and then put the results of their experiments to use, places Nazario Rizek in a distinct category of cacao growers.

Nazario Rizek is trying other methods of improving the fermentation process. In their small laboratory, which looks out onto the trees of the cacao farm, the Rizeks have begun working with inoculums, which may provide better, faster, and more even fermentation results. The term *inoculum* sounds vaguely threatening, but it simply means to introduce a benign microorganism that speeds up the natural fermenation process.

The yeasts and bacteria that convert the sugar in cacao pulp into alchohol during fermentation appear naturally—that is, during most cacao fermentation, humans don't do anything other than put the beans in an environment where bacteria can thrive. For centuries, winemakers, brewers, cheese makers, and bakers have isolated very specific strains of yeast and bacteria and added these strains at a specific point in the process. The Rizeks are attempting to do the same during cacao fermentation. The scientists who work at Nazario Rizek have isolated strains that work particularly well during fermentation, and they are experimenting with how to inoculate the fermenting beans with these strains to speed the process and produce beans that are more evenly fermented.

The Rizeks use fermentation boards at their facility, a very low-tech device that works well to show beans in various stages of fermentation. Well-fermented beans are crumbly looking with fissures and cracks.

Beans that aren't fermented have a slatey look—there's a subtle glossiness and a smoothness to the bean surface that you don't see in fermented beans. There was something both elemental and quite beautiful about the fermentation boards. Obviously these boards had been used for decades, which meant the Rizeks had been charting the fermentation of their beans meticulously for much longer than we'd been making chocolate.

JOHN

As we got further from Santo Domingo, the road narrowed and the pavement gave way to gravel and then to hard-packed dirt. The houses on either side became smaller, closer to the road, and wildly colorful. Most of them were clearly built by hand from palm wood, and slept entire families in one small room.

Every few minutes we passed another roadside stand, often just a fold-out table piled with food. People sold cashews or eggplants or even whole roasted pigs. We pulled off the road to buy fire-cooked *patatas* lined up in a homemade wooden rack; the woman handed the potatoes in through our car window, the rural version of a drive-through. We broke open the potatoes and ate them with our hands. They were pale gold inside, and had a subtle flowery flavor under the smokiness.

We were jammed into a green minivan riding through a flat, narrow valley between two steep forested mountains. Bright green rice shoots filled the flooded fields on either side of the road. The rice fields ended where the mountains began, and the ride got bumpy as we climbed uphill over a rutted dirt gully. We were heading into the mountains to meet a group of farmers who grew cacao here, traveling with Jesús Moreno, president of the Fundación Loma Quita Espuela, a foundation begun in 1990 by Jesús's father. One of the foundation's goals was to improve the quality of life for the farmers while keeping the forest intact. We were here to talk to the farmers about buying their cacao if they would ferment their beans.

Jesús sat up front in the passenger seat, turning to talk to us but mostly looking ahead to brace himself for the deeper ruts in the road. The shocks on the minivan clearly weren't designed for this kind of terrain, and in spite of our seat belts my head kept smacking the ceiling inside the van. When Robert asked why Jesús had become involved with the FLQE, Jesús unfastened his seat belt. He turned to face us, searching intently for the right words in English.

"We are from San Francisco de Macorís. My father loved so much his town. He was seeing it destroyed and decided to work very hard to save it. The last seven years of his life he dedicated, personally, to this work. When he was dying, the only thing he asked me was to help the foundation. He didn't talk about ice cream, he didn't mention business. He talked only of Loma Quita Espuela. He said, 'Please, Jesús. I want you to continue this work for me.'"

In the Dominican Republic, the two most recognizable brands are Presidente beer and Helados Bon, a chain of ice cream stores. In 1950, Dr. Alfonso Moreno, Jesús's father, began Helados Bon very modestly, making his own ice creams from local fruit. Helados Bon was the first company to franchise in the Dominican Republic and in the eighties, Bon ice cream shops swept across the country. At the same time, the rain forests surrounding Alfonso's hometown of San Francisco de Macorís shrank by sixty percent. More than six

thousand of Loma Quita Espuela's eleven thousand farmers left their homes in one decade, striking out for the United States and Puerto Rico in search of a better life. About one million legal and illegal Dominicans currently live in the U.S. They make up the largest Latino group in the United States after Mexicans, and many of the people who still live in the Dominican Republic stay afloat because of money sent to them by relatives who have left the country.

Stunned by how quickly the lush forests near his hometown were being cleared, Alfonso met with the president of the Dominican Republic to try and have the area officially protected. He bought what land he could, donating it to become part of a scientific reserve, and began meeting with the farmers who remained about how he could provide better health care and education in these rural communities while at the same time helping to preserve the forests. Because cacao grows beneath the rain forest canopy, it offers a way to keep the tall trees but still provide an income to the farmers left in this area.

Our minivan ground up a final steep hill and lurched to a stop in front of the Taller Community Center. The center is one large room, open on all four sides and sheltered by a high thatched roof. The roof supports are slender tree trunks peeled of bark, still new enough then to smell of just-cut wood. Honey-colored palm fronds cover the sloping roof, creating a fringe at eye level all the way around. Only the kitchen, set in one corner, was enclosed by thick walls, painted a cool mint green.

Victor Almánzar, director of the FLQE, hurried out to greet us, gently pulling us under the shade of the center's roof. Moving out of the harsh sun was a relief. The open room was surprisingly cool; the fronds blocked the light and the heat rose into the roof's high peak. Victor proudly told us the building was a community project, built jointly by all the farmers in this region. We sat in plastic chairs at the long wooden tables and were handed plates filled with food made just for us in the small kitchen—stewed chicken, rice with plump beans, mashed eggplants that looked and tasted like tomatillos, and thick, salted plaintain chips. We drank cups of a punch made from bitter oranges, and by the time we were sipping thimble-sized cups of strong, sweet *café con azucar,* the farmers began to arrive.

Some came on foot, some rode motorcycles, but most stood in the backs of pickup trucks that bounced and swayed up the rocky hill. More than seventy people showed up, primarily men, but a few women. The poise of these farmers impressed us. Even when ten men rode together in the back of a pickup, their dignity remained. When an older farmer arrived in a white shirt, bolo tie, and a black felt hat, Jesús signaled for the meeting to start.

One of the farmers in the back stood up and began a prayer. Everyone stood silently with their head bowed as he gave thanks for our meeting in a deep, solemn voice. Both Robert and I spoke briefly before we began answering questions—fairly sophisticated questions. Except that the questions were asked in Spanish, they were basically the same questions that would have been asked by a group of Napa Valley grape farmers.

When we asked how many in the group currently fermented their beans, fewer than ten raised their hands.

ROBERT

The biggest obstacle to fermentation was gathering a big enough pile of beans. The farmers of Loma Quita Espuela each owned small farms, only one or two hectares or even smaller. On the drive up the hill, we'd seen tiny piles of beans drying on blue plastic tarps beneath clotheslines hung with shirts. Fermenting properly requires at least fifty kilograms of beans, and few of these farmers grew that much cacao. For their beans to work for us, they'd have to cooperate and ferment their beans jointly, which meant weighing the amount brought in by each farmer and then divvying up the proceeds by weight.

There's a certain risk in throwing in your crop with the crops of other farmers. You lose autonomy and control over what you grow, a thought that's disquieting to people who've farmed their own plot of land over many generations. On the other hand, if they wanted to ferment their beans, and be paid the higher prices that well-fermented beans brought, the farmers had no choice but to ferment their beans together.

After the meeting, we went with Jesús and Victor to visit a few of the farms and to see a cacao nursery. By the standards of American agriculture, the nursery looked modest, but the young cacao trees, protected from the sun by a mesh canopy, seemed an indication of hope for these farmers.

Guatemala

JOHN

Scharffen Berger had never bought Guatemalan beans. In 2005 Peter Kocaurek, Brad Kintzer, and I went to meet a few Guatemalan cacao growers and see if their beans might work for us. We got to see several regions, because Martin Keller, a coffee grower who owns a plantation in the Santa Rosa region, offered to fly us around the country in his small plane. Martin is a fourth-generation Guatemalan farmer whose great-grandfather arrived from Germany and first planted coffee on this land in 1899, and he's recently begun to grow cacao.

FINCA SANTA ISABEL

Martin is one of those farmers who does everything right. His plantation, Finca Santa Isabel, is certified with ECO-O.K., the Rainforest Alliance's seal of approval, only the second plantation in Guatemala to earn that label. Martin has built health clinics and schools for the people who harvest the coffee beans, he's made environmental education part of the school curriculum, and he's provided his workers with electricity and running water, unusual in this area. The workers eat two thousand tortillas every day—a problem when you consider that traditionally tortillas are made over wood fires. At Finca Santa Isabel, the workers are served three meals each day, and their tortillas are made in an industrial kitchen to avoid the pollution caused by burning wood. Martin even engineered a tortilla-making machine that cuts down the kitchen staff's hours.

Without Martin and his plane, we couldn't have visited some of the more remote regions, because to stick to the roads in Guatemala would have required days of driving over hazardous mountain roads.

LAGO DE IZABAL

After Finca Santa Isabel, we visited Rick Bronson's place. From Canada originally, Rick is an archaeologist whose wife's family has lived near Lago de Izabal for decades. Over the past three hundred years, cattle ranchers have cleared the virgin rain forests that once covered this area. Rick and his wife want to put trees back on this land, and they're trying to create a model that can be used for reforestation throughout the country.

The hardwood forest the Bronsons had begun planting was still very young but small stands of mahogany, teak, and rosewood trees already topped fifteen feet. Rick will grow cacao beneath these trees to provide a cash crop while the trees mature over the next sixty years. He asked me to join him by helping him find the world's best cacao to use as the basis for his planting. I love the idea of using cacao to help finance a reforestation program.

Rick plans to start a carpentry school here, to teach a livelihood to residents of this area while using the hardwoods that come from his farm, as well as the trees thinned out as the forest matures. Rick hopes to eventually have seedlings of hardwoods and cacao in his nursery. When he has this micro-finance program in place, and he sees that a combination of wood and cacao can help bring forests back to deforested areas, he hopes to extend his model to the Mayan farmers who live further inland.

CAHABON

Cahabon, an isolated region between Coban City and Lago de Izabal, was our last stop. Martin flew us as close as he could and then kept us company for four hours as we drove a mud-spattered pickup truck up the narrow, painfully unpaved roads that wound into the mountains near the Cahabon River.

Raymond Chavez, who works with Counterpart, met us at the top of the mountain. Counterpart is a nonprofit group started in 1965 to help some of the world's most impoverished people. Ray, who is Harvard-educated, studied filmmaking at NYU, and speaks several languages, wants to help the farmers of Cahabon improve their standard of living without resorting to cutting any trees in this region.

Since the 1960s, when human populations began fanning out in Central and South America, keeping corridors of rain forest intact has been a focus for many environmental organizations. As the cities expanded, huge forests shrank into small pockets. The creatures who live within these pockets, which are virtually islands of forest surrounded by urban and suburban areas, become more vulnerable to extinction as their gene pools become smaller and smaller. Connecting these pockets of forest—creating corridors that allow animals to reproduce among a larger population as well as expanding their habitats—gives a better shot to many

species of animals and plants. Here in Guatemala these stretches of rain forest are called jaguar corridors, and Cahabon is in the center of one.

But there's also a human component to life in these corridors. It's likely that the Mayan people who live here today are descendants of the ancient Mayans. Their ancestors have lived here for centuries, but in the past fifty years, farmers like them have left their lands in droves throughout South and Central America. Both natural and manmade events—from witches'-broom in Brazil to clear-cutting of forest in developing areas such as Trinidad and the Dominican Republic—have forced many farmers to abandon a way of life passed down through generations. People like Ray Chavez try to help these village farmers improve their income and care for their families without losing their way of life or threatening the jaguar corridors. Growing cacao may be one way of preserving this way of life, because the trees can grow under the rain forest canopy and be harvested while still maintaining a habitat for many endangered birds and wildlife.

Our pickup finally pulled up the last steep stretch of dirt road and came out onto a green plateau. We had expected that maybe ten Cahabon farmers would show up to meet us, but there were easily eighty people, dozens of farmers and their families, waiting for our truck.

The women wore traditional dresses made of brightly woven fabric while the men wore mostly Western-style clothing; several of the younger farmers had T-shirts printed with the faces of Sylvester Stallone and Bruce Willis even though nobody in Cahabon spoke English. All of the farmers spoke a Mayan dialect, but a few spoke Spanish as well. We spoke in Spanish, which then had to be translated for the rest of the group.

After shaking hands all around, we were led into a small single-room building made from logs and mud. The elder farmers sat next to us while everyone else filed in and stood against the walls. Those who couldn't fit into the room hung in through the window and watched us eat. Several women ladled a spicy turkey soup into bowls. Small pots of crushed red peppers were passed down the table. We sprinkled the peppers on top the soup and took a few sips. The peppers were delicious—unlike any peppers I'd tasted in the States. By the time we'd finished our soup, I'd recovered from four hours of nonstop bouncing in a pickup truck.

As the soup bowls were cleared, I stood to thank the farmers for their welcome. Brad and Peter handed out wrapped samples of our chocolate and presented the group with copies of Maricel Presilla's book *The New Taste of Chocolate,* which was met with applause. Most of the farmers slipped the bars into their shirt pockets, but a few opened them and looked at the smooth chocolate very curiously. Although they had been near cacao trees and cacao beans all their lives, many in this village had never seen refined chocolate.

Brad went to the truck to get more samples, which weren't wrapped in paper but enclosed in resealable plastic bags. Zip-loc bags were completely unknown in Cahabon, and they created quite a sensation among the farmers and their children.

Once we'd distributed our gifts of chocolate, the leader of the group got down to business and presented me with a contract, which had already been signed and notarized. I signed the contract promising to pay for the materials for new fermenting structures, and made sure the group understood that Brad Kintzer would work with Robert and answer any fermentation questions that might arise.

The farmers then got up to lead us to where their cacao grows. Getting to see their cacao was a thrill. It had been planted on steep hillsides that at one time had been cleared—slashed and burned for corn planting. Ten years ago, the Cahabon residents began replanting the slopes. They are now covered with a lush forty-foot canopy of fleur de baba trees, which shelter the cacao trees underneath from sun and wind. To see deforested land recovering—and to see these people bringing back cacao along with the forests—was one of the most moving moments of the trip.

. . . .

The Risk in Planting Monocultures

The forest garden model helps a farmer make sure that if disease attacks his farm, not every plant will be wiped out and his livelihood won't be at risk. Planting several varieties of a cash crop as well as subsistence foods serves as a safe model for farmers in the developing world. First World agriculture has often embraced a monocultural approach to farming. A monoculture is the cultivation of one crop or a single variety of plant on forest or farmland.

The idea behind monocultures is high production. If a specific type of tomato, for example, tastes better or grows faster, then a farmer might believe planting an entire farm in that one variety would bring in more money. The problem with a monoculture is it has little defense against unforeseen diseases. If that variety is vulnerable to a pathogen, then the disease will spread from plant to plant, or tree to tree. In a monoculture, a farmer's entire field—or in the case of witches'-broom in Brazil—an entire region could be devastated. The problems in Brazil were complex: labor unrest, too-large farms, and low cacao prices compounded the region's inability to protect against the rapidly spreading disease.

On a small farm, a polycultural approach—planting several varieties of cacao alongside bananas, citrus, macadamia nut, coconut, and oil palm trees, as well as the farmer's manioc, yam, corn, and cassava—seems to be the ideal model for cacao production. Currently, about eighty percent of the world's cacao is grown just this way.

. . . .

Panama

JOHN

When Allen Herre says that he's a biologist with an interest in fungi, not many people outside of a cacao conference are going to think Allen has the world's most exciting job. But for those of us interested in cacao, the work being done by Allen and his collaborators may promise an end to the biggest threats against it—diseases like witches'-broom, black pod, and monilia. Allen and his wife, Sunshine Van Bael, live in Panama, and both of them work for the Smithsonian Tropical Research Institute to protect life in the rain forest.

Allen studies the relationship between endophytic fungi, a type of fungus that lives within the healthy tissues of plants such as cacao, and their hosts. Most of us have an automatic negative reaction to the word *fungus*, especially where food is concerned. But Allen points out that essentially all healthy plants are shot through with fungi. "Look at any plant," he says, "and what you're seeing is not just a plant but a mosaic made up of plant cells and fungus cells. In two square meters of leaves, there are more species of fungus than tree species found in the United States and Canada combined. These fungi seem to appear naturally after a new leaf opens, entering and growing between the leaf cells until reaching a saturation point at about four to six weeks when there's no room for any more fungi cells."

Scientists have known for years that the mycorrhizal fungi that live in the roots of plants help pull in nutrients and water that the roots couldn't access otherwise. Research on the role beneficial fungi play in the leaves of plants is newer.

The work done by Allen and his collaborators indicates that these beneficial endophytes can reduce the damage caused by pathogens such as *Phytophthora*, the microorganism behind black pod rot. Their initial greenhouse studies showed that cacao trees that were loaded with beneficial fungi suffered less damage when they were attacked by disease. This work may reveal that the use of fungicides can actually inhibit a plant's long-term health, but that inoculating a healthy cacao plant with benign endophytes can block harmful pathogens because they leave no starting point where the pathogens can invade the healthy tissue.

The benign fungi in plants as well as the microorganisms that attack the plants are both constantly evolving. Applying fungicides and pesticides may in fact give pathogens the advantage, because they can evolve to resist the chemicals. By shifting the balance between benign fungi and pathogens, the pathogens might be kept in check naturally.

"We think that the benign fungi—if we can apply the right ones—strengthen a plant's ability to defend itself," Allen said.

And exactly how does Allen inoculate healthy plants with benign fungi? "A big soup," he laughed. "A big, live soup." Trying to imagine what this looks like, we asked the color of the soup. "It's creamy," Allen said, and Sunshine laughed and added, "Cream of mushroom soup."

Allen says cacao is just the start of his research. "If it works with cacao, theoretically, it should work with any plant. There is no agricultural plant that isn't threatened by some sort of pathogenic disease."

ROBERT

Sunshine Van Bael is a biologist focused on bird populations in forested regions. When the bird population drops, trees suffer almost immediately as the insect populations increase. As the forest degrades, the floral cover for migrating birds also degrades, and a vicious circle begins with fewer trees for the birds and fewer birds to help the trees.

Cacao is where Allen's and Sunshine's work come together. Studies on undisturbed tropical forest remnants in the Bocas del Toro province of Panama show that the bird diversity in cacao plantations grown with a shady overstory is pretty close to the bird diversity in the undisturbed forest areas. A few species of birds—especially those that forage on the ground—don't fare as well on cacao farms as they do in pristine rain forest, but for many birds, a cacao farm provides a good habitat. Cacao, grown in conjunction with taller shade trees, might provide the floral cover that migrating birds need. The birds keep insect count down, the trees grow better and faster as a result, and the indigenous farmers can make a living selling their cacao.

If you look at the bigger picture in Bocas del Toro, cacao's importance becomes even more apparent. Until recently, the land here has been used primarily to grow bananas and cacao. Because there were no roads to Bocas del Toro, freighters would come into port, pick up bananas and cacao, and steam off. In 1996, when roads connected this region with the rest of Panama, suddenly cattle came too. Cattle may bring in more money initially, but they harm the land. The indigenous farmers in this region, choosing between competing against the huge banana companies here, growing cacao despite the many diseases that threaten it, or grazing cattle, often opt for cattle. The saddest part of the equation is that the cattle often aren't their own. Wealthy ranchers pay to rent land that has been cleared of trees. They graze their cows there, and in five to seven years, when the land has become unusable, they move their cows to a different cleared plot of land. The farmer who has cleared all the trees from his land to make room for the cattle has no way to make a living.

The runoff from the cattle also affects the region's shoreline. The coral reefs and turquoise water outside Bocas del Toro make up a 32,700-acre marine reserve. On paper, the marine reserve is protected habitat. Yet in the past few nine years, the runoff from agriculture and ranching has changed the formerly unspoiled reefs and threatened the mangroves that support reef life.

Tourists are just discovering this region, and tourism could provide a way for the indigenous people to continue to live here. However, if tree clearing and the runoff from cattle ranching continue to harm the reefs at the current rate, there won't be a destination for tourists within a few decades.

Sunshine Van Bael sees cacao, grown in a polyculture, as one way to slow the rise of cattle ranching as well as the best possible alternative to deforestation. "Cow pastures and banana farms do not provide habitat for many bird species, especially migratory birds," she says. "A cacao farm with a shady overstory can provide that habitat."

Epilogue

ECUADOR

After the Slow Food conference, the Kallari Association farmers were able to increase the overall fermentation level of their beans by fifteen percent. Their 2005 harvest of cacao brought a selling price that was fifty percent higher than they'd gotten previously for unfermented beans. With donations of European conching equipment, they've started a small chocolate factory in a high-altitude community. Judy Logback plans to offer tours of what may be the highest chocolate factory on earth.

GUATEMALA

We found a source of old criollo and were able to arrange for plantings to be carried to Rick Bronson's reforestation project in Lago de Izabal. We've begun a nursery there to propogate the plants. It will be years before we see the results, but if all goes well, we'll have an initial criollo harvest in 2011. In the meantime, Rick's farm will serve as a sort of technical support for the work we're doing near the Cahabon River.

THE DOMINICAN REPUBLIC

As we were finishing this book in August 2005, we received our first samples of beans from the farmers of the Loma Quita Espuela cooperative. Because the beans came from dozens of farms, they had a wide range of flavors, but we tasted deep, earthy notes with traces of dark cherry and tobacco. We think they'll work for our chocolate. If luck is on our side, by the time you read this, you will be able to taste a chocolate bar made with the beans fermented jointly by the farmers of Loma Quita Espuela.

CHAPTER 10

A NEW CHAPTER FOR SCHARFFEN BERGER CHOCOLATE MAKER

In August 2005, we sold Scharffen Berger Chocolate Maker to The Hershey Company. Many of our fans—even people who've known us from the very start—were surprised by the sale. Some of the people who wrote us letters, called, and e-mailed us expressed concern that our chocolate would change.

If you've read this book, you have a sense of how carefully we choose cacao, and how thoroughly we try to research its origins and even to meet the people who grow it. We applied this same curiosity and scrutiny to Hershey before we agreed to the sale, because we wanted to be certain that what was special and unique about our chocolate would remain unchanged.

Hershey has its own story, which is told very well by Joël Glenn Brenner in her book *The Emperors of Chocolate*. It was clear to us that Hershey, although a large company, operates a little differently from others. And the fact that the oldest chocolate company in the United States, with its history of milk chocolate, was interested in Scharffen Berger—compared to Hershey, we're a very small, very new company—signals a sea change in how Americans view dark chocolate.

Both of us will stay involved with Scharffen Berger Chocolate Maker. This change allows both of us to focus on what we love and what we're good at—looking for the best cacao beans we can find, and continuing our quest to make the best chocolate we can.

CONTRIBUTORS

This book would not have been possible without the help of these people, who kindly contributed recipes, advice, and time.

RICK BAYLESS

Chef and owner of Frontera Grill and Topolobampo in Chicago, Rick has shared his love for Mexican food through his restaurants, his PBS television series *Mexico—One Plate at a Time,* and his award-winning cookbooks, including *Authentic Mexican, Rick Bayless's Mexican Kitchen, Mexico—One Plate at a Time*, and *Rick and Lanie's Excellent Kitchen Adventures.* His most recent book is *Mexican Everyday.*

CAROLE BLOOM

Carole has taught pastry making and confectionery arts for more than twenty-five years and is the author of eight cookbooks, including *Truffles, Candies & Confections; All About Chocolate; The International Dictionary of Desserts, Pastries, and Confections,* and a forthcoming comprehensive baking book. Carole was a contributor to *The All New All Purpose Joy of Cooking.* She is the national spokesperson for the Chocolate Manufacturers Association.

FLO BRAKER

Author of *The Simple Art of Perfect Baking* and *Sweet Miniatures,* baking columnist for the *San Francisco Chronicle,* and a past president of the International Association of Culinary Professionals, Flo is also a charter member of the Baker's Dozen, the Bay Area baker's club that inspired *The Baker's Dozen Cookbook.*

JOANNE CHANG

An honors graduate of Harvard University with a degree in applied mathematics and economics, Joanne left a management consulting firm to start a cooking career. After years of working in New York City and Boston restaurants, she opened the much-loved Flour Bakery + Café in Boston's South End in 2000.

MICHAEL CHIARELLO

The Emmy Award–winning host of *Easy Entertaining with Michael Chiarello* on the Food Network and *NapaStyle* on the Fine Living Network, Michael is the author of six cookbooks, including *Michael Chiarello's Casual Cooking, Napa Stories,* and *At Home with Michael Chiarello.* He's the owner and farmer of Chiarello Family Vineyards, as well as the founder of the NapaStyle catalog and the Consorzio line of food products.

JIM DODGE

A renowned pastry chef and author, Jim was named to the Honor Roll of American Chefs by *Food & Wine Magazine,* has appeared on the *Great Chefs of San Francisco* and *Great Chefs of the West* television series, served as a contributing editor to *The All New All Purpose Joy of Cooking,* and has won awards for his books, including *The American Baker* and *Baking with Jim Dodge.* He is currently in management at *Bon Appétit* in San Francisco.

STEPHEN DURFEE

Winner of the James Beard award in 1998 for Best Pastry Chef and named one of the Ten Best Pastry Chefs in America by *Pastry Art and Design* in 1999, Stephen is known for creating desserts as refined as they are artistic and flavorful. After working for years at the French Laundry, Stephen is currently a pastry instructor at the Culinary Institute of America at Greystone.

ELIZABETH FALKNER

Citizen Cake, Elizabeth's restaurant and bakery in San Francisco, showcases her bold and artful combinations of ingredients. A former filmmaker, Elizabeth worked at Rubicon, Elka, and Masa's before opening Citizen Cake. She was named Rising Star Chef by the *San Francisco Chronicle,* Best Pastry Chef by *San Francisco* magazine, and one of the Ten Best Pastry Chefs in America by *Bon Appétit,* and she received a Best Pastry Chef nomination from the James Beard Foundation. Women Chefs and Restaurateurs awarded her their Golden Bowl for Best Pastry Chef and Most Inspiring Woman of 2003.

SUSAN FENIGER AND MARY SUE MILLIKEN

Susan and Mary Sue are well known for their innovative cuisine at Border Grill and Ciudad restaurants in the Los Angeles area, as well as Border Grill Las Vegas at Mandalay Bay. They have written five cookbooks together and filmed almost four hundred episodes of the popular *Too Hot Tamales* and *Tamales*

World Tour programs for Food Network, and they currently host *In the KFI Kitchen with Mary Sue and Susan,* a two-hour radio show on KFI-AM 640 Los Angeles.

HEIDI FRIEDLANDER

Heidi, a veteran of the Cleveland food and restaurant scene, owns Heidi & Karen Luxury Caterers with her partner, Karen Gorman. Heidi developed her luscious baked hot chocolate recipe (see page 58) while working as the opening pastry chef at Moxie, which has listed this popular dessert on its menu every day since it first appeared.

JASON HAMMEL AND AMALEA TSHILDS

Self-taught cooks Jason and Lea like to call the cuisine at their Chicago restaurant, Lula Café, artisanal because so much of what they serve is done by hand. Jason and Lea still share the cooking, the menu writing, finding exceptional Midwestern produce, and coming up with new ideas for fancy foods served in what they refer to as a "not-so-fancy setting," their small café in historic Logan Square.

STEPHANIE HERSH

Long-time personal assistant to Julia Child, Stephanie is a celebrated baker. A graduate of the Culinary Institute of America, Stephanie also has a master's of gastronomy from Boston University. An active member of the International Association of Culinary Professionals and the American Institute of Wine and Food, she currently writes, teaches cooking classes for children, and runs Chef Steph, her own pastry-making enterprise in New Zealand, where she now lives.

THOMAS KELLER

Chef and owner of the French Laundry, Bouchon, and Bouchon Bakery in Yountville, California; Bouchon in Las Vegas; and Per Se in New York City, Thomas Keller is also the author of the award-winning books *The French Laundry Cookbook* and *Bouchon.* The French Laundry has twice been named the best restaurant in the world in a poll by the London-based *Restaurant Magazine,* and Per Se was awarded Best New Restaurant by the James Beard Foundation in 2005. Thomas is the first American chef to be awarded three stars by the *Michélin Guide* for his restaurant Per Se.

SHARON LEBEWOHL

Sharon grew up watching her father, Abe, cook in his Second Avenue Deli. Abe began with a ten-seat place in the Village, and over fifty years, his deli became a New York City institution. Abe once served *Gourmet* editor Fred Ferretti, and as Ferretti left the deli, Abe followed him and yelled, "Don't forget, just because you write for some fancy-schmancy magazine, that cholent is Lower East Side cassoulet." After Abe died in 1996, Sharon began overseeing the deli with her uncle. A graduate of the French Culinary Institute, cooking teacher, and author of *The Second Avenue Deli Cookbook,* Sharon is currently writing her second book.

DAVID LEBOVITZ

After studying at Callebaut College in Belgium and Ecole Lenôtre in Paris, David worked with Lindsey Shere at Chez Panisse for twelve years. He is the author of *The Great Book of Chocolate,* which the *New York Times* and *Food & Wine* each listed as one of the top books of the year, *Room for Dessert,* and *Ripe for Dessert,* and he was a contributor to *The Baker's Dozen Cookbook.* Named one of the Top Five Pastry Chefs in the Bay Area by the *San Francisco Chronicle,* David currently teaches classes in chocolate and leads chocolate tours throughout Europe.

ROSE LEVY BERANBAUM

The former owner of the renowned Cordon Rose Cooking School in New York City, Rose has instructed thousands of students in the art of baking. Her first book, *The Cake Bible,* won the IACP/Seagram Book of the Year and is currently in its thirty-fourth printing. *Rose's Christmas Cookies* won a James Beard award in 1990, and *The Pie and Pastry Bible* was *Food & Wine's* choice for their Best of the Best cookbooks. Rose was awarded the Gourmand World award for Best Bread Book in the World for her *Bread Bible* in 2003.

EMILY LUCHETTI

Emily honed her dessert-making skills at the much-loved Stars restaurant. She was nominated for the James Beard award twice before receiving it in 2004. Emily was one of *Chocolatier* magazine's Top Ten Pastry Chefs in 1994 and recipient of the Golden Whisk award in 2001 from Women Chefs and Restaurateurs, as well as a Silver Spoon award from *Food Arts* in 2003 for her lifetime of contributions to the food industry. Emily is the author of *Stars Desserts* and *Four-Stars Desserts, A Passion for Desserts,* the dessert recipes in the *Farallon Cookbook,* and, most recently, *A Passion for Ice Cream.* She is currently executive pastry chef at Farallon restaurant in San Francisco.

MARVIN MARTIN

Marvin is a long-time Napa Valley chef and educator who is certified as a master olive oil taster by both the California Olive Oil Council and the International Olive Oil Council. He has worked at Robert Mondavi Winery's Great Chefs' Cooking School, has been a chef to author Danielle Steel for many years, and is currently olive oil and orchard consultant to wineries and private properties in Napa and Sonoma. He produces his own award-winning olive oils, OliOdessa, Carneros Olive Oil Company, and California Koroneiki, at The Olive Press in Glen Ellen, California, where he is a partner.

PAM MAZZOLA

Five years after opening L'Avenue with Nancy Oakes in 1987, Pam Mazzola helped open Boulevard, named Best Restaurant in San Francisco in 2000. Currently executive chef of Boulevard, Pam is coauthor of the *Boulevard Cookbook*. She travels frequently through Asia and Europe to broaden her culinary knowledge.

ALICE MEDRICH

Alice has helped us in so many ways that it's hard to imagine Scharffen Berger Chocolate Maker without her friendship, wisdom, and sound advice. One of the nation's foremost authorities on chocolate, she was invited to serve on the first board of directors for Scharffen Berger Chocolate Maker in 1998 and, with great enthusiasm, has advised us on everything from cacao tasting to recipe testing. She credits our chocolate with inspiring many of the recipes in her groundbreaking book *Bittersweet: Recipes and Tales from a Life in Chocolate*, which is one of the best compliments we've received.

When Alice opened her shop, Cocolat, in 1976, she revolutionized chocolate—first in Berkeley and soon after across the country. She is the author of five cookbooks, including *Cocolat: Extraordinary Chocolate Desserts* and *Chocolate and the Art of Low-Fat Desserts*. Her books have earned her the distinction of winning more Cookbook of the Year awards than any other author, twice from the James Beard Foundation and, more recently, from the International Association for Culinary Professionals for *Bittersweet*. She writes for *Bon Appétit*, *Food & Wine*, and *Fine Cooking*, among other magazines, and was a major contributor to *The All New All Purpose Joy of Cooking*. Alice has appeared on the Food Network in the *Chef du Jour* and *Baker's Dozen* series, and on PBS with Julia Child in *Baking with Julia* and Joan Nathan in *Jewish Cooking in America*. She continues to inspire chefs, chocolate makers, and home cooks through her writing, teaching, and consulting.

NANCY OAKES

A self-taught chef, Nancy has won numerous awards since opening San Francisco's Boulevard restaurant in 1993. She was named Best Chef in California by the James Beard Foundation in 2001, after being named one of the best chefs in California in 1997, 1998, 1999, and 2000 by the foundation; named a Best Chef in America by American Express; and named Best New Chef in 1993 by *Food & Wine,* which also named Boulevard Best Restaurant in San Francisco in 2000. Before Boulevard, Nancy ran a fifty-seat neighborhood bistro called L'Avenue, where she honed her cooking skills.

ARNON OREN

Arnon helped us open Café Cacao in our chocolate factory and took on the challenge of using chocolate in many of the savory dishes he created for the restaurant. After receiving his training in Lyons, France, Arnon worked at Oliveto in Berkeley and then spent four years at Chez Panisse before opening Café Cacao.

JACQUES PÉPIN

One of America's best-known chefs, cooking teachers, and cookbook authors, and a contributing editor to *Food & Wine* magazine, Jacques is dean of special programs at the French Culinary Institute in New York City and teaches at Boston University. In 2004, he was awarded France's highest civilian honor, the French Legion of Honor. Born in Bourg-en-Bresse, Jacques was the personal chef to three French heads of state, including Charles de Gaulle, before moving to the United States in 1959. His latest series for public television—his ninth—debuted in 2004 and is based on his most recent cookbook, *Jacques Pépin: Fast Food My Way.* His memoir, *The Apprentice: My Life in the Kitchen,* was a national best seller.

NICOLE PLUE

Nicole, who manages the pastry program at Julia's Kitchen at COPIA, attended the California Culinary Academy after earning a degree in English literature. Her first culinary job, at the Sheraton Palace Hotel, included a midnight baking shift. "I loved it," Nicole says. "It was just me, the bread, and the radio." Nicole was part of the opening team of One Market restaurant and managed both the bread and pastry programs at Hawthorne Lane, where she was named Pastry Chef of the Year by *San Francisco* magazine and Rising Star Chef by the *San Francisco Chronicle* in 1997. Nicole moved to Manhattan to help open Eleven Madison Park and Gustavino's and went on to manage dessert programs at both AZ and Pazo. *Bon Appétit* magazine mentioned her desserts in their "Best of" issue.

MICHEL RICHARD

Michel was a pioneer of French/California cuisine, before moving to Washington, D.C., where Michel Richard Citronelle became his flagship restaurant. His style is light, fresh, and intelligent, and known for witty presentations. Michel's creative recipes have appeared in numerous culinary publications, including *Food & Wine, Food Arts, Gourmet,* and *Bon Appétit,* and he has been featured in the *Washingtonian, New York Times, Washington Post,* and *Los Angeles Times,* among others. Michel is currently working on his second cookbook *Happy in the Kitchen,* to be published in 2006.

SALLY SCHMITT

Long before Napa Valley became a destination for food lovers, Sally and her husband, Don, opened the French Laundry in Yountville at a site that had previously been, by turns, a laundry and a bordello. Napa's first winemakers began coming to the restaurant regularly, starting a tradition that would continue when Thomas Keller bought the restaurant in 1994. While running the French Laundry, Sally and Don bought an old apple orchard in Philo, which their daughter and son-in-law, Karen and Tim Bates, filled with heirloom and antique apple varieties. Sally now teaches cooking classes at The Apple Farm and produces jams, chutneys, vinegars, and cider.

ERIC SHELTON

Eric made a name for himself at Aqua in San Francisco and then went on to work with Michael Mina at Arcadia. Eric met his fiancé, Ruthie Planas, at Aqua, and the couple opened an old-fashioned ice cream parlor in Berkeley called Sketch. They make their own organic gelato-style ice creams and sorbets flavored with seasonal fruits ranging from Mariposa plums to persimmons and Gravenstein apples, as well as caramel, coffee, and, of course, chocolate.

CRAIG STOLL

Craig is chef and co-proprietor with his wife, Anne, of Delfina and Pizzeria Delfina in San Francisco's Mission District. Named one of America's Best New Chefs of 2001 by *Food & Wine* as well as a Rising Star chef by *San Francisco* magazine and the *San Francisco Chronicle,* Craig was a James Beard Best Chef in California nominee in 2005. Before Delfina, Craig worked at Campton Place, Postrio, and Splendido. The turning point in Craig's career was a scholarship that sent him to cooking school in Torino, Italy, in 1992. His externship at Da Delfina, a one-star Michelin restaurant in Tuscany, helped define his cooking style.

JOANNE WEIR

Host of PBS's *Weir Cooking in the Wine Country* and *Weir Cooking in the City,* Joanne won a James Beard award for the companion book *Weir Cooking in the City,* as well as acclaim and awards for her books *From Tapas to Meze, Weir Cooking: Recipes from the Wine Country,* and *You Say Tomato,* among others. Joanne's professional experience includes years at Chez Panisse restaurant and an apprenticeship with Madeline Kamman in France, where she was awarded a Master Chef Diploma.

SHERRY YARD

Sherry has received several Outstanding Pastry Chef of the Year awards: in 2005 from *Pastry Arts & Design* magazine, in 2004 from the Women Chefs and Restaurateurs, in 2002 from the James Beard Foundation, and in 2000 from *Bon Appétit* magazine. After graduating from the Culinary Institute of America, Sherry worked at the Rainbow Room, Montrachet, and Tribeca Grill in New York and Campton Place and Catahoula in Northern California. She moved to Southern California in 1994 to become executive pastry chef at Spago in Beverly Hills. The author of *The Secrets of Baking,* Sherry has created desserts for the Grammy Awards, the Emmy Awards, and the Academy Awards®.

GLOSSARY OF CHOCOLATE-RELATED TERMS

astringency

A dry, cottony sensation felt on the inside of the cheeks when polyphenols—most notably tannins—react with saliva. You've experienced this sensation if you've ever tasted an underripe persimmon. Raw cacao beans are highly astringent but the degree of astringent qualities in the final chocolate depends on both the genetics of cacao and how successfully the growers fermented the beans. *See also* polyphenols, tannins.

baba

Just-harvested cacao beans still covered in pulp are called *babas,* a term derived from the Spanish word for slime.

black pod rot

A fungal disease, black pod rot causes cacao pods to rot and blacken on the tree before they can be harvested. The fungus responsible, *Phytophthora,* is recognized only when a dime-sized spot appears on a pod. *See also* fungal diseases.

bloom

Chocolate that has been exposed to heat and rehardened may have a white or gray film and look dull instead of glossy. This does not mean the chocolate is spoiled, but bloom does alter how the chocolate feels in your mouth. There are two types of bloom. Fat bloom is caused by exposure to heat and leaves a white, powdery film on the chocolate's surface. This film is made up of fat crystals that have come to the surface of the chocolate instead of remaining evenly distributed throughout. Sugar bloom occurs when the chocolate is exposed to moisture, usually through condensation. Sugar bloom gives chocolate a grainy texture.

Bloom is not an indicator of a chocolate's quality. Temperature fluctuations during shipment or storage may cause bloom to appear. Always keep chocolate away from sunlight, well wrapped, and in a cool place to help prevent bloom. If bloom does occur, you can restore the chocolate's color, smooth texture, and glossiness by tempering it (page 92).

bulk beans

Bulk beans are cacao beans that are available in large quantities because the trees are hardy, prolific, and resist diseases. Calling cacao beans bulk does not necessarily mean a lack of quality, but simply indicates beans that are more widely available in part because they're easier to grow. The term may also refer to beans that have single-note flavor characteristics. Single-note bulk beans form the foundation for most chocolate and are just as necessary as the premium beans with wider-ranging flavor notes. As with any cacao, bulk beans require fermentation to reach their full flavor potential. *See also* flavor beans.

cacao

The full name of the tree on which cacao grows is *Theobroma cacao.* The seeds or beans inside the pod, also known as cacao, become the food we know as chocolate. At Scharffen Berger, we use the word *cocoa* to refer only to cocoa powder, although for many English speakers, *cocoa* can refer to the tree and the beans as well as cocoa powder. (The word *cocoa* doesn't exist in Romance languages.)

cauliflory

The botanic trait of growing flowers and fruit from mossy patches on the trunk of a tree, such as cacao, as well as on the thicker sections of its branches.

chocolate liquor

Liquefied cocoa butter in which tiny cacao particles are suspended. Cacao nibs become chocolate liquor when the heat created by the friction of grinding during processing releases the cocoa butter from the beans and the cocoa butter and solid cacao particles emulsify. Chocolate liquor can be either a liquid or a solid, depending on its temperature.

chocolate maker

A chocolate maker creates chocolate from cacao beans. We chose this term as the English equivalent of *chocolatier* to emphasize the idea that Scharffen Berger chocolate starts with beans, rather than purchased chocolate liquor. People often confuse the terms *chocolate maker* and *confectioner; see also* confectioner.

cocoa

See cacao.

cocoa butter

When cacao beans are pressed or ground, the fat that's released from the beans is called cocoa butter. Like all fats found in nature, cocoa butter is composed of a variety of different triglycerides. The exact mix hinges on the genetic background of the cacao beans, where they are grown, and the season. Oleic, palmitic, and stearic acids are the predominant fatty acids in cocoa butter.

conching

One of the final steps in the chocolate making process, conching involves thoroughly mixing all the ingredients. Conching simultaneously aerates the chocolate to rid it of unwanted volatiles, decreases viscosity, and creates smoothness by effectively coating the sugar and cacao particles with cacao butter so that they slide over each other more easily. The process, invented in 1879 by Rodolphe Lindt, mellows the flavor of the chocolate and gives it a smoother, silkier texture. Lindt's original design had a roller that moved back and forth through the chocolate, and because the equipment's shape vaguely resembled a shell, Lindt called it a conche. (*Conche* is the machine, *conch* the verb form.) Today's machines don't use rollers but are usually barrels that conch by scraping the chocolate against the walls of the barrel with metal fins that jut out from a central axle.

confectioner

A confectioner is a person (or a company) who makes candy from ingredients such as chocolate, butter, nuts, cream, fruit, and spices. A confectioner buys chocolate and remelts it to make candy. A chocolate maker, such as Scharffen Berger, makes chocolate from cacao beans. *See also* chocolate maker.

criollo

A type of *Theobroma cacao* that many consider the "holy grail" of cacao because of its rarity, criollo is sought out for its flavor and lack of astringency. However, we've found that pods called criollo often turn out not to be. The word *criollo* can also mean a wild or native source, which is one reason criollo beans may be misidentified. A bigger reason is that commercially no standards apply to use of the word, and the term is often used without any scientific confirmation that the cacao actually is criollo. *See also* forastero, nacional, porcelana, trinitario.

emulsification

The process of combining two (or more) liquids or other ingredients that don't readily mix—for example, whisking oil into vinegar to make a vinaigrette. Similarly, in chocolate making, we use prolonged mixing to emulsify cacao butter, sugar particles, and solid particles of cacao. When emulsification is done correctly, the final product is very different from any of the individual components.

fermentation

To prepare them for fermentation, cacao seeds and pulp are removed from the pods and placed in a pit dug in the ground or a wooden bin or gathered into a pile and covered with banana leaves. (Even though we speak of the beans as being fermented, it's actually the pulp, not the beans, that undergoes the fermentation process.) Wild yeasts present in the environment settle on the pulp and ferment the natural sugars in it, converting them to alcohol, at which point bacteria that produce acetic acid (i.e., vinegar), as well as bacteria that produce lactic acid from the residual sugars, take over. As these acids are produced, the pH decreases and the temperature may rise, both of which lead to seed death. When the seeds dies, the internal cell walls break down, allowing previously separated compounds to combine. This results in a wide range of new compounds, a decrease in the concentration of the small polyphenol molecules most responsible for astringency, and, as a result, a marked increase in the complexity of the bean's flavor.

See also astringency.

flavor beans

Cacao beans with intense or multi-note flavor characteristics, often with more acidity and fruity flavors than bulk beans. *See also* bulk beans.

forastero

By far the most common of the three primary varieties of cacao. Because of its resistance to disease and high productivity, forastero represents close to ninety percent of the world's cacao harvest. Forastero is believed to be indigenous to the northern Amazon River Basin, in what is now Brazil. The word *forastero* means foreigner in Spanish. *See also* criollo, nacional, porcelana, trinitario.

forest garden

The typical model of a cacao farm, in which a small-scale farmer grows the food he needs for his family—for example, casaba, yams, and breadfruit—beside small-volume cash crops such as cacao or citrus, bananas, *zapote,* and macadamia nuts.

fungal diseases

Several specific diseases that can catastrophically affect cacao production. Fungi, which often spread by releasing microscopic particles called spores, are distinct from other threats to cacao such as viruses. *See also* black pod rot, monilia, witches'-broom.

ganache

A ganache is an emulsification of chocolate and any water-based liquid—cream, milk, half-and-half, even soy milk. Ganache can be thick or airy, infused with many different flavors, and/or mixed with butter. In what is perhaps its most familiar form, ganache is the center of a truffle. *See also* emulsification.

genotype

The genetic fingerprint of a plant, and the only sure way to correctly identify cacao. Because cacao's phenotype—that is, its physical characteristics—doesn't always correspond to its genotype, cacao can't be identified on the basis of sight alone. Two pods that look alike may be completely different genetically. For example, a pod that looks like a criollo pod may actually have the genetic composition and flavor characteristics of a forastero pod. *See also* phenotype.

mélangeur broyeur

In French, the word *mélangeur* means mixer and the word *broyeur* means grinder. There are several types of mélangeurs. The kind we use in chocolate making is a machine that grinds the nibs beneath large granite rollers, releasing the cocoa butter and creating chocolate liquor. *See also* chocolate liquor.

metate

A rough stone slab on which cacao beans have traditionally been ground. Metates have been used throughout South and Central America for centuries, and they are still in use in some areas today. Metates (and slaves who knew how to use them) were brought to Europe with some of the early shipments of cacao.

molinillo

A device that has been used for centuries to froth chocolate, a molinillo (shown on page 21) is usually made of a wooden rod set with movable carved wooden disks. To use it, you hold the rod between your palms and twirl it.

monilia

A fungal disease, *Moniliophthora roreri* completes its life cycle in the pods of a cacao tree, causing bumpy swellings to appear on their surface. Like other fungal diseases, monilia spreads rapidly and can catastrophically affect cacao production. *See also* fungal diseases.

monotype

Monotype means identical genetic copies or a group of plants in which every member is the same. When cacao plantations grow only one variety of cacao, described as a monocultural approach, the plantation is more vulnerable to diseases. Planting different types of trees—or establishing a polyculture—helps prevent diseases from spreading and wiping out every tree.

nacional

This type of cacao, grown only in Ecuador, and perhaps indigenous there, is known for its floral qualities. Although considered by many scientists a strain of forastero, nacional doesn't necessarily have the same flavor characteristics as other types of forastero. *See also*: criollo, forastero, porcelana, trinitario.

nib

The dark, nut-like chunks of cacao beans that remain after roasting and shelling. Intensely flavorful but not sweet, nibs *are* the essence of cacao—they are the raw material from which chocolate is made. The vast majority of nibs are made into chocolate, but, because they are now available to consumers, nibs may also be used as an ingredient in both sweet and savory foods. *See also* chocolate liquor.

phenotype

The visible traits that characterize an organism. With cacao, phenotype—the visual clues that might lead you to believe a pod is criollo, for example—doesn't necessarily correspond to the genotype, the genetic makeup of the plant. *See also* genotype.

polyphenols

A group of chemical substances found in wine, chocolate, and a vast variety of other plant foods. Polyphenols are currently the focus of many research projects examining their potential health benefits. *See also* tannins.

porcelana

An extremely rare type of criollo, porcelana beans are blond or pale pink. They make a mild, reddish-brown chocolate with delicate flavors. *See also* criollo, forastero, nacional, trinitario.

refining

A step in the chocolate-making process, refining is the final stage of particle reduction. To refine, or to make the solid cacao particles smaller or finer, gives the chocolate liquor a smoother, more uniform texture. Sugar, vanilla beans, and sometimes a minuscule amount of soy lecithin and additional cocoa butter may be added during refining depending on the type of chocolate being made.

tannins

A type of polyphenol, tannins occur naturally in many fruits and vegetables, particularly in the leaves, roots, pods, and bark or wood of the plant. *See also* polyphenols.

tempering

Tempered chocolate retains its shape, glossy surface, and melting characteristics; in other words, tempered chocolate melts at a higher temperature than untempered chocolate and requires a certain amount of force to be snapped. The goal of tempering is to enable the formation of a very specific type of fat crystal within the cocoa butter in the chocolate. This fat crystal is very stable—i.e., the crystals link together in a way that requires more force or energy to disrupt. The only part of chocolate that is actually tempered is cocoa butter.

Theobroma cacao

The Latin name for the cacao tree, which was named by Swedish botanist Carolus Linnaeus in 1753. The word *Theobroma* translates as "food of the gods" and the tree is a member of the family of tropical plants known as *Sterculiaceae*. Although other trees in the *Theobroma* genus can produce pods, no tree other than

Theobroma cacao produces seeds that can be made into chocolate. A tree in the same genus as *Theobroma Cacao, Theobroma bicolor*, for example, is grown as a food crop in Central America, but its seeds cannot be used to make chocolate.

trinitario

One of the three primary types of cacao. Trinitario, so named because it may have originated near Trinidad, is a hybrid of the criollo and forastero varieties, but it can range across the spectrum from being very similar to criollo in terms of flavor to much closer to forastero. *See also* criollo, forastero, nacional, porcelana.

white chocolate

Technically, white chocolate isn't chocolate at all. True chocolate must contain both cocoa butter and cacao particles, or solids. The nibs inside a cacao bean are made up of approximately fifty percent fat—the cocoa butter—and fifty percent solid particles. These solids give chocolate its flavor and dark color. White chocolate contains no cacao solids, which is why it lacks chocolate's flavor and color.

winnower

A machine that uses metal rollers to crack cacao beans and then a stream of air to separate the beans from the shells. The chunks of roasted cacao beans that remain once the shells are removed are called nibs.

witches'-broom

A fungal disease that can destroy a cacao tree's ability to produce pods and spreads rapidly from tree to tree. The fungus responsible for witches'-broom, *Crinipella perniciosa,* invades the plant cells, initially provoking a sprout of new leaves. As the fungus kills the cells, the tiny green sprouts all over the tree turn brown and wilt, resembling small brooms. *See also* fungal diseases.

RESOURCES

Scharffen Berger Chocolate Maker

914 Heinz Avenue

Berkeley, CA 94710

(800) 930-4528; (510) 981-4050

www.scharffenberger.com

San Francisco Store

1 Ferry Building

The Embarcadero

San Francisco, CA 94111

(415) 981-9150

New York Store

473 Amsterdam Avenue (at West 83rd Street)

New York, NY 10024

(212) 362-9734

Healdsburg Store

106 Matheson Street

Healdsburg, CA 95448

(707) 525-1150

OTHER SOURCES

Counterpart

www.counterpart.org

KALLARI ASSOCIATION

www.kallari.com

Héctor Licuy, General Coordinator

www.kallari@yahoo.es

LOMA QUITA ESPUELA FOUNDATION

(Fundación Loma Quita Espuela)

Florencio de la Cruz, Director

www.flqe.org.do

SMITHSONIAN TROPICAL RESEARCH INSTITUTE

www.stri.org

SMITHSONIAN MIGRATORY BIRD CENTER

www.nationalzoo.si.edu

WORLD COCOA FOUNDATION

www.worldcocoafoundation.org

SOURCES FOR KITCHEN TOOLS

Culinary Institute of America

www.ciachef.edu

Sur La Table

www.surlatable.com

Williams-Sonoma

www.Williams-Sonoma.com

SUGGESTED READING

Of the hundreds of books written about chocolate, these are the ones we recommend most often.

THE SCIENCE OF CHOCOLATE, by Stephen T. Beckett. Cambridge, England: The Royal Society of Chemistry, 2000.

Written for confectioners and students of food science, this textbook explains clearly and concisely the chemistry involved in chocolate making.

THE TRUE HISTORY OF CHOCOLATE, by Sophie D. Coe and Michael D. Coe. London: Thames & Hudson, 1996.

Academically sound and yet accessible, this fascinating book offers a lively view of chocolate's history.

THE EMPERORS OF CHOCOLATE: INSIDE THE SECRET WAR OF HERSHEY AND MARS, by Joël Glenn Brenner. New York: Random House, 1999.

Brenner is a journalist who researched American chocolate makers for years before writing this informative book on the founding of Hershey and Mars.

BITTERSWEET: RECIPES AND TALES FROM A LIFE IN CHOCOLATE, by Alice Medrich. New York: Artisan, 2003.

Alice Medrich explains how to cook with premium dark chocolates in a way that will inspire even novices.

ON FOOD AND COOKING: THE SCIENCE AND LORE OF THE KITCHEN, by Harold McGee. New York: Scribner, 2004.

Harold McGee clarifies the steps and chemical processes behind chocolate making and furthers our understanding of many other aspects of the science behind cooking.

THE NEW TASTE OF CHOCOLATE: A CULTURAL & NATURAL HISTORY OF CACAO WITH RECIPES, by Maricel E. Presilla. Berkeley: Ten Speed Press, 2001.

Maricel Presilla, who is a chef, cultural anthropologist, and cacao consultant, grew up in a Cuban family who grew cacao. Her firsthand knowledge infuses this book, and the sections on the different varieties of cacao are illuminating.

THE CACAO TREE: A NATURAL HISTORY OF CACAO, by Allen M. Young. Washington: The Smithsonian Institution Press, 1994.

We probably refer to this book more than any other. Young covers everything from cacao's origins and the paths by which humans transported it around the earth to his years of studying midges and cacao pollination in Costa Rica.

BIBLIOGRAPHY

The Oxford Encylopedia of Food and Drink in America. New York: Oxford University Press, 2004.

Beckett, Stephen T. *The Science of Chocolate.* Cambridge: The Royal Society of Chemistry, 2000.

Brenner, Joël Glenn. *The Emperors of Chocolate: Inside the Secret War of Hershey and Mars.* New York: Random House, 1999.

Cameron, Sarah. *Dominican Republic.* Bath, England: Footprint, 2004.

Casanova, Giacomo. *The Memoirs of Jacques Casanova de Seingalt.* New York: Random House, 1929.

Clarence-Smith, William Gervase. *Cocoa and Chocolate, 1765–1914.* Rev. ed. London: Routledge, 2000.

Coe, Sophie D., and Michael D. Coe. *The True History of Chocolate.* London: Thames & Hudson, 1996.

Grofe, Michael J. "Up From Xibalba: Death and Rebirth and the Symbolism of Cacao in the Popol Vuh." Lecture for the 23rd Annual Maya Weekend, University of Pennsylvania. April 10, 2005.

Henderson, John S. *The World of the Ancient Maya.* Ithaca, NY: Cornell University Press, 1997.

Henderson, John S., and Rosemary A. Joyce. "Brewing Distinction: The Development of Cacao

    Beverages in Formative Mesoamerica." In ***Chocolate in America: A Cultural History of Cacao,***

    edited by Cameron McNeil. University Press of Florida, 2006.

Minifie, Bernard W. ***Chocolate, Cocoa, and Confectionery: Science and Technology.*** 3rd ed. New York:

    Van Nostrand Reinhold, 1989.

Presilla, Maricel E. ***The New Taste of Chocolate: A Cultural and Natural History of Cacao with***

    Recipes. Berkeley: Ten Speed Press, 2001.

Prescott, W. H. ***The History of the Conquest of Mexico.*** 1843. New York: Modern Library, 1931.

Tannahill, Reay. ***Food in History.*** New York: Crown, 1989.

Van Bael, Sunshine. ***Project ave-Cacao: The Importance of Cacao Farms for Birds in Bocas del Toro,***

    Panama. Washington, D.C.: Smithsonian Tropical Research Institute, 2005.

Young, Allen M. ***The Chocolate Tree: A Natural History of Cacao.*** Washington, D.C.: Smithsonian

    Institution Press, 1994.

ACKNOWLEDGMENTS

FROM ROBERT

From the moment in 1994 when Bob Voorhees first suggested I look into chocolate, I have relied on others to teach, guide, and do much of the physical labor required to make chocolate. Their contributions in bringing Scharffen Berger Chocolate Maker, not to mention this book, into existence and fostering its evolution are so numerous and so critical that I am certain I have inadvertently forgotten someone in writing this acknowledgment. I began knowing absolutely nothing about chocolate, and I therefore feel safe in saying that, without the indulgence and help of the many family, friends, and acquaintances I am about to mention, the idea of making chocolate of the highest quality in the United States would have remained just that. If I were to explain in detail the role played by each person, this personal thank you would fill pages. I've therefore decided to create a loosely chronological list of everyone to whom I am extraordinarily grateful. Thank you all.

My mother, Selma Goldberg, and my sister, Nancy Steinberg. Jimmy Shuman, Rennea Couttenye, Bob Voorhees, Gayle Yamada, Agnes Ng, Sylvie Laly, Mark Fleckenstein, Julia Orenstein, Emily Luchetti, and Terry Richardson.

Matthieu Barès, Maurice and Jean-Jacques Bernachon, and the workers at Bernachon Chocolatier in Lyons, France.

Alice Medrich, Frank & Donna Katzl, Marion Cunningham, Allen Young, Michael Allured, Elizabeth Falkner, Hal McGee, Maricel Presilla, Nigel Brown, Peter Kocaurek, Raul Cabra, Ana Estrella, Carmen Elena Òtengo de Wallis, Michel Acoulon, Pam Thornton, Anita Martin, Josefina Reinoso and family, Narsai David, Joseph Schmidt, Karl Bittong, Sara Cameron, Claudia Fleming, David and Genevieve Peisch, Julia Child, Rose Levy Beranbaum, Agnes Ng, Deborah Kwan, Barbara Vick, Dana Oxford, David Lipsky, Bill Wilkinson, Maida Heatter, Marion Nestle, Ferd Puliti, Roland Sanchez, Paul Nellens, Pierre Hermé, Francois Pralus, Carole Bloom, Flo Braker, Shirley Corriher, Jacques Pépin, Joanne Chang, David Lebovitz,

Nancy Silverton, Joachim & Gertrud Bauermeister, Sherry Yard, Anne Marie Otey, Tom Gumpel, Peter Greweling, Mariella Lange & Robert Boos, Paul De Verteuil, Richard de Verteuil, Hugo Hermelink, Doralice Handal, Darlene Bucaram, Ramiro Penaherrera, Louis and Elodie Santamaria, Silvino and Ana Reyes, Karen Demasco, Jim Dodge, Rick and Deann Bayless, Kate Sullivan, and Jennifer Fite.

William Gervase Clarence-Smith, Adelaida Mejia, Jim Harris, Judy Logback, Anya Fernald, Mark Brownstein & Molly Kellogg, Jill Santopietro, Nancy Arum, Sharon Lebewohl, and all the current and former employees of Scharffen Berger Chocolate Maker.

FROM JOHN

Thanks to my mother, Marion Scharffenberger, who served our family a different dessert every day and inspired in me a love of cooking and gardening. Thanks to the generous people who helped us in the early days of Scharffen Berger Chocolate Maker: Alice Medrich, Narsai David, Elizabeth Falkner, Ric O'Connel, David Lebovitz, Julia Child, Jacques Pépin, Fran Bigelow, Martin Keller, Craig Stoll, Sally Schmitt, and Carole Bloom. Thanks to Maury Rubin of City Bakery, Karl Bittong, Mauny Kaseburg, Joan Steuer, Deborah Kwan, and Barbara Vick for helping to launch the company. Thanks to the Greenberg family of Union Confectionery Machinery with special thanks to Jimmy Greenberg. Thanks to the cacao producers who welcomed our book crew: Jo Locandro, Héctor José Rizek and the entire Rizek family, Jesús Moreno, and the staff of the Loma Quita Espuela Foundation. Thanks to the people at Scharffen Berger Chocolate Maker who've made the past nine years interesting as well as fun: Peter Kocaurek, Dylan Bigelow, Nancy Arum, Norm Shea, Jim Harris, Brad Kintzer, Frankie Whitman, Terry Shelley, Venée Call-Ferrer, Mary Younkin, and Jeni Coxe.

Thanks to those who have inspired me with their own studies of chocolate: Michael Coe, Maricel Presilla, Rosemary Joyce, John Henderson, Allen Young, and Maximilliano Wax. Thanks to the people who continue to help us work with farmers in South and Central America: Rick Bronson, Raymond Chavez and Counterpart, Arthur Demarest, Richard Hanson, Jesús Moreno, Victor Almánzar, Constanza Casasnovas Villegas, and the staff of FLQE, as well as all the people such as Judy Logback, Jonathan Kaplan, Sunshine Van Bael, and Allen Herre who contacted us on behalf of farmers and shared their insight. Thanks to Norman and Karen Painting, who took me to my first cacao farm and to Gini Choobua, the President of the Cacao Growers chapter of the Hawaii Tropical Fruit Growers.

Thanks to the people who worked on this book: Susie Heller led this project with her usual style and grace; Deborah Jones willingly hiked through rainforests with all her gear to get the cacao shots; Ann Krueger Spivack immersed herself in the world of chocolate and wrote our story enthusiastically; and Amy Vogler, an accomplished writer and cook in her own right, kept the project afloat, not only testing but also helping to develop many of the recipes in this book. Designer Adelaida Mejia took the words and photographs and added her own special touch in bringing beauty to these pages. The incredibly smart Judith Sutton made every page better. Jeri Jones and Sandra Cook worked with Deborah in studio, bringing their own brand of magic to the food shots, and Mariela de la Cerda willingly tested and even presented us with her grandmother's technique for Dulce de Leche. Thanks to agent Lisa Queen and to everyone at Hyperion, particularly Leslie Wells, Miriam Wenger, and Will Schwalbe for their kindness and enthusiasm.

Thanks to these chefs and cooks for giving us their recipes and their time: Rick Bayless, Flo Braker, Joanne Chang, Michael Chiarello, Jim Dodge, Stephen Durfee, Susan Feniger and Mary Sue Milliken, Heidi Friedlander, Jason Hammel and Amalea Tshilds, Stephanie Hersh, Thomas Keller, Sharon Lebewohl, Rose Levy Beranbaum, Emily Luchetti, Marvin Martin, Nancy Oakes and Pam Mazzola, Arnon Oren, Nicole Plue, Michel Richard, Eric Shelton, Joanne Weir, and Sherry Yard.

Thanks to the people at Hershey who took such an interest in our book, especially John Long, Stephanie Moritz, Jeff Edleman, Jim Edris, Joe Goehring, and Susan Karli. A special thanks goes to Pam Whitenack of the Hershey archives for her careful fact-checking of the Milton Hershey section.

Special thanks to Sofia and Josef Alicastro, Lotus Bell-Glover, Olivia Egan, Kendall Harcourt, and Rachel and Danny Spivack for their help with photography and tasting.

Index

Chocolate Zabaglione Trifle, 158–59

Sauce, 313